John Sloan Dickey

JOHN SLOAN DICKEY

A Chronicle of His Presidency
of Dartmouth College

by Charles E. Widmayer

DARTMOUTH COLLEGE

Distributed by University Press of New England

HANOVER AND LONDON

The preparation of this book was coordinated

by Edward Connery Lathem

Dartmouth College
Distributed by University Press of New England
Hanover, New Hampshire 03755

Printed in the United States of America 5 4 3 2 1

CIP data appear at the end of the book

Contents

Author's Note

It is not for the actors in any performance to write their own review.
Moreover, the full-bodied story of any period in the life of a complex,
*growing institution rarely gets told.**

IT IS THE PURPOSE of this chronicle of the Dickey presidency, from
1945 to 1970, to write that review and to tell that full-bodied story,
involving one of the great and formative periods in the life of the
College. Its preparation, approved by the Dartmouth Board of Trustees,
began during the presidency of David T. McLaughlin, who has maintained a special interest in it and has been kind enough to provide a
foreword.

The book's chronological coverage of events and developments of the
Dickey years is interrupted by chapters having to do with the Great
Issues Course, the refounding of Dartmouth Medical School, Hopkins
Center, and student dissent in the sixties. Telling the complete story in
each case involves both past history and a carrying forward of the
chapter into years beyond the point reached in the main-line chronicle.
We hope the reader will find this arrangement a welcome diversion,
not a distraction from the book's sequential order.

The writing and publication of this history have been coordinated by
Edward Connery Lathem, Dean of Libraries and Librarian of the College, Emeritus. His help, in large ways and small, has been immeasur-
able, and is gratefully acknowledged. Appreciation must be recorded
also for the special assistance of Kenneth C. Cramer and his staff at the
Dartmouth College Archives, in Baker Library, where most of the research was done. As may be evident to some, the author has drawn

---

* From the 1964 Convocation address of President John Sloan Dickey, summarizing the
major developments at Dartmouth College during the previous decade.

extensively on his own earlier writings in the *Dartmouth Alumni Magazine*, which he edited throughout the Dickey presidency.

Of particular importance in preparing this chronicle were the post-retirement interviews with Mr. Dickey, taped by Professor Jere Daniell as part of the College's Oral History Project, for which the Class of 1953 provided financial support.

Illustrations are from Photographic Records of Dartmouth College Library and are mostly the work of the late Adrian Bouchard.

C. E. W.

Foreword

by President-Emeritus David T. McLaughlin

JOHN SLOAN DICKEY was always a big man—by every measure. My first encounter with President Dickey occurred during the matriculation of the Class of 1954. I was surely the greenest of the "pea-green freshmen"—a Midwesterner from a small public high school who had never been east of the Appalachian Mountains or west of the Mississippi. It was for me an awesome experience to be ushered into the 1902 Room of Baker Library to meet this imposing man with the booming voice and firm handshake, who that day carefully penned his impressive signature on the certificate that formally recorded my beginnings at Dartmouth. There followed for me forty years of association with John Dickey—during this time I was, successively, a student in Hanover; an alumnus "in the wide, wide world"; then, with the passage of time, a Trustee of the College; and, finally, one sharing with him membership in "the Wheelock Succession."

Dartmouth in the aftermath of World War II was the product of John Dickey. The College in 1945 had required new direction and a fresh source of vitality, in order to extend and enlarge its leadership role in private liberal-arts education. Surely, few periods in all of Dartmouth's history were more importantly determinant of the College's future than was the quarter-century over which he presided, and few individuals in the years since the institution's founding in 1769 can have been more instrumental than John Dickey was in molding, as well as articulating, Dartmouth's character.

On numerous occasions as an undergraduate, I had the opportunity for direct contact with the President. A fair man, President Dickey was a consummate teacher. He challenged students, faculty, and administrators alike to stretch, in terms of their commitment to the "liberating arts." One instance from my student days illustrates well his conviction

9

that, given the choice, thinking men and women will choose the right course—if one has enough confidence to place in their hands the responsibility for making such a decision. As president of the Undergraduate Council, I was invited to discuss with Mr. Dickey the issue of discriminatory clauses in national fraternity charters and, also, the political obstacles that were to be confronted in addressing this situation on the Dartmouth campus. The President concluded our meeting by remarking simply, "If you do not learn to challenge injustice here, in the confines of this campus, how can you expect to exercise leadership in a more complex external environment?" The students vindicated his confidence by voting the elimination of these clauses from fraternity charters.

Throughout his presidency, John Sloan Dickey was persistent and constant in his aspirations to have Dartmouth educate men for a lifetime of fulfillment and service. Whether he was addressing the great issues of our time or the great issues of the campus, he sought to develop leaders who were broader than their heritage and stronger than their own expectations of themselves. For thousands of alumni his call for competence, commitment, and conscience was heard "the girdled earth" around.

President Dickey's accomplishments in building post-World War II Dartmouth are chronicled in this volume—significant accomplishments that speak to a style of institutional leadership that was energetic, involved, and effective. It is perhaps ironic that his final years in office were to test to the limit his creed for the College. To his credit, in the wash of social change confronting the nation and higher education in the late 1960s, Mr. Dickey never faltered in his confidence in his students—and in Dartmouth, its cause and its future.

John Dickey left office as he had served throughout his incumbency: with dignity and with pride. In my role as a Trustee, I saw him often during his post-presidential days. He was a man at peace with his accomplishments, but ever concerned about Dartmouth's role in society. Then, at the time of my own consideration of the presidency in 1981, I went to him for counsel. While we reviewed intensively the relative merits of the possibility, it was typical of his style that he never advised me as to a specific course of action. However, there was no mistaking how he felt about Dartmouth's presidency or about the measure of loyalty that was due his beloved College.

It was certainly a cruel act of fate that John Dickey became the victim of a debilitating stroke in 1982. While unable to communicate in his normal style of speaking and writing, he made his sentiments known by other expressive means. I recall that one day I accompanied him to watch an early-autumn football practice—John in his wheelchair and covered with a green blanket. At the conclusion of the practice, the entire team approached us. The captain stepped forward, greeted Mr. Dickey, and said that in honor of having two of the College's Presidents on the field, the team wanted to present us with a gift. Mr. Dickey looked at me accusingly, but as the team broke into the singing of "Men of Dartmouth," he reached up, removed the well-used 1929 reunion cap that he was wearing, and with tears in his eyes, placed it over his heart.

Those of us whose lives were touched and influenced by John Sloan Dickey, by this man who taught us to be better than we might otherwise have been, will never forget his admonition that in the Dartmouth family there are no good-byes—that, always, "the word is 'so long,' because in the Dartmouth fellowship there is no parting."

For the "students" of this great teacher and for those committed to the "liberating arts," it will ever be thus, with reference to the Dickey years at Dartmouth.

John Sloan Dickey

The Postwar College

T HE tall man in academic gown, standing to one side of the podium, had just relinquished the presidency of Dartmouth College. John Sloan Dickey, always uncomfortable when tribute was being paid to him, was listening to his successor, John G. Kemeny, deliver the citation with which he was about to confer on him an honorary Doctorate of Laws. The citation was longer than such encomiums usually are, because the occasion was being used to review some of President Dickey's major contributions to the College during the past twenty-four years—and they were numerous.

The quarter century, 1945–1970, during which John Dickey presided over the fortunes of Dartmouth College had marked, the citation declared, "the greatest progress for this institution in its entire history." His administration was, indeed, a pivotal one, deserving comparison to that of William Jewett Tucker, for turning the College in a decidedly new direction; for revitalizing and transforming the faculty and educational program to meet the requirements of a new era; for reaffirming, in contemporary form, Dartmouth's historic commitment to undergraduate, liberal arts education; and for assigning a high priority to the moral content of liberal learning.

John Dickey, as President, brought to the College a background that was both diverse and distinguished. When elected in August 1945, he was Director of the Office of Public Affairs, one of the twelve main divisions of the U. S. Department of State. Government service at the state and federal levels had occupied most of his time after graduation from Dartmouth, in 1929, and from Harvard Law School, in 1932. Despite the prospect that he might soon become an Assistant Secretary of State, he chose to accept Dartmouth's offer and to turn to a career in higher education—a career for which his appetite had been whetted by a year of teaching American foreign policy at the newly established School of Advanced International Studies in Washington.

John Dickey grew up in the small town of Lock Haven, Pennsylvania, where his father was secretary-treasurer of a woven-wire factory. His mother, Gretchen (Sloan) Dickey, was a cousin of John Sloan, the artist. Young John was the first member of his family to go to college, and by dint of taking summer courses at nearby Bucknell, to make up a deficiency in his foreign language credits, he was admitted to Dartmouth in the fall of 1925. He was attracted to the College by a magazine article by Percy Marks, onetime English instructor at Dartmouth, praising the academic freedom that prevailed there under President Ernest Martin Hopkins. Another attraction was outdoor life, something to which he was devoted throughout his youthful years in Lock Haven.

As a Dartmouth undergraduate, he was not a good enough basketball player to make the team, despite his six-foot-three height, but it was characteristic of him to remain on the squad and help improve the skills of the other players. Because he lived off campus, John Dickey had relatively few undergraduate friends until his junior year, when he and John H. Minnich '27, an engineering student, roomed together in Wheeler Hall. He then became a member and quickly thereafter the president of Theta Chi fraternity. When he graduated in June of 1929 he was chairman of Class Day and was elected to the class executive committee.

John Dickey's real undergraduate distinction was scholarship. He majored in history and received his A.B. degree, *magna cum laude*, with highest honors in that subject. Also, he was a Rufus Choate Scholar, a member of Phi Beta Kappa, and a candidate for a Rhodes Scholarship. A great deal of time was spent in the college library, and it was there that he met Christina Gillespie, a Wellesley graduate and member of the library staff, whose father taught the classics at Phillips Exeter Academy. They were married in November 1932, soon after John Dickey received his Harvard law degree and had joined the Boston law firm of Gaston, Snow, Saltonstall and Hunt (later Gaston, Snow, Hunt, Rice and Boyd).

A sociology course that he took at Dartmouth had given John Dickey an interest in criminology. At Harvard he studied criminal law under Professor Francis B. Sayre and worked part-time for the Massachusetts

Department of Correction, at Charlestown Prison, in his second and third years. When Mr. Sayre (Woodrow Wilson's son-in-law) became Commissioner of the Massachusetts Department of Correction in 1933, he asked John Dickey to be his assistant while still retaining a place in the Gaston, Snow firm. The following year President Roosevelt named Mr. Sayre Assistant Secretary of State for Economic Affairs, and Mr. Dickey took a leave of absence from the law in order to go to Washington as Sayre's assistant and as assistant to the State Department's legal adviser. His work there, at the start, was devoted mainly to winning support for and establishing the constitutionality of the 1934 Trade Agreements Act, which Secretary of State Cordell Hull was intent upon getting through Congress, to replace the Smoot-Hawley tariffs, which Hull viewed as a detriment to this country's international relations.

The bill had special significance in that it gave the President prior authority to negotiate reciprocal trade agreements without going through the treaty-making procedure of securing approval by two-thirds vote of the Senate. This stumbling block in the Senate was something Mr. Dickey dwelled upon in speeches and articles throughout most of his career. The Trade Agreements Act was successfully shepherded through Congress in 1934, and three times more, in 1937, 1940, and 1943, John Dickey was involved in its renewal. Less successful was the effort, in which he participated, to have the United States join the World Court, another goal of Secretary Hull's. This was handled as a treaty and was defeated in the Senate by seven votes, after a fierce attack upon it by isolationist forces, led by William Randolph Hearst.

In the late summer of 1936, John Dickey returned to his Boston law firm. He was succeeded at the State Department by Alger Hiss, who at the time was an assistant to the Attorney General. Except for brief returns to Washington as special assistant to Secretary Hull, in connection with renewal of the Trade Agreements Act, he devoted himself to the practice of corporation law. In 1940, however, a wartime request was made of him. Nelson A. Rockefeller had been appointed Coordinator of Inter-American Affairs by President Franklin D. Roosevelt, for the purpose of identifying Axis agents in Latin America. Since this operation was set up outside the control of the State Department, the likelihood of friction was evident. John Dickey, with his State Department connections and know-how, was asked to serve as liaison between the Department and the Coordinator's office. He carried out this assignment two days a week until the fall of that year, when he thought it best to resign from his law firm and devote full time to Washington. He remained there through the war and until called to Dartmouth.

As assistant to Rockefeller, John Dickey began work on the so-called "black list," a compilation of companies dealing with the Axis, as well as of known Axis agents or sympathizers connected with American companies operating in Latin America. In 1941 he returned to the State Department, as Chief of the Division of World Trade Intelligence. However, he still kept a connection with the Rockefeller office and with the black list, which was published that year, listing some two thousand names. In connection with the black list, he worked particularly with Dean Acheson, then holding the assistant secretaryship Mr. Sayre had filled, and thus he began a special and close friendship with him. Another State Department colleague with whom he established a lasting friendship was Archibald MacLeish, his immediate superior in developing a program of relations with the public. In congratulating John Dickey upon his election to the Dartmouth presidency, MacLeish wrote that the choice was right in every way. He added that he and Dean Acheson had long ago agreed that John was destined to be a college or university president.

In 1943 Mr. Dickey left the black-list work to be special consultant to Secretary Hull, first to oversee another renewal of the Trade Agreements Act, and then to develop a wholly new State Department division that was to concern itself with relations between the Department and the public, especially with those groups that might make a contribution to postwar planning. This was the prelude to John Dickey's becoming the first director of an Office of Public Affairs and to his assuming the role of Public Liaison Officer for the U.S. delegation to the United Nations conference in San Francisco. Forty-two organizations were invited to San Francisco as consultants to the U.S. delegation, and John Dickey was the central figure in maintaining the lines of communication with them. Mindful that the United States had failed to join the League of Nations because of the lack of Congressional involvement and of public knowledge and support, the State Department, largely at John Dickey's urging, took pains this time to emphasize public information and to welcome the input of private foreign-policy groups. The success of that public-liaison effort played no small part in this country's willingness to subscribe to the United Nations Charter. After the San Francisco conference, John Dickey returned to his Washington duties and was busy as director of the State Department's Office of Public Affairs when unexpectedly the call from Dartmouth came.

John Dickey's record as a young government official of exceptional promise attracted lots of attention from academia, foundations, and even the Rockefeller family. He had been thinking about a career change, to something other than the law, and he and his wife Chris had discussed this; but being President of Dartmouth College was far from anything he had in mind. His first inkling that he was one of the leading candidates for the job happened at an American League baseball game in Washington in July 1945. He and his classmate Dudley W. Orr, who was a Dartmouth Trustee, were together in Griffith Stadium, where the Senators were playing the Detroit Tigers. Orr pulled a paper out of his pocket, handed it to Dickey, and said, "What do you think of this letter I've just received?" John R. McLane, senior member of the Board of Trustees and chairman of the search committee for a President to succeed Ernest Martin Hopkins, had written that John Dickey was one of the men they were seriously considering, and he asked Orr to find out if his classmate was willing to be a candidate. That was the greatest surprise of his life, John Dickey later recalled, and he asked for some time to think about it. Chris Dickey was then vacationing at her family's summer place in Canada, where she received the news by letter. A trusted consultant in all her husband undertook, she was asked for her advice and had no hesitation in replying that she thought John had splendid qualifications for the job and should say yes. This turn of events clarified for the Dickeys why Mr. McLane had called on John Dickey in San Francisco during the United Nations conference and why Harvey P. Hood of Boston, also a Trustee, had made a surprise visit to the Dickey home in Washington (and had been invited to stay for a light supper of macaroni and cheese, all that Chris Dickey could hastily assemble).

Things moved rapidly from that point on. John Dickey was invited to have dinner with the Board of Trustees at the Union Club in Boston on August 9, and three days later Mr. McLane telephoned and offered him the Dartmouth job. On August 29, simultaneous announcement was made of President Hopkins' retirement and the election of John Dickey to succeed him. Prior to this public announcement only three or four persons in Hanover had any knowledge of what was taking place, and the Hanover community was flabbergasted when the news broke in a special issue of the *Dartmouth Log*, a weekly newspaper that filled in for *The Dartmouth* during the war years. That a change in Presidents could happen in such a peremptory way, without a bevy of consulting committees, was a shock to some members of the Dartmouth faculty, one of whom told President Hopkins that the faculty considered the selection procedure a slap in the face. In that day and age, however, a presidential choice could be made in such a closed way. Mr. Hopkins held firmly to the position that the Board of Trustees had the sole authority to elect the President. And remembering the contention that had occurred when his own likely election was made known back in 1916, he was determined that John Dickey should be spared that sort of experience.

The installation of John Dickey as twelfth President of the College was set for November 1, 1945. Before that, Mr. and Mrs. Hopkins invited him to spend the Labor Day weekend with them at their summer home in Manset, Maine. John Dickey expected that his visit would be filled with talk about College affairs and the job awaiting him. Instead, the conversation never touched upon such topics. Finally, when it was almost time for him to return to Washington, Mr. Dickey asked President Hopkins if there wasn't some advice he wanted to give him. Mr. Hopkins thought awhile, smiled, and said, "My only advice to you is never have anything to do with murals." This referred, of course, to the uproar among the alumni when President Hopkins gave his approval to having the Mexican artist, José Clemente Orozco, paint his now celebrated murals in the Reserve Room of Baker Library during 1932–34. President Dickey told this story many times, and he also gleefully told about the Down East photographer who came to record the informal meeting between the retiring and incoming presidents. They posed sitting on a step at the house in Manset, and after one shot, the photographer folded up his equipment and made ready to depart. "Aren't you going to take more than one picture?" Mr. Hopkins asked.

"Nope. One'll do," replied the photographer. The resulting picture was, in fact, an excellent one and appeared on the cover of the October 1945 issue of the *Dartmouth Alumni Magazine*.

The photograph of Mr. Hopkins and Mr. Dickey, posing together as if they were father and son, was an accurate representation of the relationship that was to develop between the two men. Simply put, they became intimate friends who respected and trusted each other. Mr. Hopkins made a point of not intruding upon the presidential duties and policies of his successor, but it was understood that he was always available to talk things over and to give information or his reaction to events when it was sought. President Dickey, on his part, was diligent in keeping Mr. Hopkins informed about college affairs, and through-out his administration, until Mr. Hopkins died in 1964, he regularly dropped by the home of the President-Emeritus, who continued to reside in Hanover after retirement. These visits were mainly occasions for friendly conversation, rather than for College business, and both men took pleasure in them.

The College community, which had little or no first-hand knowledge of John Dickey, was especially desirous of meeting Dartmouth's new leader. Members of the faculty and staff, and alumni residing in the area, were given that opportunity in mid-October when Mr. and Mrs. Dickey paid a three-day visit to Hanover as guests of President and Mrs. Hopkins. Mr. Dickey conferred with some of the College officers with whom he would be working, while Mrs. Dickey concerned herself with the impending business of becoming Dartmouth's First Lady and of settling her family of five in the President's House. The Dickey children coming to Hanover were Sylvia, ten; Christina, nine; and John Jr., four.

On the second evening of the visit, nearly a thousand persons at-tended a reception in Baker Library and kept those in the receiving line busy for a very long time. Although planned as a way of introducing the Dickeys to the community, the reception became equally an occa-sion for bidding farewell to President Hopkins. Earlier in the day, a campus parade by the Navy V-12 Unit had the same double character, being a salute both to the President-elect and to the man who, near the close of his 29-year administration, had successfully guided Dartmouth through the war years. The Navy V-12 review was, in fact, the last to take place before the unit gave way to NROTC when the college year began in November.

The annual fall meeting of the Board of Trustees had originally been scheduled for October 12, when Mr. Dickey was to be in Hanover, but it was postponed until October 31, so the Trustees could be present at the formal induction of the new President the next day. John Dickey's inauguration as Dartmouth's twelfth President, on November 1, 1945, was a brief affair, without the academic pomp that customarily accompanies such an event. It took place in the Faculty Room of Parkhurst Hall (the administration building) in the presence of Trustees, members of the faculty and administration, and a few family members. Mr. Hopkins, who had been elected President-Emeritus by the Trustees the night before, presided at the exercises and explained that with the effects of the war still being felt, it was deemed appropriate, with John Dickey's full agreement, to have a simple induction, in the form of a faculty meeting. He first called on Mr. McLane, as senior member and Clerk of the Board of Trustees, to present the original Dartmouth Charter of 1769 to President Dickey; and then he himself turned over the historic Wentworth Bowl, which had been given to Eleazar Wheelock at Dartmouth's first Commencement, with the request that it be placed in the keeping of each Dartmouth President who followed in the Wheelock Succession. The third symbol of presidential authority that was bestowed was the Flude Medal, traditionally worn by Dartmouth's President on ceremonial occasions. As the chain bearing it was slipped over President Dickey's head, this medal more than anything else gave evidence that he had indeed become head of the College.

In responding to the presentations made to him, President Dickey spoke only briefly. He said, in part: "Standing in the shadow of predecessors who gave this College life and strength, and in the presence of men who daily serve its cause, I have no great words of pledge or promise to stack beside their deeds and proved devotion. I do pray God, and ask each man's help, that my all shall never be less than the cause of Dartmouth, under whatever circumstance or chance, shall require."

Mr. Dickey's first act in office was a surprise to those assembled for his induction, and especially to Mr. Hopkins. Dean of the Faculty E.

Gordon Bill stepped forward and said, "Mr. President, I have the rare honor and privilege of presenting to you, at the request of the Board of Trustees and I am sure with the unanimous approval of the faculty, a candidate for the degree of Doctor of Laws, *honoris causa*. The candidate is Ernest Martin Hopkins." In his very first honorary degree citation John Dickey showed the felicitous touch that was to characterize the many citations he wrote and delivered during the next twenty-four years of his presidency. One of the sentences he used in praising Mr. Hopkins is a good example of his way with words: "The measure of your devotion and of your doing, like that of other true north-country men, will never be weighed in any man's scales."

Mr. Hopkins, partly to offset the emotion he felt, made a humorous response to this highest academic honor the College could pay him. "I have been avaricious for this degree and wondered whether I was ever going to get it or not," he said to those assembled, who only moments before had shaken the room with applause and now responded with laughter. Taking advantage of the informality which prevailed, Mr. Hopkins went on to express his great confidence in John Dickey. "I can imagine no greater happiness that can come to a man," he said, "than to feel absolutely confident that the work in which he perhaps has had a part is to be carried on in hands fully competent, and I want to say here and now what I think most of you know, that there is no confidence lacking and there is every belief that the administration which is to follow will be one of the great and one of the distinctive administrations which Dartmouth has had." Mr. Hopkins' approval of John Dickey's leadership never wavered during the nineteen years that remained for him to witness the advances made by the College.

The brevity and simplicity of the Dickey induction did not permit an inaugural address. Dartmouth Night on November 9, during the weekend of the Dartmouth-Harvard game in Hanover, therefore became a sort of second inauguration, with President Dickey speaking to the student body for the first time. The faculty and glee club occupied the stage of Webster Hall, which was packed for this initial all-College event of the Dickey administration. The President's talk, in essence, was a call for combining doing with learning.

"The historic college," he said, "has always insisted on its right and its duty to pursue the truth, without let or hindrance from prejudice or any other interest, and to make that truth known. And again, as far as I am concerned, that is well, so long as we are sufficiently humble to grant to providence, and the next generation, the possibility that the truth of the day for us may not be an eternal verity—and, also, so long as this spirit of humility is not, in practice, carried clear across the spectrum of tolerance, to the point where men of knowledge and good will become incapable of action and leave the world's doing either to those who don't know or don't care or, as in all-too-recent times, to those who do evil gladly. . . .

"I personally care not very much whether your doing be in the public service or in the ranks of the citizenry. I do want very much that this generation of educated men of Dartmouth should 'be ye doers of the word, and not hearers only, deceiving your own selves.' And remember this: there is so little time."

The phrase "so little time" was used frequently in John Dickey's addresses and writings during the early years of his presidency. The idea of good and evil contending in the world appeared even more often, and was a recurring theme throughout all the years he was in office. The concept of these opposing forces in life was the basis of his oft-stated belief that the liberal arts college must concern itself with morality.

The student body to which President Dickey spoke at the start of Dartmouth's first postwar year included some three hundred veterans who were resuming their college studies with the November term. They registered separately and were assisted by a Special Committee on Academic Adjustments. As expressed by Professor Wm. Stuart Messer, chairman of the committee, the veterans came back wanting an education rather than a degree. In recognition of their revised plans and more mature interests, the College was prepared to be as flexible as possible in making adjustments in its regular academic requirements and programs. The veterans of November, easily spotted in their casual service attire, were but the vanguard of a greater influx expected in March, when the grand total would rise to one thousand. A younger military presence in the fall was provided by a large contingent of Navy trainees, made up of 626 men in NROTC and the V-12 Unit, 206 in the V-5 aviation program, 123 Marines, and ten Navy medics.

Nothing about the veterans' return was more conspicuous, or more shattering of Dartmouth's all-male tradition, than the fifty wives who took up residence with their student husbands. To provide living quarters for the married couples, the College transformed Fayerweather and South Fayerweather dormitories into kitchenette suites and also made available apartments in several houses in town. Looking ahead to a greater demand for married-student housing in March, the College began construction of fifty prefabricated units on a site at Lebanon Street and Hovey Lane, formerly used for tennis courts. The name Sachem Village was given to this development. By fall it was joined by Wigwam Circle, a larger development located behind Thayer School, which provided two hundred units for married students. The College adopted a policy of not permitting wives to attend regular classes, but with the cooperation of the faculty some special programs were arranged for them. Many of the wives found employment with the College or in town; others took part in campus organizations; and there was of course never any lack of domestic responsibilities to be fulfilled.

The Dartmouth Trustees at their October meeting, on the eve of President Dickey's installation, approved an enlargement of the Thayer School plant, and ground was broken at once for two new wings to house the advanced programs in electrical and mechanical engineering being added to the civil engineering curriculum, which had been the mainstay of Thayer School since its founding in 1870. The new wings were scheduled to be ready by the fall of 1947. The Trustees at the same meeting named Professor William P. Kimball, who had been Acting Dean, to be Dean of the engineering school, succeeding the late Frank Warren Garran. One further action by the Trustees, announced by President Dickey in his Dartmouth Night address, was the establishment of the Ernest Martin Hopkins Scholarships, providing tuition, room, and board at the College for the sons of Dartmouth men who had given their lives in military service during World War II.

On the athletic front, the fall of 1945 saw the signing of a football agreement among the eight institutions making up the so-called Ivy League. With the creation of a committee on administration and a committee on eligibility, the signatories came closer to making a formal reality of the league that sports writers and the public had already long accepted. Besides establishing strict academic standards for eligibility and banning athletic scholarships, the Ivy Group agreed not to engage in post-season games or to schedule games involving extended absence from academic work, not to permit freshmen to play varsity football, and not to make football schedules for more than two years in advance.

President Dickey wholeheartedly committed Dartmouth to these restrictions, while still being an ardent supporter of football and other intercollegiate sports as a valuable part of undergraduate life. His ability to get to athletic events was temporarily curtailed when he was hospitalized in December after an operation to remove some of the cartilage from the knee he had injured in a softball game in Washington shortly before coming to Hanover. Despite that injury, he had managed to get through the October reception, his inauguration, and his first month in office. The two weeks in Dick's House, the College infirmary, turned out to be a shorter stay than expected, and the President was back to a full schedule well before his first meeting with the Dartmouth Alumni Council, on January 10–11, 1946.

The Alumni Council meeting had a special importance, because its primary business was a report, requested by the Board of Trustees, defining the most pressing postwar needs of the College and recommending ways of meeting them during the next two years. The report of its study committee was approved by the full Council for transmittal to the Trustees, who at their January 12 meeting voted to move ahead with all the proposals. "The Number one need of the College," the Council stated, "is to maintain, acquire, and adequately recompense the strongest possible teaching staff." Faculty compensation below the levels at sister institutions had been a Dartmouth weak point for years, and designating this as the most pressing need elicited no disagreement—certainly not on the part of President Dickey. The Alumni Council also recommended: (1) that the College build an auditorium large enough to accommodate the entire student body and faculty; (2) that the center containing this auditorium be named for Ernest Martin Hopkins; (3) that a memorial to Dartmouth men who gave their lives in the war be incorporated in the center; (4) that Wilder Hall, housing the physics department, be enlarged with up-to-date laboratories; (5) that the proposed Hopkins Scholarships be implemented with adequate financing; (6) that the Reconversion Fund of $800,000, which had been built up during the war years, be applied toward the estimated $2-million cost of the Council proposals; and (7) that the Alumni Fund for the next two years, after meeting operating deficits, be the proper means of securing a large part of the $2-million estimated as needed for immediate postwar objectives. Ironically, in view of the Hopkins Center that was finally dedicated in 1962, as a home for the visual and performing arts, the Alumni Council report of January 1946 declared: "We do not find primary appeal in a conception of making Dartmouth a North Woods center of music and drama."

President Dickey's talk to the Alumni Council was in tune with his great personal interest in public-mindedness and international affairs. He called for increased interest and activity in these fields, on the part of faculty and alumni as well as of students, and he again emphasized the shortness of time for achieving results. "The time factor," he said, "is of the utmost importance and the College, as well as the government, must be aware of it. We can no longer leave the destiny of men to work itself out over the next thousand years. We must work out certain minimum essentials of that destiny very soon. To translate this into actuality on our campus I suggest that we must be much more purposeful in the domain of public affairs. And we must quicken the pace in the sense of accelerated and intensified individual effort on the part of the student and those working with the students."

Except for the auditorium, about which his doubts were mainly architectural, John Dickey's own list of things that needed doing was very close to the one put forward by the Alumni Council. One of the first things he did after settling into the presidency was to study faculty salary records, which led him to the conviction that financial improvement for the teaching staff was decidedly overdue and, also, that the College needed to adopt a definite salary policy. In a memorandum dated January 23, 1946, and sent to the entire faculty, the President announced that the Trustees had authorized him to make permanent the temporary wartime salary increases that had been based on a three-term teaching load. He boosted faculty morale even more with the explanation that this action was but the first step in a policy of faculty compensation that would make Dartmouth competitive with the other institutions with which it was historically grouped. He made this promise, he said, because of the "apparently unanimous and strong feeling among the alumni that the maintenance and the strengthening of Dartmouth's instructional resources must have first call now and always on the free financial resources available to the College." And he made it, also, with confidence that the Alumni Fund would meet the challenge of helping to provide the necessary support.

Five months later, another memorandum to the faculty announced that, with the approval of the Trustees at their June meeting, adjustments would be made in the individual salaries of all full-time members of the faculty, to offset at least in part the increase in the cost of living since 1939. The President also disclosed that the College now had a salary policy "which will assure that teaching salaries at Dartmouth will be fully commensurate with salaries paid by the best institutions to full-time, undergraduate teachers." He pointed out that the new policy would be so administered that teachers desired as permanent members of the Dartmouth faculty would reach their maximum salaries some ten years earlier than in the past. Enclosed with the President's memo were checks covering lump-sum payments of $100 to single men, $200 to married men, and $300 to married men with dependent children. These one-time, lump-sum payments were made possible by drawing upon a reserve fund. To meet higher operating costs generally, including the new salary scale, the Trustees had already voted to raise the combined fee for instruction, general facilities, and the health service from $450 to $550, effective October 1946. With the raising of faculty salaries and the combined fee (which went up twice as much as in previous increases), John Dickey demonstrated his readiness to move boldly to solve urgent problems. That Dartmouth had come to lag so badly in faculty compensation was due in part, one suspects, to the Yankee caution and frugality of College Treasurer Halsey C. Edgerton, to whom President Hopkins and the Trustees had given a good deal of authority in financial matters. Mr. Edgerton, much to his credit, kept the College in sound financial condition, especially during the difficult war years, but he was never one to approve expenditures with any degree of exuberance.

The faculty for which President Dickey had shown such concern was badly in need of being rebuilt. It was overage and, moreover, it was top-heavy with full professors, since there was no rank of associate professor and the College had been following a practice of promoting rather generously, to make up for the low levels of compensation. President Dickey faced the prospect of having a large number of top-ranked faculty members retire within a short span of years. Dartmouth's expansion after World War I, when a surge of applications brought about the Selective Process of Admission, had resulted in the recruiting of a large number of new faculty members, most of whom would now be retiring within a few years of each other. This was an opportunity, as well as a problem. Not only could the teaching staff be rejuvenated, but a beginning could be made in changing its general character. Dartmouth under President Hopkins had been something of a maverick among the leading colleges and universities of the country, valuing teaching above all else and not emphasizing or insisting upon research and productive scholarship. The educational establishment had looked askance at this posture, leading President Lowell of Harvard to ask Mr. Hopkins, "Why don't all your professors have Ph.D.'s? Can't you afford them?"

With the Dickey administration, Dartmouth turned toward a new breed of faculty member. The description "teacher-scholar" came into vogue, and while the teaching of undergraduates, by full professors and junior faculty alike, still had top priority at Dartmouth, the creation of what might be called a professional faculty began, with John Dickey's blessing. Had E. Gordon Bill, Dean of the Faculty, continued in that office, it is not likely that he would have fully agreed with the new criteria about to be applied. Close to retirement himself, he presided over the College faculty with a loose rein and believed strongly in the educational value of supplementary programs that fell outside the academic format. He took pride in what were known on campus as "Bill's Frills"—Robert Frost, Ticknor Fellow in the Humanities; Paul Sample, Artist in Residence; Ray Nash, graphic artist and bookman; Virgil Poling, director of the Student Workshop; Douglas Wade, College Naturalist; and Ross McKenney, woodcraft mentor and adviser. However, Dean Bill became seriously ill shortly after John Dickey assumed the presidency and was on leave for more than a year, while faculty matters were entrusted to a threesome: Professors Bancroft H. Brown, mathematics; Wm. Stuart Messer, classics; and Andrew G. Truxal, sociology. He resigned the deanship in April 1947 and retired on June 30. Tragically, his condition worsened and rather than endure his remaining years in pain he chose suicide. It was with the new Dean of the Faculty that the development of a faculty of teacher-scholars would be initiated and carried forward with marked success in the period that lay ahead.

In addition to the more immediate problems of faculty compensation and rejuvenation, President Dickey at the outset wanted to introduce a stiffer academic pace, for both student and teacher; and he also wanted, as he stated many years later in an oral history interview, to have an active role in shaping the academic policy of the College. He quickly had a chance to make a major, celebrated addition to the curriculum. The Committee on Academic Policy had, before John Dickey's election, begun a study of Dartmouth's postwar curriculum, and in February of 1946 it was announced that some changes would go into effect the following fall, among them the introduction of a wider range of subjects in the first two years. The really notable innovation, proposed by Mr. Dickey himself, was the Great Issues Course, to be required of all seniors. This highly successful and influential venture, which will always be a hallmark of the Dickey administration, will be discussed in some detail later in this chronicle of events.

To the President's first-year agenda one other matter had to be added out of sheer necessity. This was the question of admissions policy, now that the number of men wanting to return to college or to enter as freshmen was growing far beyond the ability of the College to handle them in a normal fashion. Mr. Dickey recalled that the very first bit of business on his initial morning in office was a session with Director of Admissions Robert C. Strong, who said he needed some guidelines for an unprecedented postwar situation. Although the Trustees had raised the enrollment limit from 2,400 to 3,000, space was tight. The College recognized a special obligation to the men returning to Dartmouth after military service, as well as to Navy V-12 trainees with no previous college affiliation who wanted to continue their Dartmouth education as civilian students. This meant that with fewer places for regular applicants, the competition was stiffer than ever. Among this group, the sons of alumni inevitably would have less advantage than before. A good part of President Dickey's correspondence in those early years was devoted to explaining to disgruntled alumni why their sons who might have been admitted previously now fell below the College's academic cut-off point. A difficult selling job had to be done, but with the President leading it, a campaign to educate alumni about the post-war competition for admission, as well as the need to maintain the highest academic standards, gradually brought about an understanding and acceptance of the situation.

A different kind of admissions problem, mainly concerned with public relations, was one inherited from the Hopkins administration. Just three months before his retirement, President Hopkins, in response to a telegram from several New York organizations, had said he could not join in their condemnation of admissions limitations based on racial or religious grounds, if this meant that the protest was against "proportionate selection" as practiced in Dartmouth's selective process. This reply and a personal letter of explanation sent to Herman Shumlin of New York City were given to the press, which promptly led to charges of the existence of a Jewish quota and of anti-Semitism at Dartmouth. These charges were denied, and many Jewish alumni came to the College's support, but repercussions were still existent when John Dickey assumed office. He took no part in the public controversy, but he felt it was incumbent upon him to make his position clear to those in charge of admissions at the College. He instructed Dean Strong that henceforth he wished the freshman class to be selected without any consideration whatsoever of race or religion. It may not have had any relation to this particular episode, and it may indeed have come essentially from his legal and State Department background, but President Dickey was always very cautious about making statements in correspondence whenever controversial matters were involved. Rather, it was his practice to declare that the subject was very complicated and that he would much prefer to deal with it in conversation when he and his correspondent next got together. In this respect, his style differed greatly from that of Mr. Hopkins, whose propensity for candor and for writing long, detailed letters sometimes got him into hot water (as he himself was quick to acknowledge).

President Dickey delivered two Convocation addresses in 1946, one in March and another in October. Both were brief. In the first he included a favorite admonition: "Your business here is learning." He also told his student audience, reassembled for the pursuit of peace, that they would now find the pace stiffer, the purpose clearer. In the second address, advising students that "the world's troubles are your troubles," he used for the first time a closing that, with only slight variation, he employed in all the Convocation addresses he was to deliver thereafter. In its settled form, it was worded thus:

"And now, men of Dartmouth, as I have said on this occasion before, as members of the College you have three different, but closely intertwined, roles to play:

"First, you are citizens of a community and are expected to act as such. Second, you are the stuff of an institution, and what you are it will be. Thirdly, your business here is learning, and that is up to you.

"We'll be with you all the way—and good luck."

A set closing was similarly repeated by Mr. Dickey in his valedictory to the graduating class each June. In his 1946 valedictory he concluded: "And now the word is 'so long,' because in the Dartmouth fellowship there is no parting." He bade the seniors farewell in this way every year until 1969, the year before retiring, when he said, "And now, as I prepare shortly to follow you, I bid you join me in leaving our frustrations behind, to discover that in the Dartmouth fellowship there need be no parting." (This variation was prompted by the preceding year of student protest that had hurt him so deeply.)

With the March 1946 term and its higher enrollment, the College took another step toward reviving the prewar state of affairs. Two definite signs of this were the reopening of fraternities and the return of *The Dartmouth*, which had suspended publication in June 1943. Other organizations were coming out of their wartime hibernation, and to give coordination to their revival President Dickey named a student-faculty Committee on Social Organizations. One important question was the new form that student government might take. There was a growing feeling that something more widely representative of the student body than the senior-class Palaeopitus was called for. In May, radio station WDBS was back on the air and one more staple of prewar campus life was revived.

In addition to getting the spring term started, President Dickey in March made his first extended alumni tour. Accompanied by Executive Officer Albert I. Dickerson, he spoke at dinners in Cleveland, Detroit, Denver, Minneapolis-St. Paul, Chicago, and Milwaukee. Just before this midwestern tour he also had made his presidential bow in Boston and Manchester, New Hampshire, and after it he was guest of honor at Philadelphia and New York City. Prior to the string of March events, Mr. Dickey had gone to the winter commencement at Brown University, on February 24, to receive the honorary Doctor of Laws degree. This was his second honorary degree, the first having been bestowed upon him by Tufts College in October, one month before his inauguration. At Middlebury's commencement in June, a third LL.D. was conferred, and among other honors received by Mr. Dickey early in his presidency, he was elected a Fellow of the American Academy of Arts and Sciences, a trustee of the Woodrow Wilson Foundation, a trustee of the Institute of International Education, and a member of the Committee on International Political and Social Problems of the U.S. Chamber of Commerce.

The year of revival had two more additions before it ended. The regular June Commencement returned, complete with honorary degrees, which had not been awarded since 1942; and alumni class reunions, also suspended during the war, were held in six installments from late June until early August. The extended reunion plan brought forty-four classes back to Hanover, and for President and Mrs. Dickey, who played host to each group, the chance to meet thousands of alumni in a concentrated period of time was welcome, but exhausting.

The good fortune that had been attending the inaugural year was reversed in a sudden and shocking way on June 8, when Dean Strong suffered a cerebral hemorrhage and died at the age of forty-three. He had addressed a meeting of alumni officers in Baker Library that morning and was on his way back to Parkhurst Hall in the company of Dean Lloyd K. Neidlinger when he collapsed. The blow to President Dickey was particularly devastating. Bob Strong was one of the strongest pillars of the administrative staff he had inherited, and the two men had established a genuine friendship, as well as an easy working relationship. Strong was both Dean of Freshmen and Director of Admissions, and it would be difficult to say in which capacity he was the more valuable. But with admissions developing into one of the major postwar problems for Dartmouth and other colleges, the loss of his experienced and widely respected admissions director was a serious setback for Mr. Dickey. The difficulty had the virtue, however, of giving the

President the opportunity, so early in his administration, of demonstrating leadership of a very imaginative kind. He split Strong's responsibilities into two jobs, and to fill them he made two quite unexpected appointments. To be the new Dean of Freshmen he picked Stearns Morse, a professor of English and one of the best-liked and most-respected members of the faculty, who as a teacher had demonstrated a special rapport with undergraduates. And to be the new Director of Admissions he named, at some personal sacrifice, Albert I. Dickerson, then Executive Officer of the College and his own right-hand man in the President's office. As things worked out, both men were inspired choices, and the College community looked upon Dartmouth's young leader as someone who wasn't afraid to make a bold response to a big problem.

As President of the College, John Dickey had to work harmoniously not only with his administrative associates and faculty, but also, most importantly, with his Board of Trustees. Early on, he came to the conclusion that the board needed strengthening, on the side of serious interest in academic affairs. A significant first step in changing the makeup of the board took place in June 1946, with the election of Beardsley Ruml, Class of 1915, as an Alumni Trustee. Mr. Ruml, who at the time was chairman of the board of R. H. Macy and Company, as well as chairman of the Federal Reserve Bank of New York, had earned his Ph.D. degree at the University of Chicago and had been dean of that university's division of social sciences. He acquired a national reputation as author of the federal government's "pay as you go" income-tax withholding plan. Later, additional educational strength was added to the College's board with the election of John C. Woodhouse '21, DuPont scientist and inventor, who had taught at Dartmouth and Harvard. President Dickey knew, also, that the board had to acquire members with the interest and know-how for a new strategy in fund-raising, if the College was to pursue the course of seeking top-notch faculty members and paying them competitive salaries. This goal was achieved, leading in due course to the first capital-fund drive in Dartmouth's history. The Alumni Fund continued its major role in College financing, and to head it Mr. Dickey named George H. Colton as successor to Mr. Dickerson, the new Director of Admissions.

With the opening of the college year in October 1946, the two-semester calendar returned. Of the 2,800 men enrolled, about 80 percent were veterans. Housing was a problem for some of the 350 married veterans, because construction of half of the two hundred FHPA housing units at Wigwam Circle was delayed by a temporary shortage of labor and materials. All units were ready by late November, and the Wigwam population was before long enlarged by babies born to G.I. parents there. President Dickey took pleasure in presenting a signed certificate of welcome to infants born in Hanover while their fathers were students. Its Latin heading read, "From the hills a new voice is heard to cry," and the text said, "Know all men by these presents that (name) a freeborn child of this reservation is hereby extended the welcome of all the Dartmouth tribe."

The fall semester launched a revised curriculum that went into effect with the incoming freshman class. Its two main features were a wider range of subjects in the distributive requirement of freshman and sophomore years and the introduction of the Great Issues Course, to be required of all seniors beginning in the fall of 1947. To broaden the student's general education before concentration in a major field, the number of courses needed to meet the distributive requirement was increased; but to go along with this, one-semester introductory courses were created in all three divisions—the humanities, the social sciences, and the sciences.

The Committee on Educational Policy had proposed to the faculty that the general education objective be accomplished by means of two sequential interdepartmental courses in each division. This was rejected by the sciences, favored only in principle by the social sciences, and accepted by the humanities alone. The proposal was killed, but from it came a new interdepartmental course, Humanities 11–12, which dealt with classics of European literature and thought. The revised curriculum did not alter the standard or modified majors, but new divisional majors were offered in international relations and public administration. These were fields in which President Dickey wanted Dartmouth to do more, and he took special interest also in a new introductory course in international relations, taught by Professor John Masland, newly recruited to the Dartmouth faculty from Stanford.

The thinking about international relations that he brought to the

College at the outset of his presidency was well expressed by John Dickey in a letter he wrote in September 1946 to Chester I. Barnard, who had invited his ideas about future programs of the Rockefeller Foundation. "The most decisive issues of our time, that is, the next fifteen or twenty-five years," he wrote, "are international. I certainly do not wish to be misunderstood as believing that all men can or should turn their complete attention to the international aspects of our problems. Life in all its manifestations and necessary functions must and will go on. We have many pressing and highly important problems on the community, state and national level which we must keep working at, and we will keep working at them. My point is that we have got to find ways, and quickly, to bring more effective attention to those issues which, unless they are met, are going to make all other issues and efforts irrelevant. I believe that for the foreseeable future those decisive issues are essentially international."

Elsewhere in this letter Mr. Dickey gave a sharper explanation of the "so little time" theme he had used in speaking to students and faculty. "My second principal point," he wrote, "is to emphasize the time factor. During the past year I have given a good bit of thought to the purpose and problems of a liberal arts college today. This thought has necessarily come very largely from my previous experience in public affairs, particularly in American foreign affairs. My thinking boils down to something like this: the central need of human society today is to bring into better balance the utter physical power men now possess as against the moral and political control of that power. The key factor in achieving this better balance between utter power and its control—not to mention the development of its beneficial use—is time. Time is the factor which is so radically altered by recent developments that it cannot be regarded, it seems to me, as other than a new element both in public policy and, for us in the colleges, in general education." The concern stated in this paragraph of the Barnard letter was something that President Dickey used repeatedly in the talks and addresses he gave during the first years of his administration.

After his busy first year, John Dickey was able to settle down to being President in a more established way. However, he did not like to refer to himself as President. More often than not, he called himself "the fellow on this job." This tied in with his unassuming personality, and when January arrived he was to be found with other townspeople shoveling snow on Main Street after an especially heavy snowstorm. More of Dartmouth's alumni got the chance to meet him when he and Mrs. Dickey made a tour of five clubs on the West Coast in late November of 1946, after which the President by himself visited five more clubs in the Southwest. This left the Mid-Atlantic and the Southeast as the two sections of the country to which he had not yet made organized tours. Everywhere he went John Dickey won the support of the alumni, who liked his manner, the earnestness of his message about the liberal arts college, and his definition of goals for Dartmouth with regard to faculty, students, and educational programs.

While Mr. Dickey was visiting alumni clubs in the Southwest, he was named by President Truman to be a member of a special Committee on Civil Rights, along with fourteen other prominent American citizens. As the committee's work progressed, he became vice chairman, under Chairman Charles E. Wilson, president of the General Electric Company. Professor Robert K. Carr of Dartmouth's government department was chosen to be executive secretary of the committee and head of a professional staff of twelve assisting in the study. The committee's report, *To Secure These Rights*, was published in the fall of 1947 and prompted President Truman to submit a ten-point civil rights recommendation to Congress. For their work with the President's Civil Rights Committee, Mr. Dickey and Professor Carr were among those cited by the American Political Science Association and given the Franklin D. Roosevelt Foundation Award for the best publication of 1947 in the field of government and human welfare.

Awaiting President Dickey upon his return to Hanover from his extended alumni tour was the demanding academic responsibility he took on as acting director of the steering committee for the Great Issues Course. The committee had the job of organizing and planning the course to be introduced eleven months hence as a degree requirement for all seniors, including those in the three associated schools. Professor Arthur M. Wilson of the biography and government departments had the post of associate director, and as chief aide to the steering committee John M. Clark joined the staff as executive secretary. Clark, former *Washington Post* reporter and editorial writer, had been engaged in inter-American affairs in Washington, and just before returning to Hanover served with the O.S.S.

The matter of a new form of student government, replacing Palaeopitus, had become a burning issue on campus while Mr. Dickey was away, and it was hoped that he could clear up the conflict that had arisen over the way the various student interests would be represented in the so-called Undergraduate Council. The idea of the Council (already known as the UGC), with Palaeopitus serving as its executive committee, had been approved by two-thirds of the student body and by the faculty and Trustees, but its chance of success was slim until a variety of criticisms had been attended to. Some thought the Council's power was too restricted; others thought the proposed membership of 109 students was unwieldy. Another objection was the disproportionate representation of athletics, with sixteen team captains as members, compared with a single member from the Phi Beta Kappa Society. After some months of tinkering with the UGC's constitution, enough agreement was reached to permit the Council to hold its first meeting on May 19, 1947. In its initial year it managed to get library hours extended, to change the Thayer Hall meal-ticket plan, to subsidize the *Dartmouth Quarterly*, and to establish a UGC Judiciary Committee empowered to handle student disciplinary cases.

For the balance of the academic year 1946–47 the President's agenda was busy enough, but he had the good fortune to be able to give considerable attention to the detailed planning of the Great Issues Course, and he also found time to complete an article for the April 1947 issue of *Foreign Affairs*. In mid-February he went to Washington to testify before a Senate committee, in support of his law school classmate, Herbert Marks, whom President Truman had named to be general counsel of the Atomic Energy Commission. While he had the chance, he told the committee that the likelihood of getting good men into public affairs would be lessened "unless we are more careful about the charges we make against men once they accept the responsibilities of public service."

Back in Hanover, he announced the formation of a new Public Relations Council, to coordinate all the College's public relations programs, with special attention to securing wider public knowledge of Dartmouth's educational accomplishments. Sidney C. Hayward was named chairman, and three alumni advisory members were appointed by the Dartmouth Alumni Council. Also in this year, with other Ivy Group presidents, Mr. Dickey joined in an agreement to give prospective freshmen until June 15 to accept admission and financial aid. This adoption of a common deadline permitted applicants to make their decisions freely, without the pressure of the former system, which had deadlines ranging from early April to late May.

The *Foreign Affairs* article, to which Editor Hamilton Fish Armstrong assigned top position in the April 1947 quarterly issue of the magazine, was a piece of first-rate scholarship and gained for Mr. Dickey an enhanced reputation with his own faculty and the academic world in general. Entitled "Our Treaty Procedure Versus Our Foreign Policies," it dealt in depth with the three ways of entering into international compacts: executive agreement coupled with prior legislative sanction, joint resolution by Congress, and, most importantly, approval of treaties by the U.S. Senate by a two-thirds vote. President Dickey found this three-part arrangement "an unholy mess" and stated his belief that in foreign relations, policy and procedure were badly out of harmony. He was particularly critical of the Senate two-thirds rule as required by the Constitution, and he wrote that as a procedure for reaching agreement with other nations "it is neither workable nor does it enable the legislative branch to participate adequately in the formulation of positive foreign policies." The only sensible remedy, he concluded, would be a Constitutional amendment giving the "advise and consent" authority to both houses of Congress by normal majority vote. When asked about this proposal twenty-five years after he had made it in *Foreign Affairs*, John Dickey said he still stood by it as a way to bring about a more democratic method of approving international agreements.

Honors in the field of international relations continued to come to President Dickey, with his appointment to the executive committee of The Committee on International Economic Policy, which worked in cooperation with The Carnegie Endowment for International Peace. He was elected a trustee of Wellesley College in June, and before the year was out he became a trustee of the Brookings Institution and the recipient of an honorary Doctorate of Laws from Amherst College, where he was guest speaker at the annual meeting of the college's alumni council.

An administrative change that was to have far-reaching effect upon the College took place in the second spring of the Dickey presidency, when E. Gordon Bill, Dean of the Faculty, whose health had not improved, submitted his resignation. To fill the vacancy John Dickey made another of his daring, unexpected moves. A half-dozen or more senior faculty members were mentioned for the deanship, in the campus guessing game that developed. But everyone was wrong; in fact, not even close. To be the new Dean of the Faculty and his chief associate in running the academic side of the College, President Dickey chose Donald H. Morrison, 32–year-old assistant professor of government. After the news came out on April 24, 1947, the College overcame its surprise enough to reach general agreement that the President had again made a splendid choice—one that was in accord with both the new breed of faculty he desired and the direction in which he wanted the College's educational program to go.

Dean Morrison, who was soon elevated to full professor, was a 1936 graduate of West Virginia University. He then went to Princeton University, where he took his M.A. and Ph.D. degrees. After two years of teaching at Louisiana State University, he moved to Washington as a staff member of the U. S. Bureau of the Budget and worked there for three years before joining the Dartmouth faculty. Less than two years after coming to Hanover he was Dean of the Faculty. In him John Dickey saw great potential for achieving the goals that were now firmly shaping up in his mind. There can be no question that the working partnership between these two men, tragically of shorter duration than anyone expected, was one of the all-important factors in making the Dickey administration a pivotal one in the history of the College.

One other administrative staff appointment before the college year ended was that of Robert S. Monahan, who would return to the College in the fall in the dual capacity of General Manager of the Dartmouth Outing Club and College Forester. Monahan had been with the U.S. Forest Service for fifteen years and at the time of his Dartmouth appointment was assigned to the regional office in California. He had a major part in establishing the Mt. Washington Weather Observatory in 1932–33. In his D.O.C. post he assumed business oversight of the Club's outdoor enterprises, and as College Forester he had managerial supervision of the Dartmouth Grant in northern New Hampshire, including the logging operations that provided scholarship funds for undergraduates from the state.

The linking of Dartmouth's historic outdoor interests to special educational programs was extended at the start of the 1947–48 academic year, with the announcement that the College would inaugurate a new program of arctic study. The presence in Hanover of Vilhjalmur Stefansson, who was appointed Arctic Consultant, was the central strength of the non-credit program. Assisting him, with the title of Arctic Specialist, was David C. Nutt, who had taken part in a U.S. Naval expedition to the Antarctic and made many trips to the far north. World War II had created a new awareness of the Arctic and its economic and strategic importance. Dartmouth alumni, faculty, and undergraduates had for some years been involved in special projects in the far north, and it was a logical step to give that area a more definite place in the educational concerns of the College. The new program, which included seminars as well as outdoor activities, had the advantage of working informally with the newly created Arctic Institute in Montreal, headed by Lincoln Washburn, Class of 1935, and founded with President Hopkins and several Dartmouth faculty members among its sponsors. As things turned out, the venture into arctic study was the first step in developments that later included a pioneer northern studies program and the establishment in Hanover of the U.S. Army Corps of Engineers' Cold Regions Research and Engineering Laboratory.

Great Issues

JOHN DICKEY came to Hanover with a clear idea that he would be more than an administrator. His one year of teaching at the School of Advanced International Studies in Washington, just before assuming the Dartmouth presidency, had sharpened his interest in the philosophy and conduct of higher education, and he very much wanted to have a hand in academic policy and planning at Dartmouth. The faculty in the last year of the Hopkins administration had begun a review of the curriculum, but its report had not been completed, and President Dickey was on the job in time to participate in the final deliberations. His contribution, which was the one really important part of the revised curriculum, was the idea of the Great Issues Course. Unique and innovative, geared to the problems and opportunities of the postwar world, the course was the embodiment of John Dickey's thinking about higher education's responsibilities in a new era; and its early emphasis on international issues was also pure Dickey. Great Issues caught the attention of educators all across the land and had the support of the Carnegie Corporation of New York, which made a three-year grant of $75,000 to help meet the expenses of the experiment.

Great Issues was unusual in that it was a general education requirement in senior year, not in one of the earlier years of the college course. President Dickey and the Committee on Educational Policy believed that the greater maturity of seniors would be an important factor in achieving the purpose of the course, and that having this educational experience occur just before the student left college and took on the responsibilities of a citizen in the contemporary world would be ideal timing. As a third point, Mr. Dickey emphasized the value of giving the senior class a common intellectual experience — something that the curriculum did not offer after the freshman year. "Today our seniors," he declared, "leave college without a fully developed sense of common public purpose, or as Dr. Tucker used to call it, 'public-mindedness.' They lack that sense of intellectual unity which in part at least is aroused simply through the common study of live issues."

Another unusual feature of Great Issues was the enlistment of prominent men and women from beyond the campus to give the lectures that were at the heart of the three-part weekly program. The purpose of the course and the fresh thinking that went into its planning proved to be an attraction to the eminent figures of national and international reputation who accepted invitations to speak to Dartmouth's seniors. John Dickey's wide acquaintance with government leaders in Washington and with journalists and persons active in organizations dealing with international affairs was a great advantage in working out a year-long schedule of participants.

Appropriately enough, President Dickey gave the first Monday night talk to the senior class in Dartmouth Hall on October 6, 1947. The guest lecturers who followed him in the first months of the course attest to the very high quality of the "visiting faculty": Archibald MacLeish, Alexander Meiklejohn, Congressman Christian A. Herter of Massachusetts, Joseph Barnes of the *New York Herald Tribune*, Lewis Mumford, Professor R. M. MacIver of Barnard College, President James Bryant Conant of Harvard, Chester I. Barnard of the Secretary of State's Committee on Atomic Energy, and Herbert Marks, general counsel of the U.S. Atomic Energy Commission. The format called for the guest lecturer to speak to the class on Monday evening and to remain over for a discussion on Tuesday morning. These two sessions were preceded by a class meeting on Thursday morning, when a briefing was given to the seniors by a faculty member who had a particular competence regarding the subject to be dealt with. As for the 1947–48 issues, the first semester, after an introductory period, took up Modern Man's Political Loyalties, The Scientific Revolution and the Radical Fact of Atomic Energy, and International Aspects of World Peace. The second semester dealt with American Aspects of World Peace and What Values for Modern Man?

To go along with the lecture and discussion sessions, the course addressed itself to the problem of how men could keep themselves informed about issues of the day after they exchanged college for the adult world. To establish the habit of using dependable information sources, the G.I. steering committee decided to require each senior to be a daily reader of either *The New York Times* or the *New York Herald Tribune*. Other required readings, at the proper point in the course, were John Hersey's *Hiroshima*, E. B. White's *Wild Flag*, and the Acheson-Lilienthal Report, as well as such documents as the Declaration of Independence, the Communist Manifesto, and the Charter of the United Nations. For students in the course there also was the matter of learning to make a distinction between trustworthy and slanted sources of information. To that end, the steering committee set up in Baker Library a Public Affairs Laboratory, with a full-time assistant to the director, where seniors could make a comparative study of the way in which the same news was treated by different newspapers and periodicals. One newspaper offered as an example of slanted journalism was the *Chicago Tribune*, which led to a lambasting of Great Issues, President Dickey, and Dartmouth College in a series of articles by a reporter sent to Hanover for just that purpose.

Press coverage of the Great Issues Course was extensive, and editorials praising the objectives of the project appeared in the leading New York papers and elsewhere. During the first two years many visitors from other colleges and universities came to Hanover to observe the course at first hand, and the President's correspondence was considerably increased by inquiries from other college officials. In a letter to President Nason of Swarthmore, during the second year of Great Issues, Mr. Dickey wrote: "In brief, the only basic reservation which I have at the moment concerning our experience with this experiment is whether we can sustain the cooperative effort and the pace involved in it. I shall not attempt to go into this aspect of it now, but it is important to realize that this kind of course depends upon the cooperation of many of your best men in the faculty and it requires of all concerned with it an effort which is distinctly beyond that in the well-organized course which after a year or two settles into a comfortable routine."

He also wrote about student reaction to the course, pointing out that there was criticism as well as general approval. The criticism arose from the facts that Great Issues was compulsory; that it was a stiff course, surprising those who found it "a fairly high and new kind of hurdle between them and their degree in what they had expected would be a pleasant and not too strenuous senior year"; and that the organization and techniques were basically different from most undergraduate courses and demanded a greater measure of maturity and self-reliance. There was some evidence, however, that seniors took pride in a unique course that was winning Dartmouth favorable attention in the academic world. Thomas W. Braden, who had replaced John Clark as executive secretary of the steering committee, reported that one senior, when told that Great Issues was being copied by other colleges, asked a member of the committee, "Can't we do something to stop them?" Whatever the seniors might have felt at the time they were immersed in Great Issues, surveys in later years indicated that the great majority rated it as one of the lastingly valuable parts of a Dartmouth education. Great Issues continued as a significant part of the Dartmouth curriculum until 1966. In that year it was converted into the Senior Symposia, directed by a student steering committee. With no exams or papers or grades, and with no required attendance, the symposia became a poor approximation of what Great Issues had been in its brightest years.

The inauguration of the Great Issues Course was the most noteworthy event as the academic year 1947–48 began on October 2. Enrollment of 3,001, the largest in the history of the College, was approximately sixty percent veterans, but that this element of the student body was on the decline was indicated by a freshman class of 680 that included only sixty-eight men who had been in the armed services. Middle Fayerweather Hall was returned to regular dormitory status, since Wigwam Circle, Sachem Village, and South Fayerweather Hall were now adequate for housing the 270 married students on campus.

President Dickey at Convocation again spoke only briefly, urging his listeners to acquire a sense of humility, as being a large part of any man's education and "the surest solvent known for those two most persistent enemies of the educated man: pride and prejudice." He also said, "Today we use the term 'the world' with what amounts to brash familiarity. Too often in speaking of such things as the world food problem, the world health problem, world trade, world peace, and world government we disregard the fact that 'the world' is a totality which in the domain of human problems constitutes the ultimate in degree of magnitude and degree of complexity. That is a fact, yes; but another fact is that almost every large problem today is, in truth, a world problem. Those two facts taken together provide thoughtful men with what might realistically be entitled 'an introduction to humility' in curing the world's ills."

In early December, Mr. Dickey left for Havana, Cuba, to be adviser to the United States delegation at the United Nations Conference on Trade and Employment. This was the first of a number of assignments he took on for the U.S. Department of State after assuming the Dartmouth presidency. His authoritative knowledge of the Trade Agreements Act from 1934 on was the basis for some of his State Department service, but President Truman had enlisted him for the civil rights study of 1946, and later he was to be a member of the Advisory Committee of the Foreign Service Institute (1948), U. S. consultant to the Collective Measures Committee of the United Nations (1951), and consultant to the Secretary of State and the U.S. representatives on the United Nations Disarmament Commission (1952). Among non-government appointments while President, he was to become a board member of the Rockefeller Foundation, the World Peace Foundation, and the Committee for Economic Development. He became consultant to the National War College, consultant to the Naval War College, and a member of the Academic Advisory Boards of both the U.S. Military Academy and the U.S. Naval Academy. He also became a member of the American Bar Association's Committee to Survey the Legal Profession.

Before he left for Havana in December, President Dickey filled the vacancy created in his office when Mr. Dickerson was advanced to Director of Admissions. To be the new Executive Officer of the College he named Richard W. Morin, a lawyer from Albert Lea, Minnesota, who had been one of his colleagues in the U.S. State Department. Mr. Morin, after graduate studies at Harvard Law School, Oxford, and the Political Science School in Paris, had become a U.S. Foreign Service officer and during the war served with the State Department's division of public liaison, becoming chief of the division in 1944. His friendship with John Dickey became especially close after their Washington days, beginning with duck-hunting in Minnesota (which continued in the Hanover region after Morin joined the College's administrative staff).

At the close of the college year, a change took place also in the Board of Trustees. Sigurd S. Larmon, Class of 1914, was elected an Alumni

Trustee, succeeding William J. Minsch, who had served the limit of two five-year terms. The advent of Mr. Larmon, who was president of the New York advertising firm of Young and Rubicam, marked the beginning of a strengthening of the board in the area of fund-raising for the College. At the time of his election he was one of the leaders of the campaign to raise $4-million for the Hopkins Center Project, and earlier he had been chairman of the Alumni Fund. He was past president of both the Alumni Council and the General Alumni Association, and on the basis of all he had been doing for the College was expected to help bring about a more dynamic board, actively interested in the administrative and educational affairs of the College. He was also a man interested in international affairs, being a member of the Council on Foreign Relations and the executive committee of the U.S. Associates of the International Chamber of Commerce.

The Trustees meeting at which Mr. Larmon was elected also produced major news that the College would have a new Treasurer to succeed Halsey Edgerton, who was to retire on June 30, 1949, after forty-three years in the business office, thirty-three of them as Treasurer. The man chosen to take over as Dartmouth's chief financial officer was John F. Meck '33, Washington attorney and former assistant dean of Yale Law School. While serving with the Bureau of Naval Personnel during the war, he gained an in-depth knowledge of the financing of colleges and universities through his negotiating of contracts for the Navy's college training programs. In 1946 he was secretary of the special committee named by President Dickey to devise a faculty salary policy for Dartmouth. Like so many men chosen by President Dickey to assist him in the administration of the College, Mr. Meck had experience in government and foreign affairs. While carrying on his legal duties with the Washington firm of Douglas, Proctor, MacIntyre and Gates, he devoted much time to the work of the Commission on the Organization of the Executive Branch of the Government, chaired by Herbert Hoover. More specifically, he was executive secretary of the committee named by that Commission to study the organization of the federal government in the area of foreign affairs.

Mr. Edgerton served as Dartmouth's treasurer throughout the entire Hopkins administration, assuming that post the same year that Mr. Hopkins was inaugurated. An extremely prudent guardian of Dartmouth's financial well-being, he saw the College safely through two world wars and the depression years. Among his administrative colleagues he was famous for his ability to reach into any one of several tall piles of papers on his desk and pull out precisely the document he was looking for. Besides presiding over the budget, which stood at more than $3-million in 1947, and Dartmouth's assets, which had grown from $6-million to $35-million while he was Treasurer, Mr. Edgerton supervised the expansion and remodeling of the College plant for nearly three decades and with but few exceptions was right on target in his financial projections. As Treasurer for thirty-three years he was himself an asset of Dartmouth College, but the new financial era beginning with President Dickey called for new budget and investment policies and for new fund-raising efforts. The changing of the financial guard, brought about by Mr. Edgerton's retirement, happened therefore at a propitious time.

In the Convocation address that opened Dartmouth's 180th academic year, on October 1, 1948, President Dickey departed from the short, informal talks he had given in the previous two years and launched a series of longer addresses—about national, international, and College affairs—which thereafter became a regular part of the opening exercises each fall. His 1948 address was noteworthy also because it was the second step in a planned progression of subjects that Mr. Dickey developed in his Convocation talks. He chose to speak of loyalty, as a follow-up to his remarks about humility the previous fall. In succeeding years he offered his thoughts about cooperation, maturity, hunger for learning, independence, creativity, community, fellowship, and leadership. The latent teacher in John Dickey had an outlet in these opening addresses, but the extent to which he got through to his youthful listeners must have been somewhat reduced by the precisely worded and elegantly structured way in which he expressed himself in formal addresses. The high seriousness of his message was clearly conveyed, but the chiseled form of his sentences sometimes left the listener beguiled by his style, rather than instructed by the substance of what he was saying. Caution and precision in the use of words were a natural by-product of President Dickey's legal training and State Department experience, but he had his own liking for carefully fashioned expres-

sion, often embellished with alliteration, balanced phrases, and para-
dox. The Dickey style was perfect for his short honorary-degree citations, which he insisted on writing himself. Almost without exception
they were gems of concise characterization and gracious tribute.

A reading of the Dickey citations gives one a sense of the delight, as
well as the care, that he took in preparing them. There is no better
example of this than the citation with which the President conferred
an honorary Doctorate of Laws upon Robert Frost at Commencement
in 1955. Although the poet had received a Doctorate of Letters from
Dartmouth in 1933, John Dickey so greatly valued the friendship of
Frost and so much wanted the personal satisfaction of bestowing a
Dartmouth degree upon him that a second honor was voted, making
Frost the first person in the history of the College to receive two honorary doctorates. In conferring the 1955 degree, President Dickey said:

"Coming to us as you do from having a Vermont mountain come to
you (at least in name), what dare we say or do? We could speak a word
of history and say that all your academic comings and goings began
right here in 1892. Or we might talk about Pulitzer Prizes, four so far,
or even about San Francisco and whether it was actually '74 or '75 that
you began to have your say. But it wouldn't matter much on what we
started, we'd soon find you pulling on some loose thread of truth that
caught your eye in the garment of our talk, and before you finished
pulling on that thread—well, there'd be a lot of truth laid bare. In a
sense that is what we really want to say: that you have done more good
teaching than any other man we know, teaching us to like and know
that which we do not know we know—a teacher who has always sort
of known that the hardest part of getting wise is being always just a
little otherwise. And so, because ours is a love long learned, Dartmouth
dares doubt that one honorary Doctorate of Letters is enough and
herewith, otherwise than ever before, adds in witness of all left unsaid
her honorary Doctorate of Laws."

For the subject of his 1948 Convocation address, President Dickey
chose loyalty, defining it as the temper in the steel of the true man and
an essential ingredient of effectiveness in the affairs of men. He made
one of his earliest references to the "place loyalty" of Dartmouth men,
to which he was to attach such importance as one reason for the College's strength and uniqueness. "Loyalty," he said, "is that quality in a

man which carries the bond of human solidarity beyond the reaches of knowledge and belief—indeed, even beyond the normal bounds of faith itself because faith rests on the assumption that all must be well, however incomplete or imperfect the proof of the moment. Loyalty, as I have said, goes beyond that; it is based on no such comfortable assumption. To the contrary, true loyalty only comes into play under less-favorable circumstances, when all is not or may not be well." Every human institution, including Dartmouth College, has its flaws and its problems from time to time, he added, but loyalty is the "protective lubricant" that helps to offset these imperfections.

In his 1948 address, President Dickey made one of his earliest public statements against the conspiratorial nature of international Communism, which later he characterized as reason enough for dismissing any college teacher who was an avowed Communist. While many were upset by investigation into un-American activities, he stated that "many of us do not see how this democracy can avoid the responsibilities of simple self-defense against the intrusion of conspiratorial methods in our internal affairs." Thinking of his own State Department service, he said that self-defense required "unquestioned political loyalty—in the sense of loyalty to country—from those who of their free choice accept the responsibility of serving this nation as employees."

Whatever Mr. Dickey had to say about international relations or this country's foreign policy was given a respectful hearing, because of the impressive record he had left behind him at the State Department and the promise he had shown as one of Washington's rising young public servants. Something of his stature can be gathered from the November 19, 1948 issue of *Foreign Policy Bulletin*, published by the Foreign Policy Association of New York. In it John Dickey is mentioned as a possible successor to Secretary of State George Marshall and as having the backing of executives of the CIO. In this journalistic exercise he was in the excellent company of Chief Justice Vinson, Dean Acheson, W. Averell Harriman, Lewis W. Douglas, and Justice William O. Douglas.

In addition to Convocation, the annual meeting of the general faculty soon after the opening of the college year was another occasion at which President Dickey traditionally spoke. This more informal talk was in essence a report on the state of the College. It customarily dealt with such matters as finances, admissions, financial aid, plant changes, and Trustee plans and actions. At the meeting of the general faculty on October 13, 1948, Mr. Dickey assured them that faculty compensation was still of major concern to him and that the administration was cooperating with the Dartmouth chapter of the American Association of University Professors in its study of the economic status of the teaching staff. He also reported that the agenda for the fall meeting of the Board of Trustees would include consideration of a proposal that the College put into effect a compulsory, contributing retirement system, which would replace the voluntary plan then covering only a fraction of the faculty. To make a thorough study of this problem, Max A. Norton, Assistant Treasurer and Bursar of the College, had been granted leave of absence. By the end of the academic year the details and financial implications of an improved retirement plan for faculty and administrative officers were still being worked out, but the Trustees did approve the recommendation of Mr. Norton that the College underwrite most of the cost of a lesser retirement program for non-academic personnel who had been on the staff for three or more years. At the same time, the Trustees approved a revised group life insurance system that raised to $10,000 the coverage for each full-time faculty member and administrative officer. This placed Dartmouth near the top of institutions providing such protection.

In the course of his report to the faculty at the October 1948 meeting, Mr. Dickey mentioned an idea that he had been trying to sell to the Ivy Group presidents, without success. He expressed his concern that colleges such as Dartmouth were subsidizing by fifty percent the cost, to the institution, of the education of all students, even those who were perfectly capable of bearing the full cost. "It seems to me both wrong practically and morally," he said, for an institution with financial problems to accept such a situation. This was an opinion he acquired very early in his presidency, but he had no success in getting his presidential colleagues to share it. "I've been talking this point of view in every meeting of college and university officials that I attend," he said, "and for a number of years I have been getting fairly cool treatment on it." Mr. Dickey brought up the subject again when he spoke to the Dartmouth Alumni Council three months later, but he admitted that such a radical change in the tuition fee could be accomplished only with the cooperation of other colleges, and there was little likelihood of it at that time.

In October 1948 the *Chicago Tribune*, which had done a series of articles on Harvard, Yale, and Princeton as hotbeds of New Dealism, turned its attention to Dartmouth. Colonel Robert R. McCormick sent his Ottawa bureau chief, Eugene Griffin, to Hanover to see what nefarious ideas were being taught at the College. The Great Issues Course was targeted for attack before Griffin even arrived, and when he discovered that the *Chicago Tribune* was being used in the Public Affairs Laboratory as a prime example of slanted journalism, the paper's heaviest guns were let loose on Dartmouth. The College was called "the newest seat of higher indoctrination in the New Deal cult of America-last internationalism" and Great Issues was depicted as propaganda for the international views of President Dickey, also as a smear campaign against the *Tribune*. The faculty came in for a cudgeling, being described as a bunch of socialists and globalists. The College had cooperated fully with Reporter Griffin during his extended visit, and other than advising the alumni in advance that a series of vituperative articles was about to appear, it took the *Tribune* attack in stride, as Harvard, Yale, and Princeton had done. An answer on behalf of all the attacked colleges appeared in the January 1949 issue of the *Atlantic Monthly*. Entitled "Libeling our Colleges," the article was written by Louis Lyons, curator of the Nieman Foundation for Journalism at Harvard.

For faculty and staff, much better news than that found in the press came in a November memorandum from President Dickey, saying that cost-of-living bonuses would be paid that month in accordance with a vote by the Trustees at their fall meeting. To all active full-time faculty members and officers of administration who were in service on July 1 payments of $300 were made to those married with children, $200 to those married without dependents, and $100 to those not married. Staff assistants and technicians were included with $100 payments. President Dickey wrote that the lump-sum payments represented the continued desire of the College to do everything possible to help lighten the burden of adjusting to increased living costs, but he added, "I regret that it must be emphasized that the financial outlook precludes any expectation that this kind of adjustment can be made again under foreseeable circumstances, even though living costs continue high." Similar lump-sum payments had been made in July 1946, soon after Mr. Dickey became president.

Every college year runs the risk of student tragedy, and Dartmouth had to live through the repercussions of an ugly incident, on the night of March 18, 1949, which resulted in the death of Raymond J. Cirrotta, a member of the senior class. In his dormitory room in Massachusetts Hall he was visited by a group of students who had a grudge against him, and in an ensuing fight he suffered a fatal head injury. The severity of his injury was not apparent at first, but Cirrotta's roommate, who had been away from the dormitory, found him in pain when he returned to the room less than an hour after the fight. He called a doctor who in turn asked the captain of the campus police to take Cirrotta to the college infirmary without delay. There it was decided that an operation was necessary, and although a highly competent medical team at the adjoining Mary Hitchcock Hospital tried desperately to save the young man's life, they were unsuccessful. The dormitory fight had occurred about 10:30 p.m. and Cirrotta died at 5:05 a.m. of brain damage, suffered apparently when he was knocked down and hit his head.

President Dickey was out of town at the time of the tragic event, and responsibility for handling the situation rested with Dean Neidlinger, who immediately made an effort, unsuccessfully, to reach Cirrotta's parents in Linden, New Jersey. Later, through a friend of the family, he was able to telephone reports of the condition of the injured student. By 2:00 a.m. all six of the undergraduates then known to have been involved in the incident were assembled at the infirmary, and because of the seriousness of what they had done, the Hanover police were notified. It was ascertained that some of the group had been drinking before going to Cirrotta's room, but that no one could be described as having been irresponsibly drunk.

President Dickey returned to town early in the morning, a few hours after Cirrotta's death, and took charge in a very firm way. He had asked that a designated group of administrative officers be waiting for him at the President's House when he arrived. Dean Neidlinger had prepared a rough draft of a statement to be made public, but this was discarded by Mr. Dickey, who felt that because of the legal action that was sure to follow, a shorter, bare-bones statement of the facts known at the moment was preferable. The Dean's chief concern was public disclosure, the President's was doing the right thing legally. Mr. Dickey wrote out a statement in longhand, and this was the basis for a news release that the College news service telephoned to the wire services and to certain metropolitan newspapers. The news release covered the essential facts of the tragedy and identified the students involved, who by that time had been indefinitely suspended pending court and College disciplinary actions. The brevity of the announcement had one unfortunate result; it led some to charge that the College was covering up, which led in turn to a greater influx of reporters than might otherwise have occurred and to some wildly inaccurate news accounts. *The Daily Worker* played up the story to the full, charging that racial bias was the reason for the fight, and the Italian language paper *Il Progresso Italo-Americano* ran a series of critical articles, which were reprinted by other papers. At one point in the series President Dickey felt impelled to make public denial that the College had withheld information from the authorities.

The students who went to Cirrotta's room that night were involved in varying degrees. Some had not entered the room, but the entire group was suspended indefinitely. The two men who had done the actual fighting were indicted for first-degree manslaughter and tried at different times at the Grafton County Superior Court in Woodsville, New Hampshire. On reduced charges, both received suspended sentences and were fined. At the time of the first trial two more students came forward and admitted that they had been part of the group but upon advice of legal counsel had not said so immediately. They, along with the other six students, were permanently separated from the College after the Committee on Administration hearings that followed the court trials.

Complete separation for all hands, without exception, was pushed hard by President Dickey, who was morally outraged by the irresponsibility of the eight students involved. He did not agree with those who thought that within the group there were varying degrees of guilt or with those, later, who were willing to consider readmission in some cases; and he made his view stick with the Dean's office and the Committee on Administration. At other times he had stated that young men had to learn by making mistakes, but in this case he believed there could be no excuse for an act so morally repugnant and so completely the opposite of the responsible community citizenship he had been urging upon Dartmouth men.

The Cirrotta case brought to a head John Dickey's feeling that the College's disciplinary penalties were being too lightly applied and that student behavior, particularly in the fraternities, needed stiffer oversight. For Dean Neidlinger, who had perhaps the toughest and most thankless job in the College administration, this presidential attitude only added to the burden of a job he had diligently filled for fifteen years. During the last four of those years there had not been a fully compatible working relationship or meeting of the minds with the President, such as had existed in the Hopkins years. Eventually, in March of 1952, Dean Neidlinger submitted his resignation to make way for someone who, as he said, "can approach these problems with fresh interest, fertile imagination, and uninhibited confidence." To Hanover friends he more succinctly declared, "It's just that I'm tired of being the Dean."

During the first four years of John Dickey's presidency, the addition of two new wings to the Thayer School of Engineering was the only major development of the college plant. Plans to enlarge and modernize Wilder Hall, home of the physics department, had been delayed by lack of funds to do the full job, but in the fall of 1948 the Trustees decided to go ahead and erect at the south end of Wilder a two-story brick addition that in the long-range plans for the physics department would primarily serve as a shop area, but which temporarily would provide laboratory and classroom space as well as shop space. This construction took place during the fall and winter of 1948–49.

In the summer of 1949 a third plant improvement was the remodeling of Crosby Hall, from a dormitory to an administration building to house the alumni offices of the College, which for some years had occupied cramped quarters on the top floor of Parkhurst Hall. Brought together in the fall, on the first floor of Crosby, were Alumni Records, the Alumni Fund, and the joint office of the *Dartmouth Alumni Magazine* and the Dartmouth News Service. To compensate for the loss of dormitory rooms in Crosby, the two upper floors of College Hall reverted to dormitory use and the NROTC headquarters located there were moved to the two upper "decks" of Crosby. Later, the Secretary of the College, in charge of all alumni affairs, moved his office from Parkhurst to Crosby, and the growing development program also took up residence there, thus consolidating all alumni activities in one building. All these moves freed a considerable amount of space in Parkhurst Hall and enabled President Dickey to settle his top administrative corps around him in more efficient and comfortable quarters.

By returning the opening of College to September, as 1949–50 began, the College took one more step toward getting back to a prewar state of affairs. Another sign was the diminishing number of veterans enrolled. Only three percent of the entering class of 705 men had been in military service, and of the 950 veterans enrolled for the fall semester the great majority were in the senior class and associated schools. Married veterans, residing in Sachem Village and Wigwam Circle, numbered 165 and were still an exceptional segment of the student body.

Just before the College opened on September 21, President Dickey spent two weeks in Mexico, where as a trustee of the Rockefeller Foundation he made a survey of the foundation's hybrid corn-breeding program. His colleagues in this study were Dr. Thomas Parran, former U.S. Surgeon General, and Dean William I. Myers of the Cornell College of Agriculture. After Mexico and getting the College back to its educational business, Mr. Dickey could take personal satisfaction in the start of two things he had strongly favored. One was a retirement plan for faculty and administrative officers, which became effective October 1. It provided for the College's matching up to eight percent of an individual's salary each month, to be invested with the Teachers Insurance and Annuity Association. Later on, the College assumed the entire cost of sixteen percent of salary being invested for retirement. This, with life insurance, health insurance, and a plan of college tuition for faculty children, gave Dartmouth the distinction of having the broadest and most generous package of fringe benefits among all the colleges in the nation.

The other action at the start of the 1948–49 college year was the inauguration of an "added fee toward the cost of education." The $75 fee, added to the regular tuition charge of $600, was remitted for all scholarship men. This to a modest extent was an implementation of

John Dickey's strong advocacy of "the basic principle of having those who can, bear a larger portion of the cost to the College of their education." Dartmouth's move attracted a good deal of attention among other privately endowed colleges, but there still was reluctance to follow suit. The *Yale Alumni Magazine* called it "a very practical step," but then made the very impractical suggestion that a larger added fee at Yale should be voluntary.

The fall brought further administrative reorganization. One change, recommended by a special committee and approved by the Trustees at their June meeting, involved the Dartmouth Outing Club. The other, of far-reaching importance to the College, was the creation of the Dartmouth Development Council, announced by President Dickey in a special report sent to all Dartmouth men. The objective of the D.O.C. reorganization was to retain within the control of the Club all activities and responsibilities of an undergraduate character and to transfer to direct College management all those enterprises patronized by the general public—the Outing Club House, Moosilauke Ravine Lodge, the Oak Hill ski lift, and Occom Pond ice skating. Mr. Monahan, General Manager of the D.O.C., was given the new title of Manager of College Outing Properties, which did not affect his other position as College Forester. An additional change was the merging of the predominantly graduate D.O.C. board of trustees and the predominantly undergraduate D.O.C. executive committee into a new board of trustees, made up of four undergraduates and four faculty-administration members, with authority to appoint an executive director of the club, who at that time was John A. Rand.

Creation of the Dartmouth Development Council was one of the events of the early Dickey years that set the College on a new course. It recognized the fact that reliance on the Alumni Fund and class memorial funds as the primary vehicles for fund-raising was no longer adequate, if Dartmouth was to achieve a new excellence in the educational world and to carry out the developments planned for faculty, curriculum, financial aid, and plant. The College's traditional forms of fund-raising must not be jeopardized, Mr. Dickey believed. "However," he added, "with the growing awareness of the needs which confront the College today and will face it tomorrow, it is all too clear that Dartmouth must see to it that her case does not go by default in the increasingly intensive search being carried on by all institutions of higher education for private philanthropic assistance." The new Development Council, he pointed out, "has accepted the reality that college fund-raising has become a highly competitive business and that success comes only to those colleges most effectively organized for work. The source of this organization is manpower, in and out of Hanover."

Sigurd S. Larmon, whose election as Trustee had been hailed as giving the College new leadership in the effort to improve its financial resources, was named chairman of the Dartmouth Development Council. Sidney C. Hayward was appointed director and George H. Colton secretary. The Council's executive committee also included two other Trustees, four members of the Alumni Council, the Treasurer of the College, a faculty representative, and one non-alumnus. At the beginning, seven additional alumni were elected to the Council for five-year terms, to serve in special capacities.

One of the first actions of the new Council was to seek guidance from the Board of Trustees as to the most pressing needs of the College. The board gave top priority at that time to additional endowment funds and gifts for scholarship aid. Next in order came endowment for faculty and staff salaries, and then funds for plant facilities. With regard to scholarship aid, President Dickey pointed out that in 1941–42 the average cash aid awarded to an entering freshman was $395, while the comparable award for the current year 1949–50 was $700, an increase needed simply to equalize the difference in costs. For the same years, he reported that the annual cost of faculty and staff salaries, retirement, and other benefits had risen from $1.55–million to $2.68–million, and that the maintenance of growth of this magnitude was precarious without a substantial increase in endowment. Next to the new physics laboratories, Hopkins Center was stated to be the most-needed addition to the physical plant, but the board was opposed to any general appeal to the alumni for that purpose until the other priority needs had been met.

Although establishment of the Development Council marked a definite turn in the College's policy about raising money, there still was reluctance to mount a capital campaign of many millions that would take care of all three top-priority needs. Protection of the very successful annual Alumni Fund was part of this hesitation, but there also was an underestimation of Dartmouth's ability to bring off such a campaign. Perhaps Dartmouth lost valuable time while other colleges were raising millions, but once the new development program got organized and scored its share of successes, it proved to be one of the lasting contributions of the Dickey presidency.

An early step taken by the Development Council, after it had settled into its job, was the formalizing of a Bequest and Estate Planning Program in the fall of 1951. Led by Nichol M. Sandoe Sr., a committee of the Alumni Council initiated this move and established the policies and framework for its operation. The one person most deserving of credit for promoting this form of financial support was Ford H. Whelden, who for some years had pushed the idea in his own Class of 1925. When he retired to the Hanover area and took on the job of Director of Research for the Dartmouth Development Council, he was in a position to help get the plan adopted by all classes twenty-five or more years out of college. A bequest chairman became one of the regular officers of each of these classes. The potential of the Bequest and Estate Planning Program became evident in its second year, when $650,000 was realized—a 250-percent gain over the first year. Since 1951, when the program became active, the College has received $200-million in bequests, life income gifts, and other benefactions. Equally productive results have come from the attention the Development Council has given to corporations, foundations, and the parents division of the Alumni Fund.

During a fall that witnessed significant beginnings, *The Dartmouth* brought the issue of fraternity discrimination clauses to the fore of campus discussion. After a front-page editorial entitled "Where Do We Stand?" it joined forces with four other undergraduate organizations to conduct a simple poll to determine whether the student body favored the elimination or maintenance of charters restricting fraternity membership on the basis of race or religion. The poll had an excellent response from 2,359 students and found that 1,754 or 74.3 percent of them were for elimination. More referendums were to follow, but in September 1949 the first big step was taken toward the eventual elimination of any dictation by a national fraternity regarding the membership of its Dartmouth chapter. After the poll, President Dickey stated his pleasure in the initiative taken by the students, and expressed his support in terms similar to his earlier declaration: "This College neither teaches nor practices religious or racial prejudice and I do not believe that it can for long permit certain national fraternities through their charter provisions or national policies to impose prejudice on Dartmouth men in their free selection of their fraternal associates."

Near the end of the first semester, the faculty held a special meeting to consider a change in the language requirement for the A.B. degree. The existing requirement was the satisfactory completion, in secondary school and college, of the equivalent of four years' work in one foreign language or a total of five years' work in two foreign languages. Although this rule had obtained for twenty-five years, it had the possible drawback of unequal treatment, and the faculty therefore adopted the simplified proposal, from its Interdivisional Committee for Study of the Curriculum, that in order to secure the bachelor's degree "a student must have demonstrated the ability to read with understanding a representative passage in a foreign language." Each entering freshman had to take a qualifying test, on the basis of which the department concerned could either certify his language proficiency or require him to take language courses to attain it. The student was permitted to take the qualifying test at the end of any semester, and upon passing it he was excused from any further language study. In adopting the new requirement the faculty took the position that the chief value of language study was the ability to read the language with understanding. Since that time, both the purpose and methods of language study have undergone a vast change, to the point where fluency in speaking a foreign language has become as important as any other course objective.

In the spring of 1950, President Dickey was faced with the need to name a new Librarian of the College, to succeed Nathaniel L. Goodrich, who was retiring after thirty-eight years as Dartmouth's head librarian. Once again, he made a wholly unexpected choice, as daring as any he had previously made in filling major administrative positions. The person he selected was Richard W. Morin, Executive Officer of the College and Mr. Dickey's chief assistant in the President's office. Mr. Morin had no professional library training, but he had exceptional administrative ability, as well as a background in literature and the arts, plus his State Department service abroad and in Washington. However, despite his array of talents, the unconventional appointment of Mr. Morin led one professional librarian among the alumni to lodge a strong protest with President Dickey. He later wrote a letter of apology for basing his objection on false assumptions, without appreciation of the qualities of the new librarian or any knowledge of the objectives of President Dickey and Dean Morrison in picking him. Mr. Goodrich, the outgoing librarian, also had difficulty in understanding what Mr. Dickey was up to. In a letter to the President, he wrote: "Before the public announcement of my successor is made would you give me an opportunity to ask you some questions about him? The reason is this: I shall be deluged with questions, and there will be protests. I want to make things as easy as possible for him. At present, even after a half-hour's talk with him, and what Morrison has said, I feel as though all I could do would be to shrug my shoulders. I want to do better than that." In due course, all hands, within and without the College, came to appreciate the wisdom of John Dickey's choosing Mr. Morin, who as Librarian for sixteen years very capably administered the library and directed its growth in ways that were called for by the new direction in which Dartmouth was headed.

As part of that new direction, perhaps the student body was demonstrating a more adult attitude toward its educational opportunities. At any rate, the Dartmouth faculty was willing to take a chance on it, and in April 1950 it eliminated the age-old system of required class attendance and made attendance a matter between the student and the instructor. Under the new plan, as devised by the Committee on Administration, the student was informed that he was "expected to attend regularly the scheduled meetings of the course in which he is enrolled and conscientiously give these academic engagements precedence over all other activities." The instructor was relieved of keeping attendance records and filing a report of absences with the Dean's office, but he was assigned the responsibility for initiating disciplinary action because of unsatisfactory class attendance and for keeping "unlimited cuts" from weakening the educational work of the College. One part of the new regulation that students did not appreciate was the power given to the instructor to reduce a man's grade because of unsatisfactory class attendance. Letters to *The Dartmouth* decried connecting the two and argued that successfully handling the work of the course was all that mattered. During the deliberations by the faculty it was proposed that there be a separate attendance requirement for freshmen, but it was decided that the sooner the first-year men met their college responsibilities the better.

Before the college year ended, another part of prewar Dartmouth was restored when President Dickey named ten members of the Class of 1951 to be Senior Fellows, a selected group of fourth-year men permitted to pursue their studies in their own unrestricted way. And a part of postwar Dartmouth underwent a change when, in preparation for the fourth year of Great Issues, Professor Arthur E. Jensen of the English department replaced Mr. Dickey as chairman of the steering committee. The President was still lecturing in the course and was scheduled to launch another year in September with a talk on "Liberal Arts and Great Issues." Since the first years of the course guest speakers were being drawn somewhat more heavily from the academic world, but noted government figures, journalists, scientists, labor leaders, and business executives were still coming to Hanover to share ideas with the senior class.

When the United States, in June 1950, became the leading participant in United Nations military action to halt North Korea's aggression against South Korea, many uncertainties were created for the College. The main concern during that summer was the extent to which a draft of young men for military service would affect enrollment. When the college year opened in September, it was clear that enrollment for the time being would be affected very little, but the possibility that the conflict could grow into another great war gave President Dickey, the faculty, and students no reason to believe that there was nothing to worry about. Undergraduate interest in joining ROTC rose markedly, and the Navy increased to seventy Dartmouth's quota for "contract" trainees—who were men selected for NROTC after entering college, as opposed to "regular" NROTC students who won their places in a nationwide competition and entered college as midshipmen receiving Navy pay. Remembering the actions taken by Dartmouth at the outbreak of World War II, President Dickey proposed to the Trustees that application be made for both Army and Air Force ROTC units to join NROTC on campus. One reassurance that, for 1950–51 at least, there would be no drastic attrition in enrollment came from a Selective Service ruling that students under 21 were not likely to be called and that those 21 or over would be deferred until June 1951, if they remained in good academic standing. And, so, the year began with a drop of only 127 from the 2,936 men studying at Dartmouth the year before. The presence of veterans was reduced from 730 to 250, and only ten entered with the Class of 1954.

The Korean war naturally had a place in President Dickey's 1950 Convocation address, but he spoke also of the privilege of being at Dartmouth and told his student audience that amidst world problems bigger than themselves "there is a grace in the universe which stands with men who face front." That is the way Dartmouth men, at a time of national crisis, have always faced, he asserted. Mr. Dickey saw the vote by the United Nations Security Council authorizing military action against North Korea as an event of the greatest historical importance, and he saw the absence of the Soviet Union, depriving itself of a veto, as a colossal diplomatic blunder.

"I suggest to you," he said, "that in the long view of history, the core tragedy of World War II was not simply that war came again, but rather, that when it came it was not fought as a League war against the aggression of an outlaw. The United Nations is still a most dubious 'union,' but imperfect as it is in theory, structure, and practice, the fact is, I think, that the events of the last three months may conceivably have brought the world to the point where collective security can become a demonstrated reality and where, even if there must be further international strife, it can at long last be fought and won on Lincoln's basis: the preservation of a union.

"If this be a possibility within the reach of today's diplomacy, it is only so because of what appears, to me at least, to be the most colossal blunder in the history of Soviet diplomacy—and possibly better explained as a providential intervention in the affairs of men at a truly critical juncture. I refer, of course, to the fact that the Kremlin, through what must have been a bureaucratic blunder of unparalleled proportions, saw fit to deprive itself of a voice—and thereby, of a veto—in the Security Council of the United Nations at the very moment that it gave the North Korean communists the go-ahead signal for armed aggression. Here was one of those 'breaks' in life which no man could foresee and no informed person in his right mind could even imagine happening. But it did. Moreover, let it be noted that never has American diplomacy shown to better advantage than it did that night in taking this case of aggression, and the cause of peace, to a U.N. capable—for the moment, at least—of meeting its highest responsibility. And it did. It just could be that the future can be so fashioned that June 1950 will be one of the great dates in human progress. I know of no greater irony in all history than that this possibility should have come about through the fortuitous juncture in Soviet policies of the special brands of aggressive wickedness and bureaucratic weakness seemingly inherent in totalitarian government."

Despite the serious concerns forced upon it from beyond the campus, the College settled down to business, part of which was more of the administrative reorganization that President Dickey had set as one of his goals. This time the change involved the financial offices of the College. Treasurer John F. Meck announced in October that a new Office of the Comptroller was being established and that Robert D. Funkhouser, formerly Assistant Bursar, would head it. The move was made to relieve the Bursar's office of some of the multiplicity of responsibilities it had acquired over the years, with income-tax withholding, group life and medical insurance, a retirement system, and upcoming Social Security coverage all added to the collection and disbursement of College funds. Under the new division of duties, the Bursar retained primarily those of business management, while the Comptroller took over all accounting functions. Mr. Norton as Bursar and Assistant Treasurer continued to hold those positions, with the aid of LeRoy G. Porter as Assistant Bursar. The post of Assistant Comptroller was assigned to Mason I. Ingram, who had been Assistant Bursar. Some weeks after the financial reorganization, President Dickey announced that Edward T. Chamberlain Jr. would fill the position of Executive Officer of the College, which had been vacant since Mr. Morin left the President's office to be head librarian. Chamberlain, who had been Assistant Director of Admissions and then Assistant Director of Athletics, was given oversight of all activities and programs that might develop at Dartmouth in relationship to government mobilization plans. He himself had been a Navy officer in World War II and had commanded a PC boat in the Pacific.

On the evening of November 7, 1950, President Dickey took to the air waves, via Station WDBS, to inaugurate a campus radio series, "The President Reports," designed to enable him to communicate with undergraduates more often and more informally than was possible at the few formal occasions that existed during the college year. "The substantial good which I seek," he told his audience, "is a little better opportunity to get across to you as an individual Dartmouth student a few of the facts and considerations which can make your experience here a better and more meaningful one." He elected to talk about College finances in his first chat, explaining the part that student fees play in the whole financial picture and the vital role of the Alumni Fund each year. In his second radio talk, on December 13, Mr. Dickey discussed the impact of the Korean war on the College and was in a rather pessimistic mood. He expected that conditions on the campus would be drastically altered for the coming year, with student enrollment reduced by twenty-five to fifty percent, because of national mobilization. "It is the best judgment of those of us who are working on these things," he said, "that Dartmouth must plan for the worst next year, namely, the loss of a large part of the student body without anything like a full offsetting of that loss by armed service training programs." It was essential to begin planning for adjustments in programs and personnel, he stated. A drop of twenty-five percent in enrollment would mean a loss of better than $400,000 in student fees, not counting a heavy loss in dormitory rentals. Mr. Dickey spoke of Dartmouth's fine relations with the Navy during World War II and at the current time with NROTC, but he saw no prospect of any sizable expansion of the Navy unit for the coming year. He disclosed that the College had offered its facilities to both the Army and the Air Force, should they decide to establish new ROTC units in the colleges. All in all, the tone of the President's second "fireside chat" was not optimistic, but he did his best to reassure students, and the faculty and staff as well, that the College was not idle in seeking some diminution of the difficulties that an all-out war would bring.

Not long after this radio talk, Dartmouth learned by means of a newspaper story out of Washington, on January 8, 1951, that it had been chosen by the Army for an ROTC unit in ordnance. Official confirmation provided few details, except that the unit would be relatively small and would give preference to men who were planning to major in engineering or one of the sciences. Three months later, on April 21, a wire from Thomas K. Finletter, Secretary of the Air Force, informed President Dickey that Dartmouth had been selected for one of the new Air Force ROTC units, to be established on college campuses in the fall. Although the size of the unit was not given, it was expected that the Air Force ROTC would be the largest of the three units at Dartmouth. Like the Army program, it offered two years of basic training before an advanced program in one of three Air Force specialties—Flight Operations, with some fifty hours of primary flight training in senior year; Comptrollership, of interest primarily to Tuck School men and economics majors; and Administration and Logistics.

When things got under way in the fall, the total number of students enrolled in the three military programs turned out to be much larger than first estimated. The grand total was 1,094 students, of whom 580 were freshmen. The Air Force led with 520 trainees, followed by the Navy with 340, and the Army with 234. This impingement of the military upon the normal liberal arts program of the College made some members of the faculty unhappy, but all recognized that amidst the uncertainties of war the stability provided by the ROTC units was something to be thankful for.

A rumor that fifty members of the faculty were to be let go spread through the College after the Trustees had requested a review of staff requirements. To nip this false report in the bud, Dean Morrison issued a statement that thirteen faculty members would not be returning in the fall and that unless the drop in enrollment was greater than expected, the total reduction of the teaching staff would not exceed twenty. The faculty meanwhile approved the creation of a Committee on Emergency Adjustments, headed by Mr. Dickey, with authority to adjust the academic programs of individual students, to change the curriculum to meet the requirements of military training, and to decide if an accelerated program, involving a summer term, was needed.

At the beginning of the second semester President Dickey announced that an optional summer term would be offered, primarily for the benefit of entering freshmen, so they could get in as much college education as possible before being drafted or qualifying for deferment. In taking this action the College made it clear that it was not committing itself to a full-fledged accelerated program such as had been adopted during the previous war. In early May it became apparent that enrollment would be too small to justify a summer term, and it was called off. An earlier estimate of a summer enrollment of more than one thousand, including half of the entering freshmen class, had dwindled by May to fewer than 175 students. The main reason for the change was a clarification by Selective Service of the draft status of college men. It announced that it would hold to the policy of allowing qualified men to continue their studies, and to this statement was added the Congressional action setting eighteen years, six months as the minimum draft age, which meant that nearly all entering freshmen could wait until September to begin their college studies.

As one basic means of determining whether a student academically qualified for deferment, Selective Service in April announced that it would give a nationwide test prepared and administered by the Educational Testing Service, which conducted the annual college boards. The examination would be designed not to test factual knowledge, it was announced, but to test the ability to learn at the college level. Students in college would have a decided advantage, which led to an outcry that the Selective Service testing idea was undemocratic. This point of view was strongly expressed by President Conant of Harvard and President Dodds of Princeton. Mr. Dickey, although agreeing that a steady flow of college-trained men was in the national interest, expressed the fear that the new deferment plan might increase anti-intellectual feeling, directed against the colleges. In the April 10, 1951, issue of *The New York Times* he was quoted thus: "Such misunderstanding will breed irresponsible and dangerous attacks on the whole system of higher education. I agree emphatically with the objective of maintaining a flow of trained men through our colleges and universities at all times. But many of us believe that there are better ways to reach that objective. Specifically, I think that prompt action on pending manpower legislation along the lines of the bill passed by the Senate would go far toward

meeting the serious needs of the nation while avoiding the worst possibilities of a sour public attitude on deferment of those who must be
kept at work on higher education studies."

The first of the commanding officers of Dartmouth's three ROTC
units was named in late spring. Lieutenant Colonel William B. M.
Chase, a 1937 West Point graduate, arrived in Hanover to assume the
faculty position of Professor of Military Science and Tactics and to
organize his staff and program for the fall. He commanded an infantry
battalion in Europe in World War II, transferred to the Ordnance Corps
after the war, took his M.B.A. degree at the University of Michigan,
and came to Dartmouth from the Ordnance Tank-Automotive Center
in Detroit. To command its Dartmouth ROTC unit, the Air Force named
Colonel Jack C. Hodgson, who came to Hanover from Mitchell Air Force
Base, New York, where he was air liaison officer for the First Army.
During World War II he was senior military attaché to the American
Embassy in Ottawa and later commanded the U.S. Army Forces in
Canada. The third of the commanding officers was Navy Captain Mur-
vale T. Farrar, who saw World War II service aboard the battleship
Nevada and the aircraft carrier *Lexington* and was planning officer on
the staff of the commander of amphibious forces in the Southwest
Pacific. Prior to his Dartmouth assignment he was commandant of the
NROTC unit at Rensselaer Polytechnic Institute. When college opened
in the fall, President Dickey welcomed all fifteen ROTC staff officers to
the faculty as full-fledged colleagues and was pleased, as was the faculty, by their support of the liberal arts along with military education.
Colonel Hodgson was particularly outspoken in his advocacy of the
liberal arts and won plaudits by saying that anyone majoring in Greek
would be welcome in his Air Force program.

Before the college year 1950–51 closed, Dartmouth had two new Life
Trustees, and several other changes occurred. The Life Trustees, both
of whom were in their second terms as Alumni Trustees, were Harvey
P. Hood of Boston and Dudley W. Orr of Concord, New Hampshire.
Their service on the board began under President Hopkins and was to
have great importance during the Dickey presidency. Shortly before
the board changes, Trustee Larmon turned the chairmanship of the
Dartmouth Development Council over to H. Richardson Lane of Boston, a member of the Council's policy committee.

The job of getting the administrative staff advantageously settled continued with some interior remodeling of Parkhurst Hall, so that departments operating on two floors could be consolidated on one. The most important move brought Dean Morrison to the second floor in close proximity to President Dickey. Every office except that of the Registrar was involved in the general shuffle, which provided more efficient working conditions.

The opening of Dartmouth's 183rd year on October 1, 1951, was quite unusual for the number of important initiatives going into effect. Not only were the new ROTC programs beginning, but a new Department of Russian Civilization was being launched, and so was the William Jewett Tucker Foundation, an enterprise honoring Dartmouth's ninth president and something close to the heart of John Dickey. Other innovations were the shifting of Freshman Commons from College Hall to Thayer Dining Hall, the first use of Wilder Hall's new north wing (to go along with the southern wing completed the year before), and even the inauguration of the brand-new and beautified Nugget Theater on South Main Street—a far cry from the Wheelock Street structure that was the locale for movies and peanut fights for generations of Dartmouth men. The Hanover Improvement Society displayed a fine sense of sentimentality and fun when it opened its new movie palace with a Charlie Chaplin silent film and had Bill Cunningham, Class of 1919, at the piano, just as he had been when the original Nugget opened back in 1916.

Establishing a Department of Russian Civilization was one of the major curriculum developments of postwar Dartmouth. It was the culmination of more than two years' work by a special committee named by President Dickey in the fall of 1948. It offered not only the first inter-divisional major in the history of the College, but also a number of courses for general election, among them a one-semester "Introduction to the Soviet Union." Support for the program came from the Carnegie Corporation of New York, which made a three-year grant of $50,000. Part of the grant was to be devoted to training a teaching staff for a field comparatively new for an undergraduate institution and part to building up Baker Library's Russian collection. The major was not designed to develop area specialists, such as were being trained in university graduate schools, but rather to offer a program fitting into the general-education curriculum of a liberal arts college. The planning committee in its statement of purpose had said: "In view of the existing relations between the United States and the Soviet Union, knowledge of the Soviet system is an essential part of the educational experience of American college graduates. . . . The committee believes that Dartmouth has a responsibility to increase understanding in this vital area." The committee's view was in accord, of course, with John Dickey's belief about the place of the whole sweep of international relations in a liberal arts curriculum.

A special feature of the Russian Civilization major was the requirement that everyone take the intensive Russian language course, which covered two years of college Russian in one year. Like most of the courses in the Russian program, this was open to general election after the freshman year. Fifteen courses in all were included in the Russian Civilization curriculum, and to teach them the department pulled together, in addition to its own staff, top-ranking professors from history, government, economics, sociology, geography, the humanities, and the languages. To be chairman of the new department President Dickey named Dimitri von Mohrenschildt, Professor of Russian History and Literature. Newly appointed to the department to teach the intensive language course and a course in Soviet literature was John N. Washburn from the Russian Institute of Columbia University, assisted by Nadezhda Koroton, who taught Russian language, literature, and history courses in her native land before coming to America as a refugee. Signs of student interest in this new field of study were manifested in the fall when nearly one hundred men enrolled in the one-semester "Introduction to the Soviet Union" and the number of electors of the intensive Russian language course necessitated an extra section.

Dartmouth alumni who had been students under President William Jewett Tucker had for many years urged the College to create a fitting memorial to him. When the Trustees in the mid-twenties decided to go ahead with the building of a new library, it was proposed by some that the library bear the name of Dr. Tucker. When a million-dollar gift for the library was made by George F. Baker, in honor of his uncle, Fisher Ames Baker, that settled the name of the library. Later, when the idea of a Hopkins Center was approved by the Trustees, it was proposed that one unit of the building be a Tucker memorial; but President Dickey was among those who thought this inappropriate, since Dr. Tucker deserved a memorial that would stand on its own. It was Mr. Dickey more than anyone else who had the idea of the William Jewett Tucker Foundation to promote the moral and spiritual growth of Dartmouth undergraduates. Nothing could have been closer to what President Tucker hoped to do while he was head of the College, and nothing could have had a purpose in which Mr. Dickey believed more completely. Trustee Beardsley Ruml took a special interest in the foundation and had a part in working out its form and statement of purpose.

An already existing Tucker Foundation, connected with the Alumni Fund, was dissolved by the Trustees, and its modest endowment of $120,000 was transferred to the new foundation as a nucleus for building up a much larger fund. The expectation of having an endowment capable of fully funding the foundation's program has never been realized, but the College has maintained its commitment to the Tucker Foundation and has provided support from its general funds. The program to be carried out by the foundation was nebulous at the start, and to propose ways in which its purpose might be accomplished President Dickey named a planning committee, headed by Professor Francis L. Childs, who had been a student at the College during the Tucker presidency. Although religion was one component, the Tucker Foundation's general purpose was considerably broader, embracing the ethical aspects of the curriculum, extracurricular activities, and the whole range of student life. As the foundation developed, it sponsored chapel speakers, lectures and conferences, student discussion groups, tutoring in the local schools, student help for the sick and needy in the Hanover region, fellowships, and internships. Its work took students as far afield as the economically and educationally deprived neighborhoods of New Jersey, and when the Sixties arrived it played an activist role in the defense of human rights.

When President Dickey announced establishment of the Tucker Foundation at the annual meeting of the General Alumni Association on June 23, 1951, he declared that a moral and spiritual purpose had been an intrinsic part of Dartmouth College for nearly two centuries, and that it had never been set aside, however much changing conditions had modified the ways of achieving it. Once again he showed his deep concern, bordering on preoccupation, with the contending forces of good and evil in the world. "The moral and spiritual purpose of the College," he said, "springs from a belief in the existence of good and evil, from faith in the ability of men to choose between them, and from a sense of duty to advance the good."

In his Convocation address opening the 1951–52 academic year, the President commented further on the Tucker Foundation and took the occasion to tell his student audience something about President Tucker, "who led Dartmouth to the promised land of contemporary greatness at the turn of this century." He credited Dr. Tucker with "accomplishing nothing less than the founding of the modern Dartmouth and the refounding of her ancient glory and greatness, which he happily lived to see brought to fruition, far beyond his dreams, under the inspired and inspiring leadership of his disciple, the President-Emeritus of this College, Ernest Martin Hopkins.

"It is not possible on this occasion to characterize Dr. Tucker except in the most sweeping words, but of this we can be sure, he was truly a moral man who possessed and radiated the personal powers of spiritual vision, courage, and conviction. A man of God, who as a teacher was subjected to trial on a charge of theological heresy, he has left us a heritage of goodness and strength. . . ."

The bringing together, so to speak, of Dr. Tucker and John Dickey by means of the Tucker Foundation was an especially felicitous turn of events. Not only were they in accord about the essential place of moral purpose in the life and work of the College, but their two administrations shared the distinction of being pivotal ones in Dartmouth's history. With each of these two Presidents the College not only was rejuvenated, but it turned a corner and took off in a new direction, realizing its potential more fully and attuning itself to the contemporary world. In each case, also, the new direction gave the institution the chance to demonstrate fresh thinking and innovative programs and, thus, to enhance its distinction among the liberal arts colleges of the nation.

The Board of Trustees at its October meeting elected two new Alumni Trustees. They were Lloyd D. Brace, Class of 1925, president of the First National Bank of Boston, and Thomas B. Curtis, Class of 1932, a U.S. Congressman from Missouri. Their election filled the vacancies created when Mr. Hood and Mr. Orr became Life Trustees. Not counting the

President and the Governor of New Hampshire, the board was now evenly divided between Trustees elected under President Hopkins and those elected under President Dickey.

An event that took officials to the College's northernmost outpost, the Dartmouth College Grant in Coos County, New Hampshire, was the September 23 dedication of a long-needed management center for the timber and wildlife activities conducted there. The center was a gift from the Charles Lathrop Pack Forestry Foundation of New York, and Mr. Dickey was present to accept it from Randolph Pack, president of the foundation. It provided working and living quarters for the college forester and others responsible for managing the 27,000-acre grant, and it has been a serviceable and much-used facility ever since its dedication thirty-nine years ago.

The outdoor assets of the College were augmented in a most unusual way when, under the will of Colonel Henry N. Teague, Dartmouth 1900, the summit of Mt. Washington became the property of Dartmouth College. The bequest also made Dartmouth the owner of other properties which, under the corporation of the Mt. Washington Club, included the cog railway to the top of the mountain, the base station at Fabyan, New Hampshire, and the summit hotel. What the College would do with these properties was an unanswered question at the time the Teague will was admitted to probate, but there was immediate recognition of the educational value of the Mt. Washington summit, particularly in view of the College's growing interest in arctic studies. Eventually, the cog railway was sold to Colonel Teague's assistant, and after some years of owning and making educational use of the top of the mountain, the College agreed that the State of New Hampshire should be allowed to purchase it and place it in the public domain. Colonel Teague's will had two stipulations: one, that with funds realized from his bequest the College acquire a painting of Daniel Webster arguing the Dartmouth College Case before the U.S. Supreme Court; and, two, that a loan fund be established for the benefit of students at the Tuck School, from which the colonel had been graduated in 1901, as a member of its first class of three men.

The Dartmouth, which was enjoying a plentiful supply of front-page news in the first weeks of the fall semester, gave its readers something out of the ordinary in its "Vox Populi" column of October 15. The President of the College hardly ever indulged in a letter to the editor of the student daily, but there over the signature of John S. Dickey was a letter commenting on a *Dartmouth* editorial denouncing the removal of the University of Chicago student editor because of his participation in an international Communist program. Mr. Dickey felt impelled to point out that in the same circumstances at Dartmouth he "would not wager very much on the assumption that a different course would be followed here than has been followed by the official college and the undergraduate authorities at the institution in question." He went on to write: "May I just add that this departure from a strict policy of neither associating the College with nor disassociating it from individual undergraduate utterances is strictly *sui generis* and not a precedent." *The Dartmouth*, desiring the last word, responded that if the action at Chicago was right, it should have been taken by the paper itself and not by university authorities.

Returning to matters academic and administrative, the College announced that beginning with the Class of 1956 it would require all candidates for admission to take the scholastic aptitude test of the College Entrance Examination Board. The Committee on Admission and the Freshman Year, which made the decision after a lengthy study, emphasized that the requirement would not replace any part of the Selective Process, but would have its greatest value in providing supplementary information in marginal cases. The so-called SAT test was, in fact, not especially new to Dartmouth's admissions process; seventy-six percent of the freshman class of that fall had taken the college boards. More significant than the test requirement itself was the indication that Dartmouth, which had gone its own way for so many years, had taken another step toward conforming to the ways of sister institutions, especially those making up the Ivy Group.

President Dickey, who had begun his series of campus radio talks the year before, gave the first of his "fireside chats" for 1951–52 on January 10, soon after students had returned from the Christmas recess. These talks were scheduled for 10:30 p.m., when most undergraduates were in their rooms and able to listen. After speaking briefly about the administration's willingness to have an honors system, if the students really wanted one, Mr. Dickey devoted a considerable part of his talk to intercollegiate athletics, expressing succinctly his philosophy of their place in college life. "I think it is hardly necessary," he declared, "to more than say that Dartmouth believes in intercollegiate sports; we believe in the value of the will to win in honorable competition; we want good teams but we know that our fortunes will vary from year to year and from sport to sport in healthy cycles so long as, and only so long as, our teams and the teams we meet are subordinate activities in the service of the purpose of institutions of higher education. Judged by these principles, I believe the state of intercollegiate sport at Dartmouth is essentially sound and we intend to keep it that way both by attending to whatever may need attention here from time to time and by joining our sister institutions in the Ivy Group in further developing the structure of common standards and practices which has governed football play within the group since 1945." He pointed out that the College was using general funds to support the program of intercollegiate sports and that "there seems to be no likelihood that football, at least as it is played by institutions of our character, can continue to attract enough spectators to support other sports in the style to which we became accustomed in the Twenties and Thirties."

As he had before, Mr. Dickey discussed Dartmouth's finances and gave warning that the gap between College costs and the revenue from student fees would have to be closed before long. Only a little more than two months later, on March 22, he announced that by Trustee action the "added fee toward the cost of education" had been increased from $75 to $200, effective in the fall. As before, the added fee was to be remitted for all scholarship students. The basic tuition fee was $600, bringing the total annual charge for instruction, educational facilities, and the health service to $800. With the increase in the added fee, the President moved closer to realizing his earlier proposal that students who could afford to pay the full cost of their college education should be asked to do so.

Another development soon after President Dickey's radio talk about intercollegiate athletics was the announcement in February of a new football agreement reached by the presidents of the Ivy Group. Most importantly, the pact eliminated spring practice and made more stringent the existing prohibition against post-season games for both players and coaches. It also abolished the holding of off-season clinics for high-school coaches. Among other items in the agreement, football practice would begin on a common date near the first of September; possible reduction of the number of games would be studied; the principle of control of athletics by academic authorities was reaffirmed; and the eligibility rule already in effect was stiffened to state that beginning in 1954 no student would be eligible to play football if, in return for attending a given Ivy League college, his secondary school education had been subsidized or his post-college education promised by an individual or group not closely related to the family.

The Dartmouth faculty thought it also should have its say about athletics, and this took the form of a rather voluminous report that the Committee on Athletics was requested to make. The gist of the report was that the status of intercollegiate sports at Dartmouth was healthy and in harmony with the educational objectives of the College. In particular, the faculty wanted to know if the academic work of athletes was suffering. The report found no appreciable difference between the grade standings of athletes and non-athletes. Indeed, the study found that the class standing of football lettermen from 1948 to 1951 was the second highest in the Ivy League.

The faculty also gave its attention to devising a grading system that would be more precise than the letter-grade system the College had been using since 1915. A number of proposals were put forward; one was for a numerical system of nine grades from 8 to 0 and another, more detailed, was for 21 numerical grades from 20 to 0. Another proposal, quite the reverse of what the faculty was aiming at, was for three grades: honors, credit, and failure. The faculty opted for splitting the grade of C into C+ and C− and for changing the all-A point average from 4.0 to 5.0. Because of degree requirements for classes already in college, two point systems had to be planned for the fall. C+ and C− both counted as 2.0 for men then enrolled, but for freshmen entering in September the grade of C+ would be 3.0 and C− would be 2.0. Thus, by faculty tinkering, that campus celebrity, the 4.0 man, lost his academic distinction to the 5.0 man.

As the college year neared its close, the Undergraduate Council tried to get the students' final approval of an honors system, which it had voted in January and which the Faculty Council had approved. The undergraduates were not in an acquiescent mood, however, and the fifty-eight percent who voted for an honors system was well short of the seventy-five percent needed to put it into effect.

A significant addition to the Board of Trustees took place with the election of Charles J. Zimmerman, Class of 1923, of Hartford, Connecticut, as Alumni Trustee at the June 1951 meeting of the board. Mr. Zimmerman, a nationally prominent insurance executive, was another of the men nominated by the Alumni Council to strengthen the board in an area where it needed more drive and expertise. His election, filling the vacancy created by Nelson Rockefeller's completion of two terms, was to have profound influence in creating a whole new attitude toward capital fund-raising, something about which Dartmouth had been timid up to that time. He also brought a fresh conception of the level of financial support that Dartmouth alumni and friends could be expected to give. Mr. Zimmerman, former chairman of the Alumni Fund and a member of the Tuck School Board of Overseers, was managing director of the Life Insurance Agency Management Association at the time he became a Trustee of the College. Among many distinctions, he received the John Newton Russell Award, highest honor in the insurance field; was past president of the National Association of Life Underwriters; and in 1942 was chosen "Insurance Man of the Year" by the publication *Insurance Field*. Dartmouth's fund-raising sights were lifted several notches with his coming to the board.

The Trustees' June meeting also produced quite a burst of administrative changes. Notable was approval of the appointment of Justin A. Stanley, Class of 1933, a Chicago lawyer, to be Vice President of the College with responsibility for directing Dartmouth's entire development program. At the same time, the Trustees gave vice presidential rank to Treasurer John Meck, naming him Treasurer and Vice President of the College. Mr. Stanley was just completing his term as president of the Dartmouth Alumni Council. He took his law degree at Columbia University, and in addition to being a partner in one of Chicago's leading law firms he was on the faculty of the Chicago-Kent College of Law.

Among Mr. Dickey's keen interests as President was the shaping of the College's administrative staff into a better and more effective organization. The process began in his very first year when the death of Dean Strong necessitated creating two different positions out of one. The retirement on June 30 of Professor Francis J. Neef as director of both financial aid and the personnel bureau provided another such opportunity for reorganization. A new Office of Placement and Staff Personnel was established, with Donald W. Cameron named to head it. Mr. Dickerson, Director of Admissions, was assigned the additional duties of chairman of the Committee on Scholarships and Loans and given responsibility for the entire financial aid program. Mr. Hage, Assistant Director of Admissions, was named executive secretary of the scholarship committee and placed in charge of a new Office of Financial Aid. The reorganization involved no new top-level personnel, but made possible more detailed attention to the multiple responsibilities held by Mr. Neef and also produced the sort of consultative and coordinated conduct of business that Mr. Dickey had learned to value while with the State Department.

The resignation of Mr. Neidlinger as Dean of the College, submitted in March and accepted by the Trustees at their spring meeting, became effective at the end of the academic year, at which time the deanship was assumed by Professor Joseph L. McDonald of the economics department, who reluctantly gave up teaching to provide an important service to the College and to his good friend, John Dickey. This change closed out eighteen years of administrative work for Dean Neidlinger. During his tenure he had encouraged and helped fashion a more responsible student role in undergraduate governance and campus life, as exemplified by the postwar Undergraduate Council, the dormitory committees, and the revived fraternity program. The College Health Service, established in 1936 and headed by Dean Neidlinger during its first eleven years, was another of his major contributions. When the country was preparing for World War II and during the actual war years, he had top responsibility for advising Dartmouth men about military service. In tribute to him, President Dickey said: "Dean Neidlinger has been a truly devoted servant of Dartmouth. He has made contributions to the welfare of the College community and individual students which go beyond any man's knowledge and appreciation."

Professor McDonald, the new Dean, was a member of the Dartmouth faculty for twenty-nine years before turning from teaching to administrative work. He came to the College in 1923 after teaching economics at the University of Pennsylvania and the University of Minnesota.

From 1927 to 1949 he taught both undergraduate courses and at the Tuck School, where he held the title of Professor of Foreign Trade. As helpful attributes for the deanship, he was faculty representative on the Athletic Council and had a lively interest in sports and in student affairs to go along with the academic side of his job. He was popular with the undergraduates and had a sense of humor which was to stand him in good stead in handling the problems that gravitate toward the Dean's office. In choosing an older faculty member to be Dean of the College, President Dickey once again followed his own path and did the unexpected.

Vintage Years

AS the College began its 184th academic year, in late September of 1952, the national presidential race between Dwight D. Eisenhower and Adlai Stevenson was nearing its end. The Eisenhower victory held greater import for Dartmouth than anyone could have predicted; come June, the new President of the United States was in Hanover to receive an honorary Doctorate of Laws and to speak to the graduating class.

When this historic year opened, John Dickey was only a few weeks shy of having been Dartmouth's President for seven years. Behind him was a period of solid achievement. Great progress had been made toward rebuilding the faculty and meeting the need for better compensation and a long-range salary policy for both faculty and staff. The Great Issues Course, inaugurated in the fall of 1947, was in full swing and was nationally recognized as an innovative and successful educational venture. Effective, and in some instances daring, administrative appointments had been made, and the whole administrative structure was undergoing review and reorganization, particularly with regard to admissions and financial aid, the business offices, development, and public relations. The William Jewett Tucker Foundation had been established, and a new Faculty Council and a new Undergraduate Council had come into being, with specified responsibilities in the governance of the College. Of great importance was the changed character of the Board of Trustees, to which new members had brought special talents and more active concern for specific areas of the College that needed development.

Quite the opposite of what prevailed when he arrived in Hanover seven years earlier to begin being "the fellow on this job," John Dickey was now very definitely a known quantity to faculty, administrative colleagues, students, and alumni. His stamp on the College was increasingly pronounced, and his character and his way of doing things were understood and appreciated by all constituencies of the College. The faculty, which had stood and applauded when he first described the Great Issues Course to them, respected the intellectual qualities and aspirations of the President, and they were with him in his desire to advance Dartmouth's academic excellence and to have its education program give greater emphasis to international relations and public affairs.

The open-door policy of the President's office was one indication of the informal, approachable nature of John Dickey—and this side of his character was demonstrated even more strikingly by his being the only Dartmouth President in history to help build a center-of-campus ice statue for Winter Carnival. Faculty and administrators were accustomed to seeing the President peel off his jacket when he got down to business at a meeting, and eventually they were no longer surprised at his habit of keeping an unlighted cigarette in his mouth—a practice he adopted when he gave up smoking. (Almost beyond counting were the number of times people came up to him with a cigarette lighter, only to be baffled when he responded, "Thank you, but I don't smoke. I just play with cigarettes.")

The President had a sense of humor, and it was a rather endearing trait of his to begin laughing even before he had finished telling a story, and then, at the end, to slap his knee and laugh louder than anyone else. In characterizing John Dickey, friends and colleagues invariably spoke of his integrity. Associated with that quality was the fact that he was a person of great moral rectitude, concerned that good should prevail over evil.

As the academic year 1952–53 began, the College itself also had settled into its new job—that of educating men for the postwar era. Undergraduate enrollment of 2,653 in the fall of 1952 was near normal, but with more than half of these young men enlisted in the Air Force, Navy, and Army ROTC units, reminders of the war years still remained. President Dickey, speaking at Convocation, told his student audience that they enjoyed a special privilege by being in college while other American boys were fighting in Korea. His main theme, however, was "The Business of Being a Gentleman," which, he said, "has a deep and direct bearing on whether you ever become a liberally educated man."

He was talking about manners, he added, not in any foppish way, but in the sense of self-discipline, concern for others, and sensitivity, all of which are part of "the ancient tribute 'a gentleman and a scholar.'"

In John Dickey's eyes, bad manners were indefensible. They were just as prevalent among nations as among individuals, he told his Convocation audience, and in deploring them, he made one of his earliest statements condemning Communism. "Since the Bolshevik revolution of 1917," he said, "the society of nations—except for minor and illusory interruptions—has had nothing but thirty-five years of decline in the level of international manners." Soviet diplomacy had, in his estimation, "repeatedly led the nations to new lows in a type of diplomatic roughhousing which is now endemic in such relations as remain between the non-communist world and the Soviet bloc." A few months later, at a meeting of the Chicago alumni, and again in a radio talk on campus, he expressed his anti-Communist feelings more fully and more forcefully while discussing higher education and national security.

In effect when the 1952 fall semester opened was a new agreement adopted by the presidents of the eight Ivy Group institutions. It renewed and strengthened their earlier agreement to ban spring football practice and post-season games, and created a Presidents' Policy Committee that gave responsibility for athletic policy to the presidents themselves. The use of the phrase "Ivy Group" and the agreement that each member would meet all other members in football at least once every five years were seen by the press as steps toward formalizing what was already known as the Ivy League. Four years later the Ivies did establish the league by agreeing to schedule all members in football each year, and at that time the extension of the league idea to other sports began. With strict eligibility rules for players and restrictions on recruiting, the Ivy Group presidents set the highest standards in the nation for the conduct of intercollegiate athletics, in keeping with the purposes of higher education.

President Dickey on many occasions expressed his belief that athletics, properly controlled, had a valuable place in the undergraduate, liberal arts college. At the same time that the Ivy Group developments were taking place, the Dartmouth Trustees established academic control of intercollegiate athletics and vested full responsibility in the President, representing the board. This meant the end of the Dartmouth College Athletic Council as an autonomous controlling body, the sole remaining council of its kind among the Ivy colleges. Its conversion into an advisory body had been made inevitable by the Ivy Group agreement and the Dartmouth Trustees' assumption of financial responsibility for the intercollegiate athletic program. A DCAC deficit of $79,710 for fiscal 1951–52 had been covered by general college funds, and there was small likelihood that the Athletic Council could ever again be self-supporting. Under the new arrangement, the Director of Athletics became an administrative officer of the College, appointed by and responsible to the President.

At Dartmouth Night in October, the night before the Rutgers game, football had its prominent place in the program, but the gathering was primarily one honoring Daniel Webster, on the 100th anniversary of his death. It provided President Dickey with an appropriate occasion for announcing the establishment of twenty Daniel Webster National Scholarships to be awarded annually to outstanding applicants from all parts of the nation. He also announced that an anonymous gift of one million dollars would provide approximately half of the endowment for the scholarships, which were to be held for all four years and were to vary in amount according to financial need. In a few cases, it was stated, a Daniel Webster Scholar without financial need would receive a prize award of modest amount, in recognition of unusual achievement and promise as a student and citizen. The inclusion of good citizenship among the criteria for an award was one more evidence of the importance John Dickey gave to it, in his concept of the goals of liberal education. When he received an honorary Doctorate of Laws at a Wesleyan University convocation in honor of scholarship earlier that month, he was cited for his "restless preoccupation with an education that will make young men intelligent and responsible citizens" and also for "the indelible impact you have made on Dartmouth and the enduring sense of responsibility for good citizenship you will instill in scores of her sons." The Wesleyan degree was the fifth Doctorate of Laws conferred of Mr. Dickey since he had assumed Dartmouth's presidency. Those received earlier were from Amherst, Brown, Middlebury, and Tufts.

With the establishment of its Daniel Webster National Scholarships,

Dartmouth took an important step forward in its enrollment and financial-aid programs and joined the other members of the Ivy Group in offering grants of national distinction. John Dickey had pushed scholarship aid, along with faculty compensation, from the very beginning of his administration. Because the student body was so largely enrolled in ROTC, only $26,700 of scholarship money had been expended in his first year. Seven years later, at the time of the Webster anniversary announcement, scholarship aid exceeded $300,000, and all financial aid, including loans and college employment, totaled a half-million dollars. Raising endowment funds for scholarships had a high priority in the efforts of the Dartmouth Development Council, but the College was ready to use general funds to keep the financial-aid program moving ahead.

In the eyes of Dartmouth's long-suffering hockey fans, something more urgently needed than scholarship funds was artificial ice in the Davis Rink; and to their great joy the Trustees in November 1952 approved a low-key campaign to raise $110,000 to fulfill that dream. One year later, President Dickey, with puck in hand, stepped gingerly to center ice, between the line-ups of Dartmouth and Harvard players, as play began and the rink was reactivated, never again to be at the mercy of the weather outside. The Development Council, with the rink financing well in hand, moved in an entirely different direction late in 1952, when Dartmouth played a leading role in establishing The New England Colleges Fund, Inc., a regional consortium of twenty-three independent colleges seeking financial support from business and industry. The new organization was designed to supplement, not replace, the regular fund-raising programs of the separate colleges, all of them devoted primarily to liberal arts education.

President Dickey continued to look upon his radio talks over Station WBDS as an effective way to be in touch with the student body about "the life and affairs of the College in a fairly intimate, direct way." On the evening of March 13, 1953, he delivered a talk more carefully prepared than any he had given before. It dealt with American higher education and national security, and was a written version of views he had been expressing in his winter swing of Dartmouth alumni clubs. In fact, he attached such importance to the talk that he read the text of it to the faculty at an informal meeting that afternoon. It covered the relationship of Communist affiliation to teaching qualification, the invoking of the Fifth Amendment of the Constitution, and the investigative authority of the national government. This took place at the time when Senator Joseph McCarthy of Wisconsin was raising havoc with his wholesale and unsubstantiated charges of subversion and Communist infiltration in the U.S. government, the military services, colleges, and other institutions, and before he was brought down by the condemnation of the U.S. Senate in December 1954.

"I feel that any institution owes a duty to itself and to the society which it serves to be clear about where it stands with respect to the qualifications and disqualifications of its members in a matter of this sort," President Dickey stated. "If I believed that membership in the Communist Party today involved merely a matter of minority and unpopular political affiliation, I should be clear that it was not, *per se*, a disqualification for a teacher. But I do not believe that this is in fact the case. Since 1947 I have been on record that I would not knowingly be a party to hiring a person who accepts the discipline of the Communist Party. . . . I took that position and I hold it now because I believe that the evidence is overwhelmingly persuasive that a person who accepts the obligations of membership in a conspiratorial group, committed to the use of deceit and deception as a matter of policy in the pursuit of its ends, is basically disqualified for service in an enterprise which is squarely premised on the functioning of a free and honest market place for the exposition, exchange, and evaluation of ideas."

Concerning the various public agencies that deal with problems of subversion in national life, President Dickey said he could see no general basis on which colleges and universities could, as a matter of legal right, claim to be exempt from proper governmental investigation. The line between proper and improper procedures is often a blurred one, he added, but even so, the principle should be clear that institutions of higher education are not sanctuaries beyond the law, and that the cause of academic freedom is done a great disservice if doubt about that is left in anyone's mind.

As a third main point, Mr. Dickey stated it to be his position that any person who invokes the privilege of the Fifth Amendment of the Constitution when asked a legally proper question raises serious doubt about his or her qualifications for employment as a teacher. It also calls into question the quality of one's citizenship. If such a situation arose at Dartmouth, President Dickey asserted, he would feel it necessary to take steps with the Faculty Committee Advisory to the President and the Board of Trustees looking to either the suspension or termination of the employment of such a person, depending upon the circumstances.

He concluded what he obviously thought a very important statement of policy by reminding his listeners "that there is another duty, a large, positive, persuasive duty that goes with the daily work of this business, and that is to see to it that the honest and independent-minded scholar who is deemed by his colleagues to be professionally competent is not driven from the market places of higher education because his views are unpopular in the eyes of his critics."

President Dickey's talk was not prompted by any specific problem on the Dartmouth campus. Academic affairs were moving along without excitement, although headlines were made when the College in 1953 permanently acquired the celebrated Stefansson library on the polar regions. Other newsworthy events were the replacement of the unwieldy Faculty Council with a twenty-member Faculty Executive Committee and the establishment of an interdivisional Northern Studies Program, with anthropologist Robert A. McKennan as director. The Stefansson library, which had been on deposit at Baker Library since 1951, was purchased with funds given by Albert Bradley, executive vice president of General Motors Corporation. It contained 25,000 volumes, 20,000 pamphlets, and valuable manuscripts dealing with the Arctic, the Antarctic, and the permafrost areas of the world. Its addition to Baker's permanent resources gave Dartmouth an international importance in studies of the polar regions, particularly the Arctic, and a few years later the collection was to be a factor in the U.S. Army's decision to locate its cold regions research center in Hanover. For the Northern Studies Program the Stefansson library was a great asset. Students and faculty were privileged to work with materials so rare that an estimated one-fifth of the published items were not to be found in the Library of Congress. For its new program, which amplified Dartmouth's working ties with Canada, the College also had exceptional physical assets in

Mt. Moosilauke, the College Grant at the northern tip of the state, and the summit of Mt. Washington.

President Dickey at this time was scheduled to make a speaking tour of Dartmouth alumni clubs on the Pacific Coast, but since he was in need of a respite from his college duties, he and Mrs. Dickey spent a week in Mexico City and Acapulco in mid-April and then traveled to California by train. Mr. Dickey took with him the knowledge that President Eisenhower had accepted the College's invitation to receive an honorary degree at Commencement in June and that an extremely busy period of preparation awaited him upon his return to Hanover. Because of the multitude of details to be worked out, the regular Commencement committee was expanded and headed by John Dickey himself, with Vice President John Meck as vice chairman. One of the very first decisions was that the Bema, normal site of Commencement and seating slightly more than two thousand, would be wholly inadequate for the crowd of perhaps five thousand or more that would undoubtedly want to attend the Sunday morning exercises. Graduation was, therefore, shifted to the lawn in front of Baker Library, where a canopied platform was constructed and ample seating space was available. Commencement has been held on the Baker lawn ever since.

Local rumors of the Eisenhower visit were confirmed by an official White House announcement on April 29, 1953. Soon thereafter, Secret Service men began to arrive for an exhaustive scrutiny of Commencement plans and the places where the President would be, particularly the President's House, where Mr. Eisenhower was to be the overnight guest of the Dickeys. The President's special plane, the *Columbine*, made several practice landings at the Lebanon airport, to make sure it could safely land and take off there. Preparations also had to be made for the planeload of press people accompanying the President. A group of about forty were housed in South Massachusetts Hall, fed in Thayer Hall, and given the Little Theatre in Robinson Hall as a press room. The press room, as it turned out, was the scene of frenzied activity immediately after the Commencement exercises. President Eisenhower, going beyond the brief remarks expected of him, gave an impromptu address that produced headlines all over the country.

Accompanied by Sherman Adams, Class of 1920, his chief of staff,

President Eisenhower flew to Hanover from South Dakota, arriving Saturday evening about 8 p.m. (an hour late because his plane had to slow down in order to allow the press plane to land first). There was still ample daylight for cheering crowds to see him as he rode from the Lebanon airport to the College in an open car. Tanned and smiling, he stood when he reached Hanover's Main Street and was given a rousing welcome all the way to the President's House, where he and his party spent a quiet evening.

Very early Commencement morning, before most of Hanover was up and about, President Eisenhower, in the company of Mr. Dickey, Mr. Adams, and Robert S. Monahan as tour guide, took a drive about campus. Stops were made at Baker Library and at the ski jump, where Tommy Keane, the golf pro, was waiting with two sets of clubs in case the President wanted to try a hole or two of the College course. Mr. Eisenhower did not yield to the temptation, and the party headed back to the President's House to get ready for the graduation exercises. On the way they made a surprise stop at the home of Dr. John F. Gile, Dartmouth Trustee, whose illness made it impossible for him to attend Commencement and meet the President. The weather that morning was as perfect as a June morning could ever be, and the College, with its green lawns, stately elms, and Georgian architecture, was shiningly beautiful. "This is what a college ought to look like," President Eisenhower declared during his motor tour.

The thousands of seats assembled for the graduation exercises were none too many, and except for the places held for the faculty and the graduating class, the lawn in front of Baker Library was packed long before the Sunday morning exercises began. In the academic procession to Baker, President Eisenhower was escorted by President-Emeritus Hopkins. Six other honorary-degree recipients, escorted by Dartmouth Trustees, were Lester B. Pearson, Canadian Secretary of State for External Affairs and president of the General Assembly of the United Nations, who gave the Commencement address; Judge Joseph M. Proskauer, chairman of the New York State Crime Commission; John J. McCloy, former president of the World Bank and former United States High Commissioner for Germany; Grenville Clark, lawyer and distinguished citizen; Sherman Adams; and Hugh Gregg, Governor of New Hampshire.

As part of the citation with which President Dickey conferred the honorary Doctorate of Laws upon Mr. Eisenhower, he said: "The eminence of the Presidency precludes the bestowal of greater honor and all too often fends off even those words of encouragement and gentle praise on which each man's life is somewhat borne forward. May we not, however, mark this historic Dartmouth day with these few words for your remembering: no great captain ever gave to free men everywhere such confidence in the reality of their collective strength for the common defense of God's peace."

In accepting Dartmouth's invitation President Eisenhower indicated that he did not wish to make an address, but he did agree to speak briefly to the graduating class. When he rose to make his remarks to the men of the Class of 1953, he told them: "I am going to talk about fun—joy—happiness: just fun in life. And I am going to talk a little about courage." When he got to the subject of courage, the President was warming up to something more important than "a few remarks." This country, he said, is a long way from perfection. "We have the disgrace of racial discrimination. We have prejudice against people because of their religion. We have crime on the docks. We have not had the courage to uproot these things, although we know they are wrong." To the graduates in front of him he urged the courage to look at things as they are and to do something about them.

And then the President, going beyond all expectation of what he might say in a short, informal talk, electrified his audience by asserting, "Don't join the book-burners. Don't think you are going to conceal faults by concealing evidence that they ever existed. Don't be afraid to go in your library and read every book as long as any document does not offend your own idea of decency. That should be the only censorship.

"How will we defeat Communism unless we know what it is, what it teaches? Why does it have such an appeal for men? Why are so many people swearing allegiance to it? It's almost a religion, albeit one of the nether regions.

"We have got to fight it with something better, not try to conceal the thinking of our own people. They are part of America, and even if they think ideas that are contrary to ours, their right to say them, their right to record them, and their right to have them in places where they are accessible to others is unquestioned, or it is not America."

The press corps was quick to spot the significance of President Eisenhower's impromptu statement supporting intellectual freedom. As the exercises ended and the principal participants went off to the President's House for luncheon, the press rushed to Robinson Hall to file stories that would be front-page news. The reporter for *The New York Times* called the story "a bell-ringer," and his report was the lead story in the next morning's paper. What first captured the attention of the press was the connection of the Eisenhower statement to Senator McCarthy's campaign to ban "un-American" books in the U.S. overseas information libraries. It also marked the President's taking public issue, at last, with Senator McCarthy's anti-Communist witch hunt.

When the importance and national attention given to President Eisenhower's remarks became apparent the following morning, many at the College began to wonder what had impelled him to speak as he did. Several persons who had been seated near the honorary-degree group disclosed that the subject of "book-burning" came up in a conversation between Judge Proskauer and President Eisenhower on the Commencement platform while the graduating seniors were filing into their places. Judge Proskauer expressed dismay that the State Department, under the pressure and threats from Senator McCarthy, was withdrawing "objectionable" books from the U.S. Information Agency libraries abroad. The President answered that he didn't believe this could be true, whereupon Judge Proskauer sought verification from Mr. McCloy, who said it was true that books had been withdrawn or destroyed in Germany. The President was silent for a moment and, then, said he would speak out on the subject, possibly during an address he was to give in New York State later that day. Perhaps, upon further thought, he decided that Baker Library was a more appropriate setting, and so his remarks were made at Dartmouth. Judge Proskauer, when President Dickey talked with him some time later at a New York dinner, confirmed that he had been the catalyst for the book-burning portion of President Eisenhower's impromptu address.

All in all, the Commencement weekend had gone wonderfully well, the result of detailed planning by a great many persons and the blessing of perfect June weather instead of the rain that had been forecast. President Dickey had been at the heart of the whole business; and Mrs. Dickey too, with her gracious manner and quiet efficiency, had handled her role of hostess admirably. Having the President of the United States as your house guest, with Secret Service men on the alert, inside and out, around the clock, was not an easy situation to cope with. In an article about Dartmouth's First Lady, written for the *Dartmouth Alumni Magazine* by Margaret Beck McCallum, Mrs. Dickey was persuaded to talk about having President Eisenhower as a house guest. Once the Eisenhower visit was confirmed, she recalled, "We had FBI and the Secret Service everywhere. Woodbury had to be cleared out completely because they thought it was too near our house, and our whole second floor was cleared. President Eisenhower slept in my bedroom and his valet in Sukie's and all the Dickeys moved up to the third floor.

"The night before the Commencement, Jack Bowler, Sherman Adams, and Mr. Eisenhower spent the evening talking with John, and later John and Mr. Eisenhower went on talking well into the night in John's study. I discreetly sat out in the morning room to be out of the way. And then the President sent his military aide to fetch me in to join them for an hour. It was very thrilling.

"We could hear the Secret Service men all the night before, rustling in the shrubbery around the house. I went into the garden early Commencement morning to pick a few fresh flowers, and there they were, under every bush! When Tina took Rusty (their golden retriever) out for a quick run, one of them said, 'My God, was *he* there all night?' I don't know if he thought Rusty was a threat to the President."

After Commencement, a resolution of thanks from the Board of Trustees and a personal word of appreciation from Mr. Dickey were conveyed to all the members of the seventeen different committees involved in making the Commencement plans. In return, a message bearing fifty-one signatures was sent to Mr. Dickey, with the salutation "To the Boss." It stated, "You are appreciated too," and then went on to say, "Without your leadership, without your warm and homey hospitality, without your right words and dignified representation of Dartmouth's deepest significance, all the pretty tickets in the world, all the rope in New England, all the policemen in New Hampshire, and all the Simmons mattresses in Hanover could not have made Commencement 'right' for the President of the United States, for the public, or for the Dartmouth family." And so, on a note of mutual congratulation and mild euphoria, one of the special years in the annals of Dartmouth history came to a happy close.

For a few days of carefree, outdoor relaxation after the strenuous weeks culminating in Commencement, President Dickey headed for the Dartmouth College Grant in northern New Hampshire. It had become his custom to go there with a few fishing friends at the close of the academic year. The previous June, for example, he had as his guests President Conant of Harvard; Edward Weeks, editor of the *Atlantic Monthly*; Laurence Whittemore, president of the Brown Company, which was logging the Grant for its paper mill; Trustee John F. Gile; and John Meck, the College Treasurer. Of all Dartmouth's presidents, John Dickey was the one who had the greatest personal interest in the Grant and who most frequently enjoyed the outdoor life there.

The Dartmouth College Grant, a forest area of 26,800 acres, was voted to the College by the New Hampshire legislature in 1807, with the provision that income from logging it be used to provide scholarships at Dartmouth for indigent youth of the state. To this original grant the College in 1985 added a few thousand adjacent acres from the tract known as the Academy Grant. The educational and recreational use of the area, available to Dartmouth students, faculty, and alumni, had the strong support of President Dickey, and some of his happiest and most relaxed days while carrying the burdens of the presidency were the ones he spent there. He loved the simplicity and informality of outdoor life and was glad to shed the business suit of a college president for the rough attire of an outdoorsman. This preference was sometimes evident in Hanover as well as in the Grant, to the consternation of some of the town's more strait-laced residents. A particularly striking portrait of John Dickey, painted in 1948 by Elmer W. Greene and now hanging in Baker Library, shows him wearing a plaid, open-necked shirt and looking every inch the hunter and fisherman he was.

Love of these sports began for John Dickey when he was growing up in Lock Haven, Pennsylvania. At the Grant he was mainly interested in fishing the Dead Diamond and Swift Diamond Rivers, although he occasionally went there in the fall for bird shooting. His association with the Grant was so firmly established that after his retirement from the Dartmouth presidency a part of it was named for him. Across from the Management Center a brass plaque on a granite boulder bears this inscription: "JOHN SLOAN DICKEY AREA, named in honor of John S. Dickey '29, Dartmouth College President, 1945–1970, in recognition of his love for and dedication to the out of doors. The area includes the Diamond Peaks, Diamond Basin and the Gorge. Dedicated September 17, 1976." A corner of the living room in the Management Center is known as the Dickey Corner and is decorated with photographs and memorabilia of him. That is where he preferred to sleep, although as boss of the whole layout he could have had any private quarters he wanted.

A perennial fishing mate at the Grant was Edward Weeks of the *Atlantic Monthly*, who wrote an article, "Fishing the Grant with John Dickey," for the special issue the *Dartmouth Alumni Magazine* published on the twentieth anniversary of the Dickey presidency. Mr. Weeks began his warm tribute to his friend thus: "One of the unpremeditated purposes of the Dartmouth Grant is to cool off the President after the rigor and festivities of Commencement. All Dartmouth Presidents are anglers—I assume it is a qualification for the job—but the two I have known should be classified as addicts. I never had the delight of fishing with President Hopkins, though we talked it whenever we met. But John Dickey has taken me up to the Grant for many a June and my love for the place and for the man has increased with each outing."

Besides the Grant, the other prime place of outdoor recreation for John Dickey was Swanton, Vermont, where the Dickeys had a cottage on Lake Champlain. There the family spent a month or so each summer, and there the President, with companions, could repair in duck-hunting season, which he looked forward to just as much as to fly-fishing. The two men with whom he most often hunted were classmate F. William Andres of Boston and Richard W. Morin, who came to Hanover to be Executive Assistant in the President's office and then Librarian of the College. The Connecticut River, closer to home, was another favorite spot for duck-hunting.

The cottage at Swanton doubled as a place where President Dickey could work without interruption, and it was there that he wrote most of his Convocation addresses and Commencement valedictories and honorary-degree citations. For his address opening Dartmouth's 185th year in September of 1953 he chose the topic of maturity, as a follow-up to the previous year's talk about manners and the attributes of a gentleman. Maturity, he said, is "that ultimate self-discipline which rules a free man." He told the students that nothing within their power was more important at that time than the measure of maturity that they could contribute to the national character. "I do believe," he said, "that you will have the really great experience of crossing the threshold of maturity in the company of your country."

At the start of the new college year Mr. Dickey announced further administrative reorganization, involving the incorporation of the venerable Department of Buildings and Grounds into a new Department of Plant and Operations. Richard W. Olmsted, with the title of Business Manager for Plant and Operations, was given general responsibility for the College's physical plant and the operation of dormitories and dining halls, and also for housing and purchasing. Five other appointments or promotions were made to assist him in the areas of maintenance, purchasing, and heating-plant engineering. Newly added to the college plant, to be supervised by the reorganized department, were the buildings and land formerly belonging to the Clark School, which had existed in Hanover for many years. They were purchased from the Cardigan Mountain School, which had acquired them in the spring. Most valuable of the seven buildings included in the purchase was the three-story brick dormitory on North Main Street, which was renamed Cutter Hall in memory of Victor M. Cutter, Class of 1903, a Dartmouth Trustee from 1933 to 1951. The large frame building at the corner of Elm and North Main Streets, now the site of Kiewit Computation Center, was named Fairbanks Hall in honor of Professor Arthur Fairbanks, who taught art at Dartmouth and was director of the Boston Museum of Fine Arts from 1907 to 1925.

President Dickey found himself making a lot of public announcements that fall, but none was more popular than the news that Robert A. "Red" Rolfe, Class of 1931, would be coming to Dartmouth on July 1 as Director of Athletics. The former third baseman of the New York Yankees, teammate of Babe Ruth, Lou Gehrig, and other Yankee greats, was named to succeed William H. McCarter, who after seventeen years in the athletic post was resigning to become Editor of Dartmouth College Publications.

In a radio talk to the College on December 15, 1953, Mr. Dickey announced the establishment of a Commission on Campus Life and Its Regulation. This was preceded by his discussion of the importance of the quality of one's social experience in college, particularly in the dormitories, and the need to find ways to improve it. The commission was instructed to give its attention to dormitory life and to review and appraise the entire body of rules and regulations governing the social life of the campus, something that had not been done since 1946, when the Navy V-12 Unit left at the end of the war and Dartmouth again became primarily a civilian college. Whether social privileges in the dormitories should be equal to those allowed the fraternities was one of the fundamental questions for the commission to consider, Mr. Dickey stated. Personally, he admitted to having serious misgivings about granting the same privileges in two such different situations.

One week after his radio talk President Dickey was hospitalized in the college infirmary with phlebitis. He was permitted to return to the office after a three-week stay, but on January 24 he had to return to Dick's House for another three weeks, because of a recurrence of his leg ailment. He was well enough to speak at the annual Boston alumni dinner in mid-February and at Alumni Fund dinners in Boston and New York in March, but his scheduled trips to more distant alumni centers were cancelled on his doctor's advice.

A fringe benefit of considerable importance to full-time faculty members and administrative officers was announced by President Dickey following the January meeting of the Board of Trustees. For many years Dartmouth had followed the practice of remitting tuition for the enrolled sons of members of the faculty and administration. In order to have a more equitable system, the Trustees voted to provide scholarship aid also to faculty daughters and to sons not attending Dartmouth. The amount of such aid was $600 a year for four years or the difference between that sum and any scholarship aid being received from the college attended. In addition to this program, Dartmouth became a participant in the Faculty Children's Tuition Exchange Plan, under which seventy colleges agreed to exchange students on a tuition-free basis.

That undergraduates could make a positive contribution to the educational program of the College was demonstrated in that same January when at the instigation of the Academic Committee of the Undergraduate Council the faculty voted to drop age-old Hygiene 1–2 as a freshman-year requirement and replace it with a course called "The Individual and the College." Hygiene 1–2 had been a degree requirement for decades and was celebrated in Dartmouth song variously as "Bowler's smut class" or "Pollard's smut class," so named for the doctors who taught it. In backing the one-semester course for freshmen, the Faculty Committee on Educational Policy stated that "there is a clear need for a more effective way of helping undergraduates to make the transition from home and secondary school to life in a residential college." In the words of the Committee, the course had three objectives: "the first portion of the course is concerned with the student's most effective use of his academic opportunities at Dartmouth; the second with selected topics of physical hygiene; and the third with topics concerning the attainment of maturity, as indicated in social responsibility and in a wholesome emotional and social outlook on life and its problems." Several years of work by the Academic Committee of the Undergraduate Council had paid off. One of the students involved was the Council president, David T. McLaughlin '54, who was destined to be Dartmouth's President from 1981 to 1987.

Student initiative again was the major factor in action taken to rid the Dartmouth fraternities of nationally imposed membership restrictions based on race, religion, or national origin. In a referendum conducted by the Undergraduate Council in March 1954, ninety percent of the 2,248 students voting supported the elimination of fraternity discrimination. Most of them backed the proposition that any fraternity chapter that did not within six years eliminate discriminatory clauses from its charter would be barred from all fraternity activities, including rushing. Fewer students backed a second proposition that the chapters be allowed, without a deadline, to continue their efforts to get the national fraternities to drop discriminatory clauses. The Dartmouth Trustees, at their spring meeting, accepted and approved the Undergraduate Council's recommendation that the 1960 deadline be adopted.

At his inauguration, John Dickey receives the Wentworth Bowl, symbolic of the presidency, from President-Emeritus Hopkins. John R. McLane, senior member and clerk of the Board of Trustees (center) witnesses the transfer.

President Dickey joins townspeople in clearing Main Street after a heavy snowstorm, January 1947.

J.S.D. entertains Dean Acheson, a Great Issues lecturer, at Winter Carnival, February 1948.

The President with (l to r) Dean of the College Lloyd K. Neidlinger, Dean of the Faculty Donald H. Morrison, and Dean of Freshmen Stearns Morse.

Mr. Dickey meeting with senior class officers in the President's Office in the fall of 1950.

President Eisenhower, with senior cane, leaving Hanover after Commencement, June 1953. With him are Sherman Adams, his chief of staff, and John Dickey.

President Dickey conferring the honorary degree of Doctor of Laws on Robert Frost, June 1955.

The Dickey family in 1955, on the tenth anniversary of J.S.D.'s presidency. Behind John and Christina Dickey are (l to r) John Jr., Sylvia, and Christina. Rusty, the family's golden retriever, was included.

John Dickey and President Eisenhower at a Dartmouth Grant cookout in June 1955.

The Dickey signature is added to the matriculation certificate of Peter Bulkley '59, in September 1955.

President Dickey receiving an honorary LL.D. at Harvard in June 1956. John F. Kennedy is among those in front row.

The Dickeys greeting Commencement guests at the President's House in June 1956.

J.S.D. and Mr. Hopkins aboard a bulldozer at ground-clearing for the Hopkins Center, October 24, 1958.

John Dickey duck hunting with classmate Bill Andres, 1959.

It was felt that progress during four years under the second option had been too slow. Only one chapter had succeeded in eliminating discriminatory clauses without severing its national ties. One other chapter had left its national organization and gone local.

President Dickey was pleased with the responsible role that student government was playing in the affairs of the College, and this to some extent brightened the period when he was forced into inactivity by his two extended stays in the college infirmary with phlebitis. In February he had named J. Ross Gamble to be his Special Assistant. Mr. Gamble had been with the Dartmouth Development Council since 1950, and development activities continued to be his primary concern, along with special assignments for the President. Within the year he was named Director of Development, taking over leadership in that area from Justin A. Stanley, who resigned as Vice President of the College in order to return to law practice in Chicago.

The Dickey administration was now in full stride, and the 1954–55 academic year, the President's tenth, was filled with significant developments. Mr. Dickey himself defined the years from 1945 to 1954 as a period of postwar adjustment and the years after that as a period of planning, growth, and looking ahead, particularly to the College's bicentennial. He opened the year with an especially interesting Convocation address that emphasized his preference for calling the liberal arts "the liberating arts." President Dickey had made this substitution on numerous occasions and was to continue to make it, but it did not catch on as he perhaps hoped it would. In his address he said, "Ours is the task to free, as well as to nourish, men's minds. This is why, as I have sought to understand Dartmouth's obligation to human society, I have come increasingly to think of our commitment of purpose as being to the *liberating* arts, rather than just the liberal arts. It is the active, liberating quality of these arts, I believe, that makes them the best bet for Dartmouth's purposes."

Although Dartmouth's bicentennial was fifteen years away, the Dartmouth Trustees at their October meeting took the first official step to prepare for it, by approving the creation of a Trustees Planning Committee, under the chairmanship of Trustee Harvey Hood. To serve as the committee's executive director, Mr. Dickerson was granted a year's leave of absence from his duties as director of the offices of admission and financial aid. Mr. Chamberlain, Executive Officer of the College, took over part of his work as Acting Director of Admissions. The charge to TPC, as it came to be known, was to review College operations from stem to stern and to prepare the blueprints for desirable development in the years leading up to 1969. The TPC came to have sixteen sub-committees. Mr. Dickey headed the first one, having to do with Dartmouth's purpose, and Trustee Dudley Orr was chairman of a sub-committee considering the optimum future size of the College.

In explaining the Trustees Planning Committee to the Dartmouth Alumni Council, President Dickey said: "We came to the point a year or so ago where it seemed to the Trustees, to myself and my administrative associates, and to many of you with whom we conferred, that Dartmouth was ready to begin a systematic, organized, sustained effort to plan her future in all critical areas of college life and work, so that come 1969 we would not simply hold a year of vain self-congratulation about what we were going to do in the third century, but that come Dartmouth's bicentennial in 1969, Dartmouth would celebrate because she had *produced* an undergraduate educational operation that was worthy of celebration as she moved from her second to her third century."

One member of the central TPC was Professor John P. Amsden, whom President Dickey had earlier named chairman of an Advisory Committee on Plant Planning. That committee was asked to make a study of the College's plant needs over the next fifty years. One of its top assignments was to take a new look at the Hopkins Center project, since changed conditions had raised doubts about the original idea of a large auditorium conjoined with a theater, a student union, music department headquarters, and a faculty club. Professor Amsden announced that his committee would review the entire project with regard to size, location, and activities within the center.

Later in the college year, after the Trustees' spring meeting, Mr. Dickey announced the first substantial building program of his administration, including the go-ahead for the preparation of preliminary Hopkins Center plans. Major items in the program to be carried out over the next year or two were new dormitories to house 230 men; alterations in two existing dormitories, Topliff and Middle Massachu-

setts; new faculty housing; and enlarged dining facilities in Thayer
Hall, in order to carry out the recommendation of the Commission on
Campus Life that sophomores, as well as freshmen, be required to eat
in Thayer. The plant program also called for some classroom improvements, the rebuilding of certain heating mains, and the remodeling of
locker-room facilities in Alumni Gymnasium.

Besides establishing the bicentennial planning committee, the Dartmouth Trustees at their fall meeting voted that the head of the Tucker
Foundation should have the rank of dean and that the foundation's
advisory committee should begin the search for the person to fill that
post. At the same time, approval was given to a one-year campaign to
raise $300,000 in support of the Tucker Foundation program. Alumni
leaders of the fund-raising effort were Charles E. Griffith as chairman
and Louis E. Leverone as vice chairman. The 1955 goal was viewed as
the first step in raising a substantial fund for both physical facilities and
endowment.

The fall Trustee agenda behind him, President Dickey was in New
York at the end of October to take part in the Charter Day convocation
closing the year-long celebration of Columbia University's bicentennial.
There he received an honorary Doctorate of Laws as one of the forty-
eight distinguished citizens from this country and abroad who were
given degrees. He was in the company of the Queen Mother of Great
Britain, West German Chancellor Konrad Adenauer, Belgian Foreign
Minister Paul Henry Spaak, Adlai Stevenson, and U.S. Chief Justice
Earl Warren.

President Dickey was without a right-hand man in his office after
Mr. Chamberlain left to be Acting Director of Admissions. In January
the vacancy was filled by Thomas E. O'Connell who became Executive
Assistant to the President. The former Undergraduate Council president came to the College from Philadelphia, where he had been administrative assistant to that city's director of commerce. Another
newcomer to the College staff, announced about the same time, was
Bob Blackman as head football coach. The choice of the head coach of
Denver University was preceded by several weeks of criticism of Dartmouth in the press because the contract of Coach Tuss McLaughry had
not been renewed. Because of several losing seasons in a row, sports
columnists charged, Dartmouth was bowing to alumni pressure, was

adopting a win-or-else policy, and was being unfair to McLaughry, one of the best-liked and most-respected coaches in the country. The Dartmouth Athletic Council answered that a new chapter in football had been under consideration for at least three years and had been discussed with McLaughry during that period, and the end of his five-year contract was deemed to be an appropriate time to carry out the contemplated change. As things turned out, the arrival of Coach Blackman marked the beginning of one of the greatest eras of football success in Dartmouth's history. Coach McLaughry remained at Dartmouth as Professor of Physical Education, an appointment backed by President Dickey and approved by the Trustees at their April meeting.

At their spring meeting the Trustees also filled a vacancy on the board, electing Dr. Ralph W. Hunter, Class of 1931, of Hanover to be a Life Trustee. He took the place of Dr. John F. Gile, who had died, and thus continued the tradition of having a resident of Hanover, in addition to the President, on the board. Dr. Hunter at the time was Medical Director of the College, a staff physician at the Hitchcock Clinic, and a member of the Medical School faculty.

Among the reports heard by the Trustees was one concerning the discussion Dartmouth officials were having with the Army Corps of Engineers about locating the country's principal cold regions research and engineering laboratory in Hanover. The Army planned to consolidate the work of the Snow, Ice and Permafrost Research Establishment located in Wilmette, Illinois, and the Arctic Construction and Frost Effects Laboratory in Waltham, Massachusetts, both civilian organizations under the Corps of Engineers. Dartmouth's chances of being chosen for the combined laboratory were enhanced by the academic personnel involved in the College's pioneer Northern Studies Program, by the availability of the Stefansson collection, and by the geographical assets of the College. The Thayer School of Engineering was another reason for locating in Hanover. It took a long time for Washington hurdles to be cleared, but it was finally announced, in the summer of 1957, that CRREL would be located in Hanover, and Congress at that time included an appropriation of $2,496,000 in the military construction bill it passed. Construction was to begin in June 1958, with January 1, 1960, as the target date for completion. The College made available some land it owned on Lyme Road, where the Record Farm formerly existed.

The heart of President Dickey's educational philosophy is to be found in the phrase "competence and conscience," and this got some national attention when he was featured on the cover of the *Atlantic Monthly* for April 1955 and wrote the lead article for that issue. His subject was "Conscience and the Undergraduate." For John Dickey the moral aspect of liberal learning continued to be a subject of intense interest, but when speaking of moral and spiritual purpose he much preferred the word *conscience*. This was used a great many times in his addresses and writings, and when teamed up with *competence* was a striking example of his fondness for alliteration. The main theme of President Dickey's article was that concern for choosing the good and rejecting evil is the historic and unique characteristic of an institution of liberal learning, as distinct from professional and technical institutions, or graduate schools of arts and sciences, where development of a special competence is the primary mission.

"Without attempting here the impossibility of conclusive proof," he wrote, "I suggest that the American liberal arts college (including the church colleges) can find a significant, even unique, mission in the duality of its historic purpose: to see men made whole in *both* competence and conscience. Is there any other institution at the highest level of organized educational activity that is committed explicitly by its history and by its program to these two goals?" The creation of competence at every level of education is commonplace, he added. "We could hardly stop it if we would. The appetite for self-interest will keep enough of us hungry for ever larger portions of competence. It is the job of the college to keep competence civilized." As a further point, he declared, "To create the power of competence without creating a corresponding sense of moral direction to guide the use of that power is bad education."

President Dickey admitted that a good deal of his own thinking about moral purpose in liberal education came from his exposure to Dr. Tucker's writings. Perhaps his adoption of the word *conscience* came from the same source. In his article he included this quotation from Dr.

Tucker: "Seek, I pray you, moral distinction. Be not content with the commonplace in character any more than with the commonplace in ambition or intellectual attainment. Do not expect that you will make any lasting or very strong impression on the world through intellectual power without the use of an equal amount of conscience and heart."

As the college year moved toward its close, announcement was made of further improvement in faculty and staff salaries. This was to be financed by an increase in tuition from $800 to $900, plus a general fee of $80 for the health service, student activities, and other services. The combined cost of tuition, room and board was estimated at $1,650, which put Dartmouth roughly in the middle of the Ivy Group.

The announcement about salaries was made jointly by Treasurer John Meck and Dean of the Faculty Donald Morrison, who himself became news when he was promoted to the newly created position of Provost of the College. Along with this important administrative innovation, effective July 1, it was announced that in September the position of Dean of the Faculty would be filled by Professor Arthur E. Jensen of the English department. Three other major administrative appointments, all to begin on July 1, 1956, were those of Mr. Dickerson to be Dean of Freshmen, Mr. Chamberlain to be Director of Admissions, and Robert K. Hage to be Director of the Office of Financial Aid. Mr. Dickerson's deanship was delayed until Professor Stearns Morse relinquished that post in order to return full-time to the teaching of English.

The naming of Dean Morrison to be Provost gave him an even stronger voice in the academic affairs of the College, and it was a recognition of the central role he had played in rebuilding the faculty and improving the educational program during his eight years as faculty dean. President Dickey found him a thoroughly compatible coworker and relied upon him heavily, not only in faculty and academic matters, but in all phases of administering the College. Not one to delegate authority readily, he gave Morrison an unusual degree of responsibility and had confidence in his thinking and in his implementation of policies decided upon. Creation of the position of Provost was intended to provide the President of the College with an officer of major stature who could assist in the overall supervision and coordination of academic programs in the undergraduate college and the three associated schools, and who could represent the President in educational policy matters. Separated by only two rooms on the second floor of Parkhurst Hall, the two men were in daily touch and enjoyed both the philosophical and pragmatic aspects of running a college.

Trustee Beardsley Ruml also had a close working relationship with Provost Morrison. As expressed by Mr. Dickey, "They hit it off and worked hand in glove." Mr. Ruml had been elected to the Board of Trustees because of his educational experience and curriculum interests. He and Morrison collaborated on a small book, *Memo to a College Trustee*, published in 1959 by The Fund for the Advancement of Education. It was a report on the financial and structural problems of the liberal college, and caused something of a commotion in academic circles by backing the board of trustees as the locus of final responsibility and authority and by asserting that the trustees should find some mechanism other than the collective faculty to which to assign responsibility for the curriculum. Competing, self-interested departments within the collective faculty are not likely ever to devise a good liberal arts curriculum, the authors wrote.

John Dickey's annual June fishing trip to the College Grant became a very special one in 1955 when President Eisenhower joined the party for lunch. The President had been the guest of his Secretary of Commerce, Sinclair Weeks, in Lancaster, New Hampshire, and was on his way by motorcade to a fishing club in Maine. His visit lasted only an hour and a half, but he thoroughly enjoyed it and had the fun of donning a Dartmouth Outing Club jacket and cooking his own trout. The President declared that cooking trout was one thing he was good at, and calling for cornmeal, salt and pepper, he wrapped the prize catch of the previous day in aluminum foil and broiled it on the coals of the outdoor fire. Those who had a taste of it admitted that Mr. Eisenhower was not overstating his skill. Tom Dent, the Dartmouth soccer coach, who quickly struck up a nickname friendship with the President, made Ike laugh by asking him if he was available to be the cook on Dent's next fishing trip. The President also took a great liking to Sam Brungot, the Norwegian fire patrolman at the Grant and a North Country character. Quite a large group had been invited by President Dickey to enjoy broiled trout, cornbread, beanhole beans, salad, and pie which made up the menu. Among those at the party were President-Emeritus Hopkins, Sherman Adams, Sinclair Weeks, Senators Norris Cotton and Styles Bridges of New Hampshire, Senator Fred Payne of Maine, Governor Lane Dwinell of New Hampshire, Edward Weeks, Robert Cutler, Laurence Whittemore, Edmund Ware Smith, and James Hagerty, plus a sizable contingent from the College, including Stewart Sanders '56, undergraduate head of the DOC. A lively account of Mr. Smith's participation in the Grant gathering appears in his book, *A Treasury of the Maine Woods*.

The inexorable march of college semesters resumed in the fall of 1955 with the largest enrollment in the history of the College, slightly ahead of the total in 1947, when men flocked back to their studies after the war. The grand total of 3,007 included a record undergraduate enrollment of 2,793. To these men President Dickey, in his convocation address, spoke of the Trustees Planning Committee and the comprehensive review that was being undertaken in anticipation of the bicentennial. As a very succinct description of the spirit in which the TPC was beginning its work, he said, "The anniversary date is 1969–70, but the target of our planning is today and the tomorrows between now and that time. The Trustees of the College have decided that Dartmouth's bicentennial should mark not merely the completion of two centuries, but rather, that it should also be the culmination of fifteen years of sustained rededication and refounding, a unique period of intensive planning and development aimed at bringing this institution to a running start of preeminent performance when it enters a third century."

For John Dickey that autumn marked the tenth anniversary of his assuming the office of President, and high praise was voiced for what he had achieved in the first Dickey decade. At the regular meeting of the full faculty in October he undertook his own review of the ways in which Dartmouth had been strengthened, while mentioning also some of the College's unfulfilled needs. On the plus side, he began with the gains that had been made in faculty salaries and in faculty recruitment. The percentage of entering freshmen receiving scholarship aid had risen from seventeen percent for the Class of 1949 to twenty-five percent for the Class of 1959, and progress was being made toward the goal of thirty percent. Mr. Dickey cited the new enrollment efforts sponsored by the Alumni Council and the steady growth of the for-malized development program which began in 1949. His summary included the Great Issues Course and the fact that the College was ready for a major curriculum review. Other accomplishments were the start of a five-year building program, creation of the William Jewett Tucker Foundation, student government progress, organizational changes in the College's administration, and, most recently, establish-ment of the Trustees Planning Committee. An editorial in *The New York Times* said, "The College has been strengthened physically, financially, and intellectually under Mr. Dickey's imaginative leadership." Praise was widespread, and in a personal tribute that meant a great deal to him, more than one hundred of John Dickey's classmates gathered at a dinner at the Dartmouth Club of New York and presented him with a gun, chosen in all probability by his hunting companion, Class Pres-ident Bill Andres.

Dartmouth's commitment to raising faculty salaries was rewarded by a bonus grant, when the Ford Foundation distributed $260-million to hundreds of four-year liberal arts colleges to assist them in increasing faculty compensation. Dartmouth's grant of $2,079,500 was the thir-teenth largest and was set at that figure because the College was one of the institutions for which "accomplishment grants" were added in recognition of efforts on their own to improve faculty pay. The basic grant was restricted to endowment for ten years, but the accomplish-ment grant could be used for immediate, pressing needs, on the theory that those needs had been passed over in order to free funds for the faculty. Although the Ford Foundation money was to be paid out in two annual installments, the second half not until July 1, 1957, the Dartmouth Trustees voted to put into effect, on July 1, 1956, the salary increases that income from the entire grant could be expected to pro-vide; and a portion of the 1956 Alumni Fund was earmarked to help finance that action. Coming on top of the $200,000 of salary increases the previous July and the normal salary adjustments made each year, the enlarged salary budget made possible by the Ford Foundation grant constituted a major step forward in President Dickey's program to make Dartmouth more competitive in recruiting and retaining topnotch teacher-scholars. At the same time that the Ford Foundation made its grant to the College, it also gave $250,000 to Dartmouth Medical School endowment as part of some $21-million distributed, for instructional purposes, to forty-four privately supported medical schools in the United States.

As far as Dartmouth skiers were concerned, an important accomplishment that should have been claimed for the first Dickey decade was the decision to create a new ski area on the northeast slope of Holt's Ledge in Lyme, thirteen miles north of Hanover. Oak Hill in Hanover had become too small and too tame for a college with Dartmouth's reputation in the ski world, and a planning group headed by Treasurer John Meck succeeded in bringing off the new development, which included four trails from novice to expert, a Pomalift capable of carrying 800 persons an hour, and base facilities. A limited campaign to raise $150,000 was successfully carried out by Mr. Meck and the College development office, and the slope was officially dedicated January 19, 1957, although it had been in use for some time before that. In a contest to find a name, Dartmouth Skiway was the winner. It was submitted by Miss Pauline Case, secretary to the Secretary of the College. Her prize was a lifetime pass (which has increased greatly in value since the opening year when lift rates were thirty-five cents a ride or $3.50 for all day). To manage the Dartmouth Skiway the College named Howard P. Chivers, former captain of the Dartmouth ski team and a member of the U.S. Olympic team in 1940. He filled that position for twenty-seven years until his death in 1984.

A month after the Skiway dedication, the Brundage Lodge was ready for use at the Holt's Ledge development. It was the gift of Mr. and Mrs. Charles E. Brundage, in memory of their son, Marine Lieutenant Peter Brundage '45, who was killed while leading his platoon in the fighting on Okinawa. Young Brundage had been a leader in the DOC, director of the Winter Sports Council, and head instructor for Cabin and Trail. The ski lodge bearing his name features a large observation lounge and a snack bar, plus ground-level rooms for waxing, first-aid, the ski patrol, and the management.

While skiers were having their fun, President and Mrs. Dickey on February 10, 1956, sailed from New York on the *S.S. Independence* for three months abroad, their first extended vacation since his taking office. The trip was made under the auspices of the Carnegie Corporation of New York and involved visits to universities and educational institutions in Greece, Italy, Switzerland, Germany, Holland, and Denmark, concluding with a month's residence in Great Britain. Mr. Dickey managed to meet with U.S. Foreign Service officers in the various countries, as well as with Dartmouth alumni—who, according to the President, were everywhere. The Dickeys returned to Hanover on May 22, in time to get ready for the annual June meeting of the Board of Trustees and another Commencement.

At the board meeting, Lloyd D. Brace, Class of 1925, an Alumni Trustee, was elected a Life Trustee, to fill the vacancy created by the retirement at 70 of Mr. McLane, who had served on the board for thirty years. At the Trustees' following meeting, Orvil E. Dryfoos, Class of 1934, was elected to fill out Mr. Brace's alumni term, and John L. Sullivan, Class of 1921, was elected to fill out the term of Mr. Larmon, who had resigned. (Mr. Larmon wanted faster action on his proposals that the board should have more than twelve members and that it should have someone other than the President of the College serve as its chairman. Both of these changes were eventually adopted.) With the retirement of Mr. McLane, only Mr. Hood and Mr. Orr remained as Trustees who had begun their service under President Hopkins.

President Dickey on June 14 received an honorary Doctorate of Laws from Harvard University. Among those honored at the same time were Senator John F. Kennedy, Supreme Court Justice Felix Frankfurter, and Secretary of Commerce Sinclair Weeks. In September another honorary LL.D. was conferred upon him by Princeton at a convocation marking the bicentennial of Nassau Hall. The Princeton LL.D. was Mr. Dickey's ninth honorary doctorate.

The late summer of 1956 saw the start of construction of four new dormitories that would house a total of three hundred students. Not only were they the first major plant additions of the Dickey administration, but the four-building complex, on the former Clark School playing field off Choate Road, marked the introduction of modern architecture to the campus and embodied a new concept of dormitory life as recommended by the Commission on Campus Life. Interconnected by glassed-in bridges, each pair of dorms was designed to have a ground-level apartment for a resident faculty member, as well as a large common room for social activities. The student rooms were grouped in eight-man suites, each containing a living room and a variable combination of double and single study-bedrooms. President Dickey explained that the new dormitories, erected at a cost of $1.5-million, were being built not to permit an increase in the size of the student body, but to relieve the crowded conditions in existing residence halls. He also made it known that Topliff Hall, after renovation, would be divided into two units and that once the new dorms were built the remodeling of Massachusetts, Wheeler, Richardson, and South Fayerweather Halls would be undertaken, all part of the plan to have the dormitories play a more positive role in the educational and social life of the campus. The first of the new dorms, occupied in February 1958, was named Little Hall in honor of Clarence B. Little, a Trustee for twenty years and a benefactor of the College. The other three, ready for occupancy the following fall, were named Bissell Hall, for George H. Bissell, pioneer oil man whose name was on the building to be torn down for the Hopkins Center; Brown Hall, for Albert O. Brown, Dartmouth Trustee for twenty years and former Governor of New Hampshire, whose 1938 bequest of $500,000, now quintupled in market value, supports the Hopkins Center; and Cohen Hall, for William N. Cohen, Justice of the New York State Supreme Court, whose gift of $1-million provided funds to pay part of the board, and thus reduce the working hours, of students earning their meals at the Dartmouth Dining Association.

In enumerating the things that had given Dartmouth College its individuality and unique institutional character, President Dickey often cited its location, its adventurous beginning, its fight for independence in the Dartmouth College Case, its refounding under President Tucker, and the carrying out of Dr. Tucker's vision by President Hopkins. He also liked to speak of the strength the College had in people, place, and purpose—another instance of his fondness for alliteration.

In his address opening the 1956–57 academic year, Mr. Dickey elected to discuss purpose and independence and especially place. "Dartmouth is committed," he said, "to the liberating arts as the best bet for the liberation of men from both the meagerness and the meanness of mere existence. This sense of purpose to see men made whole in the largest measure, makes the liberal arts college different from other educational enterprises and, as with any true purpose, it pervades all that we do here. However, I should like now to focus our awareness not on our purposes, but on that other pervasive influ ence that gives Dartmouth her individuality and character: the place itself. . . .

"As I have come to know this College in relation to her sister institu tions, I have concluded that probably more than any other major Amer ican college Dartmouth's character flows from the place and cir cumstances of her founding. If we would understand our College and her influence on us, it is important to remember that the founder of this College deliberately placed it in an outpost position on the northern frontier. . . . Any stranger to Dartmouth's story would need to know only of her frontier founding and of the adversity and dedication at tending the early years, to make shrewd guess that here was an institu tion where early example and continued circumstance would foster an uncommon quality of independence, resourcefulness, and fellow ship."

The freshmen in Mr. Dickey's audience were the largest entering class in Dartmouth's history, numbering 805 men. It was the first class to come under the wing of Albert I. Dickerson, former Director of Admissions, who had now assumed the position of Dean of Freshmen after being on leave from his regular duties for two years to serve as executive director of the Trustees Planning Committee. The TPC job vacated by Mr. Dickerson was taken over by Mr. O'Connell, Mr. Dickey's executive assistant, who continued in that post with reduced responsibilities. The fall also saw another reorganization of the busi ness and plant operations of the College. The short-lived Department of Plant and Operations was abolished, and Mr. Olmsted, its manager, was named Business Manager of the College, responsible for the plant and new construction, and for managing student and faculty housing, the Dartmouth Dining Association, the Hanover Country Club, the Skiway and other auxiliary activities. In the reshuffling, the old Depart ment of Buildings and Grounds was revived, under James D. Wilson as supervisor, and its headquarters near the heating plant were named McKenzie Hall in honor of Alexander A. McKenzie, who headed the department from 1898 to 1904 and is believed to have been the first college officer of that kind in the country.

The Dartmouth Board of Trustees at its October 1956 meeting took an action of historic importance when it decided that the time had come for the College to mount its first capital-gifts campaign, to raise the millions of dollars needed for plant projects and for endowment to increase annual operating income. The decision to go ahead with a 200th Anniversary Development Program broke, once and for all, the pattern that Dartmouth had previously been following in its fund-raising efforts. It did not come easily, because annual giving had been a dependable and increasingly successful way to obtain financial sup-port, and there was no telling what would now happen to this core of the College's development program. President Dickey himself ap-proached the capital-campaign proposal with caution. One Trustee who argued strongly for taking the plunge was Mr. Zimmerman, then chairman of the Trustees' committee on development. Not surprisingly, he was the unanimous choice to head the national campaign.

Preliminary to their October action, the Dartmouth Trustees had sought the advice of the professional fund-raising firm of Marts and Lundy, which brought in the report that Dartmouth had fallen behind other ranking colleges and universities, in not making a comprehensive effort to raise capital funds, and that the potential for raising the kind of money needed to realize the ambitious bicentennial plans did exist among alumni, friends, corporations, and foundations. The thinking at the outset was that upwards of $25-million would have to be raised over the next twelve years, leading up to the 200th anniversary in 1969. The first stage, it was decided, would be a two-year campaign to obtain the money needed for priority plant projects, among which the Hop-kins Center was foremost, and for further improvement of faculty salaries. The goal for this two-year campaign was not immediately determined. Marts and Lundy thought that $12-million was an achiev-able figure, but Mr. Zimmerman and the College's development officers believed that a higher goal was needed and could be reached. The figure finally settled upon was $17-million, and the success of the campaign that began in the fall of 1957 proved that $17-million was indeed the right objective.

To inform the Dartmouth family about the impending capital cam-paign, President Dickey mailed a statement to the entire alumni body. "This historic step was taken neither lightly nor in haste," he wrote, once again emphasizing what a departure from long-standing policy this campaign was going to be. A private college, he explained, depends for its life upon three different kinds of giving: an annual fund to help meet current operating costs, bequests to build endowment, and capital gifts to build and replace plant. Dartmouth's development program had great strength in the first two areas, but in the third area, he stated, "We have never had a comprehensive capital-gifts campaign and we have had no major plant gifts during the past quarter century. The studies of the Trustees Planning Committee and its Advisory Committee on Plant Planning make clear that progress on the plant front is now imperative."

In March of 1957, while plans for the capital campaign were being formulated, a top-level change in the development office became necessary. Ross Gamble, Director of Development and Special Assistant to Mr. Dickey, resigned for reasons of health. To take his place as Director of Development, President Dickey named Mr. Colton who for one year had been Assistant Director. Operational responsibility for the impending campaign was a large order, but Colton brought to his new post twelve years of experience with various phases of Dartmouth development work, including three years as head of the Alumni Fund and six years as Executive Secretary of the Dartmouth Development Council. When he reached retirement in 1976 he was Vice President of the College. Along with the Colton appointment, the President also named Ford Whelden to be Executive Secretary of the Bequest and Estate Planning Program, a steadily growing development activity of which he was a founding father.

Not long after it had added the capital campaign to the College's fund-raising strategy the Board of Trustees took another action of far-reaching importance, this time an action bringing about a fundamental change in the educational program. The board approved the recommendation of the faculty that the then-existing system of two semesters of five courses each be replaced by three terms of three courses each. The new calendar, to go into effect with the academic year 1958–59, was designed to have the long Christmas and spring vacations come between terms, thus eliminating the fragmentation that obtained under the two-semester system and making possible within each term a continuity and an unbroken concentration not possible under the old calendar. The number of weekly class hours for each course was increased from three to four, and more time was made available for independent work. The requirement for the degree was reduced from forty to thirty-seven courses, and although the number of electives open to a student was also reduced, qualified men were permitted to take two additional courses without charge.

Although the three-term plan received the most attention in press coverage of Dartmouth's new educational program, this was but the mechanism for achieving the broader purpose of giving the student more responsibility and more time for self-education. "The primary objective," the faculty report stated, "is a determined effort to increase the student's responsibility for his own education and to shift the emphasis from teaching to learning." Dean Jensen put it more informally when he defined the purpose as "less dependence on two time-honored crutches: the professor and the textbook."

The program approved by the Trustees included a great deal more. It instituted an independent program of general reading for the first two years and one of independent reading prescribed by the major department in the last two years; an increase in the humanities distributive requirement from two to three courses, two of them to be sequential; modification of the English requirement, allowing qualified freshmen to be exempted from English 1 and to meet that requirement in a more advanced course; modification of the foreign language requirement, establishing proficiency as the equivalent of three terms of study at the college level; continuation of ROTC, with three-fourths of the military courses counting toward the A.B. degree (and with ROTC cadets, therefore, required to take thirty-nine courses instead of thirty-seven to fulfill the degree requirements); and an adjustment of the Great Issues Course to the new calendar, by having the course meet twice weekly throughout senior year and count for credit as a single course.

"Three-three," as the new plan quickly came to be known, was only the fourth major revision of the curriculum in nearly 190 years of Dartmouth history. The first occurred in 1880 when electives were permitted in a limited way, after a conservative faculty had rejected them a decade before. The second, under President Tucker, took place in 1902 when courses in freshman year were largely prescribed and those in the remaining three years were entirely elective, with the proviso that the student have a major of six courses in one department and a minor of four courses in a department of each of the other two divisions. The third and most famous revision took effect in the fall of 1925, based on a nationwide study of the liberal arts college made by Professor Leon Burr Richardson. The major in junior and senior years was given prime emphasis; the comprehensive examination was introduced; the first two years became a period of introduction to various fields of study, with the requirement that courses be elected in all three divisions; honors work was permitted for highly qualified students; and the A.B. became the only Bachelor's degree awarded by the College. This 1925 curriculum remained basically unchanged until the faculty and Trustees approved the three-term, three-course program for 1958.

Any committee undertaking a comprehensive study of a college curriculum is likely to travel a rocky road, and the review at Dartmouth was no exception. More than two years of work, argumentative and often frustrating, went into the report that was finally adopted by faculty and Trustees. It began with the Trustees Planning Committee sub-group dealing with educational program planning and headed by Trustee Dudley Orr. Joint meetings with the faculty Committee on Educational Policy eventually led to consolidation into one committee, under the chairmanship of Professor William A. Carter of the economics department. The first report of the joint committee was presented in March 1956, but six meetings of the general faculty failed to win support, and agreement of any sort appeared doubtful. However, the joint committee put things on hold, went back to work in September, and came up with a revised report that finally won approval at the general faculty meeting the following March.

At the time of adopting the three-three program, the College also began a new foreign study plan that permitted language majors to study abroad. Juniors majoring in French, German, or Spanish could spend the spring term at one of the selected university towns, where they had the guidance of a Dartmouth faculty counselor and where they lived with a native family as a means of developing their ability to speak the language. Russian and Italian were later added to the plan, and as the College entered more fully into a four-term academic year it became possible to study abroad for two consecutive terms. From the modest beginning in 1958 there eventually came into being a varied and greatly expanded program of foreign study, not necessarily in languages, as well as such off-campus opportunities as public-affairs internships. At its fullest development, decades later, foreign study for academic credit found Dartmouth undergraduates in France, Germany, Italy, Spain, Mexico, England, Scotland, Russia, China, Kenya, Nairobi, and Central America. The new academic calendar provided unusual flexibility for electing off-campus study for a term or two, but the comings and goings could be confusing and they worked against class solidarity. The problem has led the College, at this writing, to require each undergraduate to spend the entire freshman and senior years on campus.

While attention was focused on these major happenings of the year, other matters had to be considered and acted upon. Moderate-cost rental housing for junior members of the faculty and staff was a problem never fully solved. As a partial answer, the College teamed up with Mary Hitchcock Memorial Hospital to build thirty duplex units, housing sixty families, on Lyme Road north of the golf course. The hospital's participation in the $600,000 project was one way of meeting its need for local housing for residents, interns, and other staff personnel. The development came to be known as Rivercrest, and its construction was well timed, since Wigwam Circle and Sachem Village, which provided inexpensive housing during the war years, were about to be razed.

Good news for the faculty was contained in a spring announcement by President Dickey that a substantial increase in faculty and staff compensation would take place July 1, in the form of an extension of retirement and insurance benefits. The College, he announced, would henceforth bear the full cost of the retirement plan and would pay sixteen percent of the individual's salary into the retirement fund, without requiring the matching payment of one-half as before. At the same time, group life insurance coverage for faculty and administrative officers was increased from $10,000 to $20,000, at no added cost to them. By these compensation moves, coupled with the faculty children's tuition plan, the College continued to have the most generous package of fringe benefits provided by any college in the country. For non-academic employees also, group life insurance coverage was increased and the College assumed full cost of their separate retirement plan. For all, the Trustees' actions resulted in more "take home" pay, and it also had the virtue of giving maximum retirement protection to those who had been unable to afford it. Funding of these greater benefits came from an increase in tuition, voted by the Trustees at their spring meeting. Tuition of $900, plus a general fee of $80, was replaced by a "combined fee" of $1,170.

President Dickey, who had had a whole string of executive assistants since assuming office, acquired a new one in the person of Franklin Smallwood, who came from Washington, where he was administrative assistant to the Atomic Energy Commission's general manager for research and development. He took the place of Mr. O'Connell, who resigned his Dartmouth post to accept appointment by Governor Harriman as administrative deputy in the New York state budget bureau.

The President, immediately after Commencement, was deluged with inquiries from alumni and friends about a news story that referred to him as "retiring president of Dartmouth." This premature designation was caused by a Boston wire-service deskman who misconstrued Mr. Dickey's valedictory to the graduating class to be his own valedictory to the College. The mistake was corrected, and even had its good side by creating evidence that the Dartmouth family valued John Dickey's leadership and did not want it to end.

President Dickey, speaking to the Dartmouth class officers at their annual May 1958 meeting, characterized the academic year 1957–58 as "a vintage year" in the history of the College. Some of the things that justified that claim were a hugely successful Dartmouth Convocation on Great Issues in the Anglo-Canadian-American Community, marking the tenth anniversary of the Great Issues Course; the New York dinner gathering of more than two thousand persons to honor President-Emeritus Hopkins on his eightieth birthday; reexamination of the entire Dartmouth curriculum, in preparation for the three-term, three-course program going into effect in the fall; the largest amount of money Dartmouth had ever raised in a single year, thanks to the first year of the capital-gifts campaign; the ongoing review of all aspects of the College taking place under the auspices of the Trustees Planning Committee; and one of Dartmouth's best year-round records of athletic success, highlighted by a football team that missed an undefeated season by but one game, a ski team that won the national championship, and a basketball team that won the Ivy League title and then went on to reach the third round of the NCAA tournament.

The Dartmouth Convocation on Great Issues in the Anglo-Canadian-American Community extended over three days, September 5–7, 1957. The caliber of the participants from three nations attracted press, radio, and television attention such as the College had rarely had before. From Canada came Prime Minister John Diefenbaker; President Sidney E. Smith of the University of Toronto (who before he left Hanover had a new title, acquired by his acceptance of Mr. Diefenbaker's invitation to become Canada's Minister for External Affairs); James D. Duncan, chairman of the Hydro-Electric Power Commission of Ontario; and Edgar W. McInnis, president of the Canadian Institute of Public Affairs. From Great Britain came Sir Harold Caccia, British Ambassador to the United States; Sir Geoffrey Crowther, managing director of *The Economist*; Arthur L. Goodhart, Master of University College, Oxford; and Sir William Haley, editor of *The Times* of London. From the United States came Sherman Adams, chief of staff to President Eisenhower; Henry Cabot Lodge, U.S. Representative to the United Nations; Paul G. Hoffman, U.S. Delegate to the United Nations General Assembly; Lewis W. Douglas, former U.S. Ambassador to the Court of St. James's; Hanson W. Baldwin, military affairs editor of *The New York Times*; Allan Nevins, Columbia University historian; Clarence B. Randall, adviser to President Eisenhower on foreign economic policy; and Arthur Hays Sulzberger, publisher of *The New York Times*. Mr. Douglas served as convocation chairman, and Dean Arthur Jensen was chairman of the College's steering committee.

At the opening assembly in Webster Hall, President Dickey spoke of Great Issues and said, "The theme of the convocation was chosen for many reasons, some historical, some geographic, but basically because we believe that there is nothing more important today than that the people of these three nations should talk to each other, as members of a community, about the issues that both divide and unite them. This talk should be responsible and candid, as befits the talk of men and women of good will discussing any community problem."

Besides the opening assembly, there were three panel discussions and a final assembly at which Ambassador Caccia, Mr. Lodge, and Prime Minister Diefenbaker were the speakers. There was special anticipation of Mr. Diefenbaker's address, since he was making his first visit to the United States since taking office. He spoke quite candidly of some of Canada's grievances, citing the trade imbalance between Canada and the United States and the disquiet in his country over the external ownership and control of Canadian industries. He called for a more equal partnership, but said that he spoke not in a spirit of truculence but in a spirit of cooperation between good neighbors. At the outset of his remarks, Mr. Diefenbaker called the Dartmouth convocation a great contribution to understanding among the three participating nations and added, "It represents, I believe, a milestone in our relationship. Indeed, in the last few days Dartmouth College has become a cathedral for freedom and its maintenance among the three nations represented."

The stature of the convocation was enhanced by greetings and good wishes sent by President Eisenhower; Prime Minister Harold Macmillan of Great Britain; former President Harry S. Truman; Hugh Gaitskell, leader of the British Labour Party; Sir Oliver Franks, former British Ambassador to the United States; and John Hay Whitney, U.S. Ambassador to Great Britain. In presiding at the third panel discussion, Sir Geoffrey Crowther mentioned the attractive convocation emblem designed by John Scotford and pointed out the small circle marking Hanover's location on the world map. "Whether that is intended to suggest that this campus is, as indeed for these few days it is, the hub of the Western World, or that Hanover is a target of some kind, I'm not quite sure," Sir Geoffrey quipped.

The most colorful event of the three-day program was the gathering in the Bema on Saturday afternoon for the awarding of honorary degrees to the eight participants from Canada and Great Britain. Two other events that Mr. Dickey described as "family affairs" were the dedication in Baker Library of the Charles Ransom Miller Public Affairs Laboratory of the Great Issues Course and the ceremony at which seventeen distinguished Dartmouth graduates were given Alumni Awards. Arthur Hays Sulzberger gave the dedicatory address for the public affairs laboratory, which was named for Charles Ransom Miller,

Class of 1872, a native of Hanover, who was editor of *The New York Times* from 1883 to 1922. Sherman Adams, who received one of the Alumni Awards, was the principal speaker at that Friday evening event.

Throughout the three days, attendance was large and enthusiastic. Among the thousands who heard the addresses and discussions were more than six hundred alumni, who were housed, with their wives and families, in the dormitories. The convocation was on an extremely ambitious scale, but when it was all over, there was general agreement that it had gone off with near perfection and that one more major achievement could be credited to John Dickey's imaginative leadership. The international character of the convocation was especially important to him. His State Department experience gave him a lifelong interest in foreign affairs, and American-Canadian relations were becoming his specialty.

In order that Dartmouth students, at the opening of college two weeks later, might have some sense of what had happened on the campus, Convocation was held in the flag-decked setting of Alumni Gymnasium, where the final assembly of the international gathering had occurred. "We are meeting here today, rather than in the all-too-limited facilities of Webster Hall," President Dickey said, "in order that as many members of the College community as possible may touch and sense, at least momentarily, something of the alternating forces of independence and unity which, within the context of three wonderful days of creative discussion, made history both here and beyond Dartmouth. This special Convocation marked both the tenth anniversary of the Great Issues Course and the midpoint between twelve years of postwar Dartmouth and the twelve years ahead as this College enters a unique period of sustained planning aimed at bringing it to a running start of preeminence, in all respects, when it enters its third century of educational service in 1969."

A new administrative appointment made known at the start of the college year was that of Fred Berthold Jr., Professor of Religion, to be the first Dean of the Tucker Foundation. In that position he was assigned responsibility for all matters, other than academic courses, concerned with religion and the moral purpose of education at the College. The deanship placed him in charge of chapel and other worship services in Rollins Chapel, and more broadly involved him in cooperative programs with faculty members and with the community churches attended by students. Dean Berthold had received both his bachelor of divinity degree and his doctorate from the University of Chicago and had been on the Dartmouth faculty for eight years. Another major appointment announced by President Dickey was that of Dr. S. Marsh Tenney to the newly created position of Director of Medical Sciences at Dartmouth College, in which role he assumed responsibility for developing a new educational pattern at Dartmouth Medical School and raising the necessary capital funds. Dr. Tenney had come to Dartmouth the year before as chairman of the Physiology Department, after being on the faculty of the University of Rochester Medical School.

Funds being raised for the Medical School were not part of the two-year capital campaign launched in the fall of 1957. The organizational phase of the latter was advanced by the naming of fourteen alumni to be regional leaders across the country, under the general chairmanship of Mr. Zimmerman. For the long-range 200th Anniversary Development Program, of which the two-year campaign was a part, President-Emeritus Hopkins agreed to be honorary chairman and Sherman Adams honorary co-chairman. Among nine honorary vice-chairmen were Conrad Hilton, Gerard Swope, Mrs. George F. Jewett of Spokane, former Governor Channing H. Cox of Massachusetts, and J. Frank Drake, former chairman of Gulf Oil Corporation.

President Dickey, while finding his alumni speaking schedule greatly expanded because of the capital campaign, had managed to engage in a study of this country's international security and defense structure, under the auspices of the Rockefeller Brothers Fund. The report of the 24-man panel, released in January 1958, called for a reorganization of the Department of Defense with a single Chief of Staff under the President and Secretary of Defense, and also for an increase in military and education budgets and for the elimination of inter-service rivalry. Henry L. Kissinger was staff secretary for the panel. An item of both family and College interest was the announcement by President and Mrs. Dickey of the engagement of their younger daughter Christina, a senior at Smith College, to Stewart P. Stearns Jr. '54, son of Mr. and Mrs. Stewart P. Stearns '22 of Belmont, Massachusetts. At the time, their elder daughter Sylvia was a student at Wheelock College, and their son John Jr. was a year and a half away from entering Dartmouth in the Class of 1963.

Billed as the greatest Dartmouth gathering ever held outside Hanover, a king-sized dinner took place February 5, 1958, at the Waldorf Astoria Hotel in New York City, honoring President-Emeritus Hopkins on his eightieth birthday. The birthday part of the tribute was comparable to the traditional disregard of an actual natal date in celebrating the birthday of the British monarch, since Mr. Hopkins had been born on November 6. But the observance was only slightly belated, and the Dartmouth family was always in favor of any event honoring "Hoppy." The New York planning committee was eager to show that Dartmouth could do things in the grand manner, and leaders of the capital-gifts campaign saw the dinner as a stimulus to support from the alumni. The turnout was tremendous, and some 2,200 persons packed the grand ballroom and balconies, as well as the adjoining east foyer, of the Waldorf. President Dickey jokingly commented that the planning committee's claim to staging the largest Dartmouth gathering ever held outside of Hanover was questionable, if you included football crowds, but he said it was certainly true if you added "indoors" to the claim or, better still, if you called it "the greatest Dartmouth black-tie gathering ever held anywhere." All in all, the scene was resplendently festive, with candlelight and green and white decorations. The corps of assistants from Hanover was headed by Sidney C. Hayward and Warner Bentley, who brought along the Dartmouth glee club, the Barbary Coast Orchestra, and the cheerleaders.

Nelson Rockefeller, chairman of the planning committee, presided at the dinner and was a speaker, along with President Dickey and Trustee and Campaign Chairman Zimmerman. Sherman Adams, who delivered the main tribute to Mr. Hopkins, read a special, hand-written message from President Eisenhower, and presented him with a full-sized replica of the silver Wentworth Bowl. Mr. Hopkins was greeted with a prolonged and sentimental ovation when he was called upon to speak. In his brief remarks he chose to be light-hearted; otherwise, he said later, he would have wept. One of the stories he told was how back in 1916, the Governor of New Hampshire, with a slip of the tongue, had referred to his inauguration as President of the College as "another millstone in the history of Dartmouth College."

President Dickey, in his address, said that his part in the tribute to Mr. Hopkins would take the form of "a report from the front on how goes the fight for liberal learning which you, as the eleventh in the Wheelock Succession, so gallantly led forward in a campaign of nigh thirty years' duration." He spoke of personal and institutional purpose in American education and chose to relate this to the problem that had been created by the Soviet Union's successful launching of Sputnik only a few months before, in October 1957. What disadvantage existed in this country's pluralistic educational purpose versus the monolithic purpose of the Russians? "To be exterminated by someone with inferior purposes but superior weapons is certainly neither a desirable nor noble end, let alone a promising prospect for liberal learning," he said. "Let us be clear, such an outcome is not necessary. But let us also be clear that if the best of American education now panics and loses its sense of great purposes, American power will assuredly lead, as Soviet power today leads, to what great power without moral restraint has always led—a very dead end."

Commenting upon an issue that was still alive decades later, President Dickey added, "If I may be permitted one unqualified certainty tonight, it is that only disaster can come out of any attempt to conquer and control outer space for national purposes. Any such universal arrogance must surely bring down on all of us commensurate catastrophe. President Eisenhower requires the dedicated service of every educated man on earth behind his wise proposals to forestall this ultimate folly." He concluded by declaring that the only way the arms race could be won was by ending it. "We cannot know how far off this day may be; we can only know that bringing it nearer remains the prime civilizing business of liberal learning today." The address was one of John Dickey's most thoughtful, and it gave to the program the note of serious educational concern that was not at all inappropriate for the festive occasion.

With their black ties and dinner jackets put away until another special occasion occurred, the College staff went back to work in Hanover. An early February announcement made known the Trustees' approval of an upgraded scholarship plan for the sons and daughters of faculty and administrative officers. The plan increased the annual tuition grants from $600 to the amount of Dartmouth's tuition (then $1,170) at colleges of the children's choice, and it also eliminated the old requirements that sons must first apply to Dartmouth and be denied admission and that daughters and sons going elsewhere must first apply for tuition exchange or scholarship grants at the other colleges. The scholarships were available for four years, so long as the recipients were enrolled in the undergraduate programs of colleges offering the Bachelor's degree in liberal arts and sciences and remained in good academic standing. Dartmouth's edge in fringe benefits was thus increased even more.

Another development that gave Dartmouth a claim to uniqueness was the inauguration, on March 4, 1958, of radio station WDCR, the country's only non-profit, commercial station completely run by students. Permission to operate the 250-watt commercial station on a frequency of 1340 kilocycles had been granted by the Federal Communications Commission the previous summer. The Dartmouth Trustees had backed the application for a commercial license and had authorized a loan to build a transmitting tower on Chase Field and to purchase needed studio equipment. Advertising revenue was expected to make the station self-supporting. Under its old call letters WDBS, the student station, with its 100-man staff, had been one of the best managed and most responsible student activities on campus, and its friends looked upon the FCC license as a well-deserved reward for past performance.

The position of Vice President for Development and Alumni Affairs, which had been vacant since Justin Stanley resigned in 1954, was filled in April 1958 with the appointment of Orton H. Hicks of New York. Mr. Hicks, chief of 16 mm. operations for Loew's International Corporation, was an Overseer of Tuck School, past president of the Dartmouth Alumni Council, and New York regional co-chairman for the capital-gifts campaign. Under him Mr. Colton continued to serve as Director of Development and operational head of the campaign. Progress in the first year of the fund drive was steady and was given a boost in April by a grant of $500,000 from The Spaulding-Potter Charitable Trusts of Manchester, New Hampshire. The gift, to be used toward the cost of one of the major units of the Hopkins Center, was in memory of Huntley N. Spaulding, Governor of New Hampshire and a Dartmouth Trustee during his term of office, 1927–1929. The grant was eventually applied to building the Spaulding Auditorium within the Center. Later in the spring, Mr. Zimmerman, the national chairman, announced that the special-gifts phase of the campaign had produced more than $7.5-million of the $17-million being sought, and that the general canvass of alumni and others would begin in September.

Meanwhile, in the separate campaign to raise $10-million to finance an expanded educational program at the Medical School, great encouragement was provided by a grant of $1.5-million from the Rockefeller Foundation. Two-thirds of the grant was for strengthening teaching and research, and the remainder was to help construct a projected medical science building. By the end of the college year, Dr. Marsh Tenney was able to announce that the campaign total stood at $4.3 million.

A Medical "Refounding"

A MAJOR problem facing John Dickey in the early years of his presidency was the state of the Dartmouth Medical School. Consideration was even being given to closing it down. Although the School held the distinction of being the fourth oldest medical school in the United States and had been part of the College since 1797, its plant was antiquated; its full-time faculty numbered only six, aided by part-time teachers from the Hitchcock Clinic and the College's Faculty of Arts and Sciences; its student body was not large enough to provide the level of tuition income needed for a going enterprise; and its offering of only the first two years of medical training, excellent as it was, was an obstacle to full accreditation. Moreover, virtually no research was being done to supplement and keep up to date the instruction given in the basic medical sciences of the first two years. Another part of the problem was the financial drain on the general funds of the College, which at that time was providing about $150,000 annually to keep the School in existence. The consensus among those concerned with the Medical School's parlous state was that Dartmouth either should get out of the medical-school business completely or should make an all-out effort to rebuild the School, even to the extent, perhaps, of reviving the four-year M.D. course that had been discontinued in 1914. One thing clear was that the latter option would require a great deal of money, for new plant, additional full-time faculty, the inauguration of research programs, and endowment. The situation obviously called for a careful, in-depth study.

All three of Dartmouth's associated schools—engineering, business administration, and medicine—were included in the sweeping review of the College's strengths and shortcomings that was inaugurated by the Trustees Planning Committee in 1954, as part of the development program leading up to Dartmouth's bicentennial. In the case of the Medical School, because of the crucial question regarding its future, the survey was not entrusted to a formally constituted TPC subcommittee. Dean Morrison in 1954 began studying the situation and making informal reports. As a next step, the opinions and advice of outstanding medical educators from outside were sought and made the basis of recommendations that finally reached the Board of Trustees in June of 1957. These consultants included Dr. Alan Gregg, Director of Medical Sciences for the Rockefeller Foundation; Dr. George P. Berry, Dean of the Harvard Medical School; Dr. Robert F. Loeb, Samuel Bard Professor of Medicine at Columbia University; and Dr. W. Barry Wood, Vice President of Johns Hopkins University. To round up all the findings and discussion reports and to make a final recommendation, the Dartmouth Trustees appointed a special committee of three Board members, headed by Harvey Hood and including Dudley Orr and Dr. Ralph Hunter. The committee's report, submitted on June 7, 1957, was the basis on which the Trustees decided to "refound" the Dartmouth Medical School as an enlarged, modernized, and quite different associated school—one that would be more in the mainstream of the whole College and would have closer ties to undergraduate instruction in the biological sciences.

The outside authorities were in agreement that Dartmouth's two-year medical school had strengths worth preserving and that, if provided with new facilities, an enlarged faculty, greater student enrollment, and adequate financing, its educational program, anchored in the basic medical sciences, could serve as a much-needed prototype for similar two-year medical schools. Such schools, it was pointed out, would have the dual virtue of filling the third- and fourth-year vacancies that attrition created in the four-year medical schools and also of helping to train more physicians without the enormous cost of establishing additional four-year schools. Dartmouth's medical students were readily accepted for advanced placement in the country's leading schools, and the high quality of their basic training was recognized, particularly by the Harvard Medical School, to which the majority of each Dartmouth class transferred. Serious consideration was given, in fact, to a proposal that Dartmouth and Harvard might work out a cooperative arrangement whereby all the men who successfully completed the two-year program in Hanover would move on to their final two years in Cambridge.

Having made the decision to keep the Medical School alive, President Dickey and the Trustees moved quickly to carry out the proposals of the Hood committee. The Trustees agreed to meet the Medical School's expenses for 1957–58, but stipulated that thereafter the School would have to raise the funds needed for its expanded program. A three-year goal of $10-million was set, and this effort was to be entirely apart from the capital campaign the College itself was then conducting. To direct the refounding program and to lead the drive to secure the necessary funds, the Trustees named Dr. S. Marsh Tenney, Dartmouth 1944, to the newly created position of Director of Medical Sciences at Dartmouth College. Dr. Tenney had joined the Medical School faculty the previous year as Chairman and Professor in the Physiology Department. He came to Dartmouth from the University of Rochester School of Medicine, where his research in cardio-pulmonary physiology was supported by grants from the National Heart Institute and the U.S. Air Force. Tenney had taken a strong stand in favor of creating a new Dartmouth Medical School on the historic foundation of the old one, and it was his spirit and dedicated work that, more than anything else, brought about the achieving of the expansion goals.

In association with Dr. Tenney's appointment, Dr. Henry L. Heyl, Executive Director of the Hitchcock Foundation in Hanover, was named Assistant Director of Medical Sciences for Research and Planning. In that position he had responsibility for administering sponsored research within the School. Also serving under Dr. Tenney was Dr. Rolf C. Syvertsen, who continued as Dean.

At the end of the first year of the new organization, in June 1958, a total of $4.3-million in capital funds had been raised, and this was encouragement enough to push along the planning for a seven-story medical science building, which would be the focal point of the whole Medical School operation. Included in the grants received were $1.5-million from the Rockefeller Foundation, $1-million from the Commonwealth Fund, $1-million from the U.S. Public Health Service, and $800,000 from the Ford Foundation. Before ground was actually broken, in the summer of 1959, additional grants had come from the Fannie E. Rippel Foundation and the James Foundation of New York, plus alumni gifts raising the interim total to more than $5-million. By that time, twenty-five basic medical scientists had been added to the faculty, which temporarily carried on its work in scattered quarters, including the old Medical Building, dating from 1911.

The new central building of what was destined to be a cluster of Medical School structures was located in close proximity to the Mary Hitchcock Memorial Hospital. Its design provided one floor each for the six departments of the School—anatomy, physiology, pharmacology, pathology, biochemistry, and microbiology—and a top floor for an animal house and animal operating rooms. Teaching and research activities were closely related in the design of the building. Some idea of the Medical School's aspirations can be derived from the approved architectural plans, which, aside from administrative offices, called for space for a basic medical-science faculty of thirty-five, a part-time clinical faculty of fifty-five, a doubled student enrollment of ninety-six, thirty research fellows, and seventy-five residents and interns. The estimated cost of the building was $3.5-million.

After covering the cost of a new Medical Science Building, the $10-million capital campaign was intended to provide endowment for faculty salaries. The rapid growth of the full-time faculty to thirty members could not, however, be wholly attributed to the campaign. Many of the new professors were term appointees supported by outside research grants. In the first year of the Medical School's restructuring, research money exceeded $200,000, and for the year 1959–60 outside grants totaling $600,000 financed forty different research projects. This was a far cry from earlier days, when only a modicum of clinical research was carried on through support from the local Hitchcock Foundation; and it was the most dramatic evidence that a remarkable metamorphosis was taking place. Prominent among the research scholars added to the faculty were Dr. Manuel Morales, chairman of the Biochemistry Department; Dr. Robert E. Gosselin, chairman of the Pharmacology Department; and Dr. Shinya Inoue, chairman of the Cytology Department—all men of national reputation in their respective specialties. A three-year grant of $230,000 from the National Science Foundation, enabling Dr. Inoue to study the submicroscopic structure of living cells, was the sort of thing that was now happening at the School. Work at such an advanced level opened the possibility of offering, later on, the

Ph.D. degree in some departments; but the College's Trustees were not about to take that idea seriously while the School still had the unfinished task of getting itself fully transformed.

Despite the emphasis on newly introduced research programs, the central purpose of the Medical School remained the training of physicians. The question of concentration on research and advanced work in the basic medical sciences, as against priority for the education of medical students, later became the cause of a faculty schism, but that fight was a half-dozen years away. To help determine specific ways in which the Medical School should develop, the Dartmouth Trustees approved the appointment of a Policy Committee, headed by Dr. John P. Bowler, then chairman of the Hitchcock Clinic and Professor of Surgery at the Medical School. The committee's other members were three of the outside medical educators who had participated in the early study of the School's future—Dean Berry of Harvard, Prof. Robert F. Loeb of Columbia University, and Dr. W. Barry Wood of Johns Hopkins University—as well as Dr. Waltman Walters, senior surgeon at the Mayo Clinic. One recommendation made by both the Policy Committee and those involved in the early investigations was that the Medical School should break away from the practice of having each entering class drawn entirely from the Dartmouth senior class. The projected doubling of enrollment made it desirable to seek students from other colleges. For Dartmouth applicants, the School still permitted qualified students to begin medical studies in senior year. And there was no change in the requirement that every applicant, whether from Dartmouth or elsewhere, must present a record of undergraduate studies in the liberal arts.

Ground was broken for the new Medical Science Building in the summer of 1959. Construction moved ahead with unusual dispatch, and enough of the building existed to make possible a dedicatory ceremony there on September 9, 1960, as part of the three-day convocation devoted to "The Great Issues of Conscience in Modern Medicine" (described elsewhere in this chronicle). Dr. Tenney, who had been given the additional title of Dean of the Dartmouth Medical School, following the death of Dean Syvertsen, presided at the ceremony and expressed the hope that all the activity within the new center would be characterized by the morale, camaraderie, and *esprit de corps* of the old Medical School. President Dickey and Trustee Harvey Hood also took part in the program, which had as its principal speaker Dr. Ward Darley, Executive Director of the Association of American Medical Colleges. Dartmouth, Dr. Darley said, had "the opportunity, almost the mandate, to establish the two-year school as a significant part of this nation's system of medical education and this upon the basis of ideals and educational standards that are badly needed when we are struggling to keep pace with rapid medical progress. In fact, I do not think I exaggerate when I compare the importance of Dartmouth's opportunity of 1960 with that which confronted Johns Hopkins in 1893."

On January 31, 1961, the first-year students in Dr. Inoue's histology class launched the educational use of the Medical Science Building. The School's administrative offices had moved in some time before, and by mid-February all the departments were settled in their new quarters. To pick a comparable improvement in campus facilities, one would probably have to go back to the time when Baker Library took over from old Wilson Hall.

Meanwhile, the Medical School's capital campaign was slowly but steadily moving ahead to its $10-million goal. The chairmanship of the drive had now been assumed by John Brown Cook, with Dr. John L. Norris as co-chairman. About the time that faculty, students, and administrators were occupying the Medical Science Building, the W. K. Kellogg Foundation made a gift of $500,000 to build an adjacent teaching auditorium. Six months later, just before the start of the 1961–62 academic year, announcement was made of a gift of $325,000 from the Strasenburgh family of Rochester, New York, to build a badly needed dormitory for medical students. Strasenburgh Hall, sited not far from the Medical School's main structure, was designed to house eighty students. The donors had a long connection with medicine, through research and marketing of pharmaceutical products. Three sons of Edwin G. Strasenburgh, head of the family firm, were Dartmouth graduates: Robert J. II '42, David M. '49, and R. John III, Tuck '70.

The Medical School was in the news again in December, when President Dickey announced that Dr. Gilbert H. Mudge, Associate Dean of the Johns Hopkins University School of Medicine, would succeed Dr. Tenney as Dean, effective June 1, 1962. Dean Tenney had expressed the wish to give up his administrative duties, in order to devote himself fully to research and teaching, as Chairman and Professor of Physiology. Dr. Mudge, in addition to being Dean, was named Professor of Experimental Therapeutics, a subject he taught at Johns Hopkins. Dean Tenney's four years of leadership, with the strong backing of President Dickey, was generally acknowledged to have been the most important factor in the successful transformation of Dartmouth's medical school from an institution of precarious existence to one with an assured future.

When Dean Tenney relinquished his administrative duties the total raised in the Medical School's capital campaign stood at $6.8-million. Most of this money came from foundations, and further foundation support, near the close of the 1961–62 academic year, made possible the addition of two more units to the Schools' mushrooming plant. The Charles A. Dana Foundation gave $400,000 toward constructing a library that would house 60,000 volumes from Baker Library dealing with the medical and life sciences and would provide expansion space for shelving double that many. The Dana Biomedical Library, as it came to be named, was a three-story building having, in addition to stack space, a general reading room, a rare-book room, individual and group studies, and study carrels throughout the stack areas. Charles A. Dana, whose name the library bears, was a New York lawyer, industrialist, and philanthropist.

The Dana Foundation gift was followed, shortly afterward, by the announcement that the Gilman Foundation was contributing $1-million for establishing a biomedical center that would facilitate collaboration between the medical scientists of the Medical School and the life scientists of the College's Department of Biological Sciences. Combined with a grant from the National Science Foundation, earmarked for research and instructional facilities, the gift from the Gilman family of New York and Gilman, Vermont, produced the five-story Charles Gilman Life Sciences Laboratory. This building became the core structure of the Gilman Biomedical Center, which consolidated the Medical Science Building, the Dana Biomedical Library, the Kellogg Medical Auditorium, and Strasenburgh Hall. When ready for occupancy in the fall of 1964, the Gilman Laboratory provided the Medical School and the Department of Biological Sciences with eight large teaching laboratories; two dozen constant-temperature and environment rooms; twenty faculty offices, each with its own research unit; a lecture hall; seminar rooms; and a top-story greenhouse. At its dedication on October 30, 1964, Charles Gilman Sr. was accompanied by his two Dartmouth alumni sons, Howard L. Gilman, Class of 1944, and Charles Gilman Jr., Class of 1952. All three, at that time, were affiliated with the Gilman Paper Company. The 1962 announcement that the laboratory would be built came at an opportune time. Enrollment of medical students was doubled to ninety-six that fall, and the new facilities were urgently needed.

The Dartmouth Medical School was the beneficiary of a strong national interest in medical research and education, and its financial resources continued to grow in the first half of the decade of the Sixties. The Richard King Mellon Charitable Fund gave $250,000 to augment faculty salary funds, and from the James Foundation of New York, an early supporter of the revamped School, came a second and larger grant of $2-million. This was followed by $1-million from the Irene Heinz Given and John LaPorte Given Foundations, to endow professorships in cytology and pharmacology. Somewhat later, $300,000 was received from the Commonwealth Fund, another early supporter, to establish a Department of Medicine. This particular period of the School's history closed with the announcement that Dr. Mudge would resign from the deanship on September 1, 1965, but would continue to serve as a member of the faculty. To be Acting Dean, President Dickey named Dr. Ralph W. Hunter, Associate Clinical Professor of Neurology and a member of the Dartmouth Board of Trustees. Dr. Hunter filled the position for only four months before turning the responsibilities of Acting Dean over to Dr. Tenney, who agreed to return to that familiar administrative job until a new Dean could be chosen.

Beneath the surface of the Medical School's impressive progress there had been simmering among the faculty a sharp difference of opinion about the School's priorities. This burst into the open in the spring of 1966, when six professors resigned because, they charged, those administering the School were unwilling to push ahead in expanding staff and facilities for research and education in the basic medical sciences. Specifically, the resigning group wanted a greater commitment to developing the graduate program in molecular biology, for which the

Departments of Cytology, Biochemistry, and Microbiology were responsible. Another, but lesser, bone of contention was the School's tenure policy, which was criticized as being too frozen.

The dissident group came from the three departments directing the graduate work in molecular biology, and included Professors Shinya Inoue, R. Clinton Fuller, and Andrew G. Szent-Gyorgyi. Their colleagues in the five other departments took the position that an increased emphasis on graduate and post-doctoral work would destroy the School's institutional balance and would go against its primary purpose—the education of medical students.

The controversy and faculty resignations were widely reported in the press, which erroneously in some cases depicted the conflict as one between research and teaching. It was more a matter of the Ph.D. versus the M.D. The departing faculty members made a public statement: "We came to Dartmouth to fulfill a unique opportunity for education and research in the basic medical sciences. To those of us who are leaving it has become apparent that we cannot effectively accomplish this purpose here. We disagree with the way the medical school is being administered and the direction it is taking."

Dean Tenney, in responding, said that the Medical School had to maintain a balance among all its departments if it was to adhere to the purpose for which it was refounded. He conceded that facilities for graduate students in the basic medical sciences were not as extensive as desired, but he added: "The Medical School is doing all it can to grow in a balanced and orderly way, and these things take time and money. You cannot do everything overnight. Too rapid growth leads to instability, and unilateral growth jeopardizes other programs."

On the issue of tenure, Dean Tenney pointed out that many of the faculty positions and programs at the School were financed by outside grants. "It is the policy of the Medical School," he said, "not to award tenure to a man unless we have the money to insure his salary through retirement. This means endowment, not research money."

Comment was also provided by Provost John W. Masland, who had nothing but praise for the way the Medical School was fulfilling its purpose and for the quality of its medical education. "It was unfortunate," he said, "to have differences at the Medical School carried to the point where the faculty was finally forced into a choice between the medical program or the graduate program. This is a professional school and the graduate and medical programs go together. You also cannot have one at the expense of the other. This is the view shared by the great majority of the Medical School faculty." And if a final word were needed, the Dartmouth Board of Trustees provided it with a resolution that included the statement: "The primary purpose of the Dartmouth Medical School is the education of medical students, but with full recognition that this purpose can be accomplished only in an environment which provides optimum opportunity for scholarly endeavor, including the accumulation and advancement of knowledge through research and other essential educational activities." The wording was doubtless the handiwork of President Dickey.

The educational purpose to which the Dartmouth Medical School was committed was further confirmed when President Dickey, in May of 1966, announced that the new Dean of the School would be Dr. Carleton B. Chapman, Professor of Medicine at the University of Texas Southwestern Medical School in Dallas, who was an internationally known cardiologist and a former president of the American Heart Association. The Dartmouth Trustees simultaneously approved in principle the medical faculty's proposals to expand the curriculum, faculty, and plant in order to accommodate an enrollment of 168 students. Particularly significant in this increased enrollment would be the inclusion of twenty students in each of the third and fourth years engaged in an experimental tutorial program leading to the M.D. degree. The increase in the instructional staff was proposed for the "core faculty," meaning those supported by Medical School funds, rather than by outside grants. Some of the added faculty were needed to staff the full-time Departments of Medicine, Surgery, and Psychiatry that had now been established with Trustee approval. Dean Chapman was to arrive just in time to take on responsibility for implementing the faculty's innovative program.

Formal approval of reviving the M.D. degree (not awarded since 1914) was voted by the Trustees at their June 1968 meeting. Although their approval was contingent upon getting the necessary new financing, the Trustees were encouraged by four gifts amounting to $4.25-million, given to Dartmouth's Third Century Fund and designated for the Medical School. The largest of these gifts, $1.75-million, was made by Mr. and Mrs. Martin J. Remsen. Also contributed was $1.5-million from

Mr. and Mrs. Foster G. McGaw in memory of James D. Vail, Mrs. McGaw's first husband; and $250,000 from James C. Chilcott, for a teaching auditorium-laboratory. The Vivian Beaumont Allen Foundation gave $650,000 to endow the Nathan Smith Professorship of Medicine and an additional $100,000 for scholarship support. Dean Chapman estimated that an additional $14-million in endowment funds was needed to make the M.D. program viable.

The so-called Dartmouth Plan for Medical Education would be phased in over the next six years, Dean Chapman explained. One objective was to shorten the time required to produce a doctor. By admitting a student after three years of undergraduate, pre-medical education and operating the School on an eleven-month academic year, the nine years traditionally required to go from freshman year in college through the completion of an internship could be reduced to seven years. One of the features of the proposed plan was an open clerkship at the Dartmouth-Hitchcock Medical Center in the third year of medical study and an internship under the direction of the Medical School in the fourth year. Classroom time was to be reduced in favor of more independent work. Students not concentrating in surgery, for example, would no longer spend long hours dissecting cadavers. Instead, by means of a self-teaching viewer, they could watch full-color films depicting the dissection of any area of the body. In addition to its streamlining proposals, the Dartmouth plan hoped that the students' early experience with patients at Hanover's Mary Hitchcock Memorial Hospital would encourage more M.D.'s to choose the practice of rural medicine.

With these advances in the making, on top of all that had already been accomplished, the Dartmouth Medical School was scarcely recognizable to those who remembered it from the time when John Dickey became Dartmouth's President and wondered whether the Medical School could be saved. Getting the funds for the revived M.D. program was something Mr. Dickey had to leave to his successor when he retired, and he expressed regret that the timing worked out that way. But even before the M.D. program began in the fall of 1970, the Medical School was truly and solidly refounded, to be counted as among the major achievements of the Dickey administration.

Some Educational Changes

THE College's 190th year began in September 1958 with a strong sense of new things happening. The prime cause of this feeling was the launching of the three-term, three-course curriculum. Students who had been carrying five courses in each of two semesters came back to a drastically revised program that called for greater concentration in fewer courses and a much higher degree of independent, self-directed learning. For the faculty as well, the new plan was a departure from the old reliance on lectures, textbooks, quizzes, and hour exams. More than a year had been spent reorganizing courses, majors, and class procedures, in order to be ready for three-three. The seminar-tutorial became an important adjunct to lectures and independent reading, and in some courses, such as English 2, the student group selected its own study project. In short, college was no longer to be an extension of secondary school, with lecturer and textbook as the main props of learning, but was to be a cooperative effort in which the student, with faculty guidance and help, was to depend primarily upon himself for acquiring an education.

President Dickey in his Convocation address spoke of the College as "a community of learning" composed of students and faculty, and said: "We can all share the satisfaction of knowing that the new educational programs we move into here at Dartmouth today, reflect the conviction of our fine faculty as to how this College can be most responsive to its opportunities; they are not a mere reflex response to someone else's challenge. As with any new effort, we shall meet unexpected, as well as foreseen, difficulties in our new program; but even in such difficulties, you who are here today as students will have the supreme educational experience of learning *with*, rather than from, fine teachers." He also made the point that "he alone teaches truly who, in the same moment, is himself learning." This synthesis of teaching and learning

135

was a theme that Mr. Dickey had developed in June when he spoke at his daughter Sylvia's graduation from Wheelock College in Boston. In his remarks to the future teachers in Sylvia's class, he referred extensively to Rodgers and Hammerstein's musical, *The King and I*, and quoted from the song, "Getting to Know You," which was sung by Gertrude Lawrence in the role of the teacher of the King's children. *The King and I* was a great favorite of John Dickey's, and in his Convocation address of 1955 he had quoted another of its songs: "Whenever I feel afraid / I hold my head erect / And whistle a happy tune, / So no one will suspect / I'm afraid." The President had conferred an honorary Doctorate of Humane Letters on Oscar Hammerstein at the 1952 Commencement and had used the occasion to express, in his citation, the delight he took in the words of the gifted librettist.

New to the College as the year began were the Choate Road dormitories, all four of which were fully occupied for the first time. A faculty resident for each pair of dorms implemented a concept that had been introduced in a smaller way in Cutter Hall. Although the Choate Road group was constructed to relieve the crowding in the existing residence halls, the Trustees, looking ahead to an undergraduate enrollment of three thousand, authorized the preparation of plans for three more dormitories, to house an additional three hundred students, contingent upon approval of a $1.7-million loan from the U.S. Housing and Home Finance Administration, which had provided funds for the Choate Road group. Wigwam Circle, west of Thayer School, would make way for these dormitories, and early summer was the hoped-for time to begin their construction.

Not yet completed, but on the way to joining the new things on campus, were additions to the east and west wings of Steele Hall, the chemistry building. Together with added laboratories and faculty offices, the renovation provided an improved ventilation system and modern equipment, all to be ready in the fall of 1959. Perhaps not noticeable, but the newest of all new things, was the College's landmark smokestack—whose slow-motion plume of smoke on sub-zero days was watched to tell how cold it was. For safety reasons, it was torn down over the summer and rebuilt. The $700,000 cost of improving Steele Hall was one component of the capital-gifts campaign, which at the opening of the college year had reached $10-million toward its

$17-million goal. Another $100,000 was earmarked for two modest additions to Baker Library, one to provide more space for the Stefansson Collection, and the other to provide new quarters for rare books and the College Archives.

A major curriculum development inaugurated in 1958 along with the three-three program was the addition of a new Department of Engineering Science. An unusual feature of the department was its drawing upon the faculty of the Thayer School of Engineering, headed by Dean William P. Kimball, to teach the undergraduate courses. In cooperation with the Departments of Mathematics, Physics, and Chemistry, the Department of Engineering Science offered a four-year major, which had the aim of integrating engineering studies with the basic physical sciences, in line with the demands of modern engineering. After the major, the student could take a fifth year at Thayer School, leading to a professional engineering degree or a B.S. degree in the combined field of engineering and business administration, or, as a third option, a Master's degree in engineering science. The whole program required a strong underpinning of liberal arts. (Nearly forty percent of the undergraduate courses were to be in the humanities and social sciences.) This adherence to the liberal arts as the foundation for professional studies was a reaffirmation of the educational philosophy that had made Thayer distinctive among engineering schools ever since its founding in 1870.

The engineering science program was the outcome of several years of study by a special committee, which began its work in 1954 at the instigation of the Trustees Planning Committee. At that time, whether Thayer School could be maintained much longer was a matter of concern to the Trustees. Enrollment was small and the expense was growing; the educational program, along the traditional lines of civil, mechanical, and electrical engineering, was not keeping up with the kind of engineering that was developing in the technological world; and research was not a strong point of the School, although the work of Professor Millett Morgan on the ionosphere and of Professor James Browning on the nature of combustion was well known. It was decided that a critical evaluation of the engineering school needed to be made.

The *ad hoc* committee appointed by President Dickey in 1954 was headed by Dean Morrison and included three outside consultants on engineering education, in addition to Thayer School faculty and alumni and members of the College science faculty. The three members from outside were Gordon S. Brown, head of electrical engineering at the Massachusetts Institute of Technology; Dean S. C. Hollister of the Cornell Engineering School; and John A. Hutcheson, vice president of the Westinghouse Electric Company. The consulting group played the key role in the evaluation of Thayer's educational program, and in effect operated as a sub-committee within the main committee. It was their opinion that "Dartmouth has a golden opportunity to do two things at once. The first is to train well-rounded men, and the second is to give them a training in the physical sciences that will qualify them for the kind of engineering competence that will have the greatest social value in the future with the maximum potential for creative leadership. Very few schools now do this."

Dean Kimball, speaking for the Thayer School staff, was pleased with the outcome of the study, as well as the prospect of increased enrollment and a much brighter future for the School. Of the new educational plan itself, he said, "The program meets the two most significant emerging trends in engineering education and practice. These are the orientation of undergraduate engineering education toward basic and engineering sciences and the emphasis on 'systems' engineering, which requires close teamwork among engineers and scientists of different disciplines."

After the Thayer School program had been in operation for two years, the Dartmouth Trustees reviewed the situation and decided that the School should be allowed to grow into full graduate-school status, eventually offering the Doctor of Engineering degree. This second phase of the rejuvenation of Thayer School awaited the arrival, in 1961, of Dean Myron Tribus, under whom the School made great advances. The Board of Overseers, which was reorganized in 1957 and enlarged from five to nine members, acquired more members from outside the College. In the late Sixties it was enlarged again, to fifteen members, including the President, the Provost, and the Dean. One of the Overseers at the time of the TPC study was John C. Woodhouse, a top research scientist for the E. I. DuPont de Nemours Company and a former teacher of chemistry at Dartmouth and Harvard. He was elected to the Dartmouth Board of Trustees in 1960 and was ever a strong supporter of Thayer School.

John Dickey when he took over the Dartmouth presidency felt that all three associated schools needed to be lifted to new levels of scholarly endeavor and that they should be brought more into the mainstream of the College proper, instead of being viewed as just tagging along in their isolated ways. Funds given by Trustee Albert Bradley spurred more research and publication at Tuck School, and rejuvenation and expansion of the Medical School followed the great effort that went into saving that institution. Thayer School was the associated school that seemed to some to be the most distant from the mainstream that President Dickey had in mind, but with the establishment of the new engineering science department it suddenly acquired a closer relationship to the undergraduate college than the other two graduate schools had. It was one of the significant improvements achieved during the Dickey presidency that all three associated schools acquired greater distinction in their fields and became a more integral part of the whole College.

The Trustees at their fall meeting raised tuition from $1,170 to $1,400 for the academic year 1959–60. President Dickey explained that salary increases already in effect for 1958–59 were being financed in part by an Alumni Fund Faculty Salary Reserve, which would be exhausted by the end of the year. During the thirteen years of the postwar period, beginning with a tuition fee of $550 in 1946, Dartmouth's combined fee had been raised six times to reach the $1,400 announced for 1959. Although this averaged only a little more than $65 a year, the increases were becoming progressively larger and the latest two-year jump of $230 was the biggest the Trustees had ever voted. At the same time, financial aid provided by the College had been growing, and for 1958–59 it totaled more than $1-million. Of this amount, $62,000 was being expended in scholarship grants for the sons and daughters of faculty and administrative officers, under the more generous program put into effect that year.

The fall's major event was a four-day convocation on "Education for Moral Responsibility," November 13–16, marking the installation of Professor Fred Berthold as the first Dean of the William Jewett Tucker

Foundation. In a sense, it was the formal inauguration of the Tucker Foundation itself, which had been established in 1951 but had not been fully operational pending the naming of a dean. The convocation brought to Hanover some of the leading educators and religious leaders of the country. Addresses were given by Lewis Mumford, author and philosopher; Philip E. Jacob, professor of political science at the University of Pennsylvania; Gordon W. Allport, professor of psychology at Harvard University; and Charles P. Taft, vice president of the National Council of Churches of Christ. Discussion groups were led by Edward D. Eddy, provost of the University of New Hampshire; Dr. Kenneth Underwood, professor of government at Wesleyan University; and by undergraduates from Wellesley, Princeton, and Dartmouth. At the opening installation ceremony in Rollins Chapel, the sermon was preached by the Reverend Henry Pitney Van Dusen, president of Union Theological Seminary. For the worship service which closed the convocation on Sunday morning, the guest preacher was the Reverend David A. MacLennan, minister of The Brick Presbyterian Church of Rochester, New York. Dean Berthold spoke briefly at the installation ceremony and also conducted the Friday morning chapel service. His installation had been delayed one year after his appointment, in order that he might be on leave to finish his book *The Fear of God*, a study of religious anxiety.

In late November of 1958 the Dartmouth chapter of the American Association of University Professors made public an unofficial scale of Dartmouth faculty compensation, compiled by means of a survey that elicited anonymous replies from more than two hundred faculty members. It was College policy not to give out such information, since a unique package of fringe benefits was part of compensation, and when base salaries alone were compared, as was the practice of the national AAUP, Dartmouth's ranking was not fairly presented. The Dartmouth chapter felt, however, that its survey would benefit faculty morale and would produce information to which the faculty was entitled.

The average compensation for full-time faculty, combining base salary and fringe benefits, was found to be $11,072 for full professors, $9,357 for associate professors, $7,508 for assistant professors, $6,315 for instructors qualifying for the 16 percent annuity benefit, and $5,532 for instructors not so covered. "The Dartmouth salaries are not at all ones to be concealed," the survey committee said. When compared with standards set by the national AAUP, Dartmouth's average figures were rather good for all ranks except that of full professor, where compensation ranged from a low of $8,867 to a high of $14,667.

The phlebitis that had plagued Mr. Dickey for years flared up again, and on December 10, 1958, he underwent leg surgery and had to remain in Dick's House for two weeks, before being allowed to go home for Christmas. Being hospitalized prevented him from participating in the Dartmouth Polar Conference held in Hanover on December 18–19. In conjunction with the conference, the Committee on Polar Research of the National Academy of Science, headed by President Laurence M. Gould of Carleton College, held its regular meeting in Hanover. Dartmouth's conference had the joint sponsorship of the College and The New World Foundation. Its main topic of discussion was the need for polar research centers in the United States, after the international cooperation experienced during the International Geophysical Year. A very distinguished group of scientists, government officials, and military officers came to Hanover, and the College added to its reputation as one of the recognized centers of polar studies in the country.

President Dickey, although somewhat lame, returned to his office on a part-time basis in January. Unfortunately, early February found him back in the hospital, this time for another operation to remove some cartilage in one knee. It was not until March that he was back to a normal schedule. One of the first events in which he fully participated was the annual Pentagonal Conference, for which he was host to the presidents and top administrative officers of Amherst, Bowdoin, Wesleyan, and Williams. The conference was initiated by President Hopkins in the 1930's and was held each year, on a rotating basis, at one of the five campuses. Its relatively small size and the candor and informality with which discussions were conducted made it a favorite event for all the college officers involved.

Among the academic advances Dartmouth was making in this second decade of the Dickey presidency, nothing was more impressive than the growing excellence and reputation of the College's mathematics program, developed under the chairmanship of Professor John G. Kemeny, who had come to Dartmouth from Princeton in 1954 with the rank of full professor. He and his colleagues in the department had not only modernized courses and revamped undergraduate instruction, but they themselves were greatly engaged in research and in the writing of textbooks that were widely used in higher education. Largely in recognition of this excellence, the Alfred P. Sloan Foundation gave the College $500,000 to establish the Albert Bradley Center for Mathematics and Mathematical Research. Mr. Bradley himself made a substantial gift toward the Center, which was to be housed in a new building on Elm Street, just north of Baker Library. (Mr. Bradley was for many years an associate of Mr. Sloan, whom he succeeded as chairman of the General Motors Corporation's board.) With the Sloan Foundation grant, the capital-gifts campaign chairman was able to announce in mid-February that the drive had passed the $13-million mark.

In this year that was witnessing one new thing after another, the admissions office contributed its bit by initiating an "early acceptance" plan, which permitted highly qualified secondary-school seniors to complete their applications in the fall or early winter and, if successful, to receive immediate certification of admission. In return, the admitted student had to commit himself to Dartmouth and drop applications to all other colleges. Those applying for early admission and not getting immediate acceptance were not handicapped in any way, but were reconsidered in the regular pool of applicants in March and April. During the first year of the admissions office's new system, eighty-eight men were granted early acceptance.

A year that was going so well was dealt a stunning blow by the sudden death on March 17, 1959, of Provost Donald Morrison, at the age of 44. He died in his sleep of a heart attack at the Princeton home of his former teacher, Professor John F. Sly, chairman of Princeton's department of politics. He had spent the previous day meeting with foundation executives in New York City and then had gone to stay overnight with Professor Sly. When he did not respond to efforts to awaken him the next morning, his worried host entered his room and found him dead.

The loss to the College was "beyond the reach of words," as President Dickey expressed it. Provost Morrison for nearly twelve years had spearheaded the educational advancement of the institution, rebuilding the faculty, pushing research activity, helping to establish new courses and departmental policies, and directing the faculty deliberations and compromises that led to the adoption of the three-term, three-course program. One of his greatest contributions was the part he played in saving a declining Medical School and in turning it into a first-rate center of clinical instruction and basic-science research. At the time of his death he was devoting a great deal of his time to the development of a new Medical School curriculum and was vice-chairman of the Trustees Planning Committee.

For President Dickey the death of Donald Morrison was a great tragedy and an immense personal loss. It deprived him of the administrative associate with whom he worked most comfortably and upon whom he relied with the greatest confidence. This close relationship had begun when Professor Morrison moved into Parkhurst Hall as Dean of the Faculty, and it continued in an even fuller way when he became the Provost of the College. John Dickey's need of the kind of support he got from Donald Morrison was indicated by the choice of a close friend, Librarian Richard Morin, to come into the office temporarily, to be his special assistant and to help with affairs of the office of the Provost.

Before the end of the academic year the College had a new Provost. In June it was announced that John W. Masland, Professor of Government, would fill the position, and that Leonard M. Rieser, Associate Professor of Physics, would have the newly created post of Deputy Provost. Professor Rieser, while continuing to teach, had special responsibility for academic affairs within the Division of the Sciences. Professor Jensen, Dean of the Faculty, continued to be responsible for educational policy and personnel in the Divisions of the Humanities and Social Sciences, and he also assumed responsibility for institution-wide planning preliminary to the introduction of a fourth academic term in the summer, as had been approved in principle by the faculty. Provost Masland, an expert on national security policies, came to Dartmouth from Stanford one year after John Dickey became President. Like Mr. Dickey, he had earlier served with the U.S. State Department and at the San Francisco conference at which the United Nations charter was drafted. As one of his three books, he wrote with Professor Gene M. Lyons of Dartmouth a study of ROTC, a work that had great influence in the academic world and the military services.

Another major administrative change took place at the close of the 1958–59 college year. Joseph L. McDonald retired as Dean of the College and to take his place Mr. Dickey named Thaddeus Seymour, Assistant Professor of English. Dean McDonald, after teaching economics for twenty-nine years and serving as Dean for seven more, retired amidst universal praise for his understanding relations with students and his loyalty to the College. Dean Seymour, whose undergraduate days were divided between Princeton and Stanford, had the same rapport with students as a teacher and counselor. Engaged in a variety of departmental activities, he still found time to help out in the admissions office and to coach the Dartmouth crew. And to add to his cachet on campus, he was a skilled magician and the owner of an antique Packard touring car with a fold-down top. Dean Seymour ultimately went on from his Dartmouth job to be president of Wabash College in Indiana and, then, of Rollins College in Florida.

Winding up what was by any standard an extraordinary year, National Chairman Zimmerman announced that Dartmouth's capital-gifts campaign had achieved its $17-million goal and would most certainly exceed it, since the campaign was being kept open until December 31, in order that alumni might have the whole tax year in which to determine the full amount of their gifts. Success in the fund drive enabled the College to activate some of the projects the campaign was designed to finance. The leading component, of course, was $5-million to be added to the $2.5-million previously raised for the Hopkins Center. Another priority component was $3-million to provide current-use and endowment money for continuing the improvement of faculty compensation. A third component was $2-million for the new mathematics-psychology facilities, for which plans were being drawn; and a fourth was $3-million for a proposed auditorium-arena and athletic facilities. Since the Alumni Fund had been integrated with the capital campaign, the sum of $2.5-million was earmarked to maintain that vital support for two years and to cover campaign expenses. From campaign funds the College had already expended $700,000 for additions and renovations at Steele Hall, and $100,000 for enclosing and developing two courtyards of Baker Library. And funds were now in hand or pledged to make possible other classroom and laboratory improvements. In addition to these main components, construction was scheduled to begin in July on a new $3.5-million medical sciences building, financed by the Medical School's own fund campaign. In all, new construction and renovations authorized by the Trustees had a price tag of $15-million, of which $12-million came from the College's fund drive. It was the greatest burst of plant expansion in thirty years, and a great deal more was to come in the remaining years of the Dickey administration.

President Dickey did not share the attitude of those purists in the academic world who held "bricks and mortar" in contempt. He had referred to this in his 1957 Convocation address, when he said, ". . . any man or any enterprise that must choose between essential ingredients of strength is not a candidate for true greatness, let alone preeminence. The college that must long make choices as between men and facilities will soon find it has done so at the ultimate expense of both. The price of greatness is never stated in one or the other of two essentials. For us it means *both* first-rate men and first-rate facilities."

Over the summer, excavation for the Hopkins Center at the southern end of the campus produced what was unquestionably the biggest hole dug in Hanover since the glacier retreated northward. To those most concerned it was a reassurance that the center was actually going to happen, and to students, faculty, and townspeople it was a place of endless fascination as the vagaries of the weather and the pile-drivers provided a daily sidewalk show. North of the campus, near the hospital, large-scale construction was progressing on the new seven-story medical sciences building. Each of the Medical School's six departments—anatomy, physiology, biochemistry, pharmacology, pathology, and microbiology—was to occupy its own floor, with the top floor allocated to an animal house and animal operating room. The School's administrative offices also were to have space in the building. The Medical School's fund drive, which had the medical sciences building as its major component, had reached slightly more than half of its $10-million goal when the fall semester began.

With the opening of the college year in September 1959, the College had in place an LPG-30 high-speed digital computer, which was welcomed especially by those who had been traveling to M.I.T. to get computer help with their research problems. Very few saw this one computer for what it was—the forerunner of a mushroom growth of computers and computer science that was to give Dartmouth a special distinction among American colleges. The LPG-30 was purchased with funds from the Alfred P. Sloan Foundation grant for the Bradley Mathematics Center, and until that building was ready the computer was housed in the tabulating center in the basement of College Hall. Professor Thomas E. Kurtz, who was to be director of the Albert Bradley Center, was in no danger of being caught out on a limb when he predicted that the faculty would find the LPG-30 a useful research tool and that "students would also become familiar with computers' possibilities that they might find useful in college work and in their later careers."

A personnel change in the President's office had occurred during the summer with the appointment of Gilbert R. Tanis of the development office to be Executive Officer of the College. In this position he became the principal assistant to President Dickey and the person responsible for liaison between the President's office and the Board of Trustees. He succeeded Frank Smallwood, who left Parkhurst Hall to become Assistant Professor of Government. Mr. Tanis had come to Dartmouth from the International Paper Company in 1951, to be an associate in development, and since 1957 he had been the President's special assistant for corporate giving.

In September, with ten years to go to the bicentennial, the College entered upon "what could be Dartmouth's most decisive decade," as President Dickey saw it. This evaluation was stated in the President's Convocation address, which once again picked up the topic of the previous year's address and moved on to an allied subject. Mr. Dickey elected to add fellowship to his 1958 discussion of community, declaring it to be "perhaps the highest expression of that interdependence out of which we create our community." He had nothing good to say about "blatant conviviality or sentimentality," but he was willing to run the risk of talking about fellowship, he said, because of the real need in America, especially in education, to build an effective two-way bridge between the individual and the group, and because of his wish "to pay unashamed tribute to what the Dartmouth fellowship means to this enterprise of higher learning."

The President deplored "the extent to which our time has pushed its abhorrence of commitment," and went on to say, "Commitment to any human cause, sooner or later, tests a man's capacity for loyalty. This is simply to say that anything human is perforce imperfect and from time to time has troubles and need of help. A college is 'Exhibit A' of this proposition, and Dartmouth is no exception. The extraordinary resiliency of this College, whatever her problems, has often been noted by the leaders of other institutions. I suggest to you that such built-in strength is anchored in a loyalty that from generation to generation has recognized, as all true loyalty must, that the ongoing College is always greater than either its triumphs or its failures. Such is the loyalty of fellowship. Loyalty only to that which is believed perfect is no loyalty at all."

One of the major sub-committees formed under the aegis of the Trustees Planning Committee was the one named in the spring of 1958 to study the organization of the Board of Trustees. It was chaired by Mr. Hood, senior member of the board and chairman of the TPC, and included President-Emeritus Hopkins among its members. In the report it submitted fifteen months later, the committee recommended that the board be enlarged from twelve to sixteen members by adding two Life Trustees and two Alumni Trustees, and that the College seek the New Hampshire legislature's approval of eliminating the charter requirement that at least five Trustees be residents of the state. It also recommended that the chairmanship of the board not be restricted to the President of the College, as had in practice been the case since 1822, and that the standing committees of the board be realigned to conform to the administrative organization of the College. The committee urged retention of the mandatory retirement age of seventy for Trustees and saw no reason to change the existing schedule of meetings in October, January, April, and June. It did, however, propose that the board and Alumni Council meet jointly in Hanover every other year to hear reports and hold working sessions.

At their meeting following the presentation of the report on organization, the Trustees adopted the proposed realignment of standing committees. The board now had an executive committee, an investment committee, a budget committee, an educational affairs committee, a building and grounds committee, an alumni and public affairs committee, and a trustees planning committee. A bill authorizing the enlargement of the Board of Trustees to sixteen members was introduced in the New Hampshire legislature in February 1961 by Professor Fletcher Low, one of Hanover's representatives to the General Court. It was passed by both houses in April and was signed into law by Governor Wesley Powell. (It was not until March of 1967 that the legislature passed a bill eliminating the Dartmouth charter requirement that five members of the board be residents of New Hampshire.) The increase in the size of the board permitted spreading the workload, yet kept the board small enough to maintain its character as a working board that made decisions as a whole.

The report of the committee on Trustee organization was one of fifteen that had been completed since the Trustee Planning Committee began its work in 1954. The institution-wide scope of TPC planning was underscored in a five-year summary of what had been reviewed and recommended, prepared by Frank Smallwood, TPC secretary, and printed in the April 1960 issue of the *Dartmouth Alumni Magazine*. The sub-committees he listed included those dealing with College purpose, College size, plant planning, development, the educational program, admissions and financial aid, the Medical School, Thayer School, Tuck School, alumni relations, athletics, non-athletic activities, Dartmouth Outing Club, student health, community environment, transportation, financial arrangements with the associated schools, and use of the plant by other than undergraduates. Some of the recommendations that were quickly implemented have been mentioned in the chronicle of the Dickey administration up to this point. The three-term, three-course curriculum is one, the engineering science program is another, and new plant construction still another.

The very first report presented to the Board of Trustees was prepared by President Dickey and dealt with Dartmouth's purpose. In it he cited those elements of purpose inherited from the past that should still guide the College: "(1) An over-riding sense of public obligation. The work of the College proceeds on the historical assumption that the ultimate obligation of this institution is to human society. (2) A commitment to the liberal arts as the best educational foundation for the fullest possible development of individual goodness and competence. (3) A commitment to the primacy of undergraduate education." Mr. Dickey concluded his report with the statement: ". . . the liberal arts college, more than any other institution in American life, is directly concerned at the higher levels of education with the development in all its products *both* the will and the capacity to serve the public good regardless of how the individual makes his own living. If Dartmouth annually can put six hundred such public-minded, competent citizens back into the home communities of our forty-eight states during the next fifteen years, she may be able to make a truly decisive contribution to the perpetuation of the human heritage which all education holds in trust. That, at this point, should be her ennobling aim."

A second early report submitted to the Trustees had to do with the future size of the College. The sub-committee, headed by Trustee Dudley Orr, proposed that there be a planned increase of 400 undergraduates, bringing enrollment, exclusive of graduate students in the three associated schools, to 3,000 in the early 1960's. This was recommended on the assumption that the necessary personnel and facilities would be available by then. The report stated that going beyond 3,000 was not desirable, although it recognized that future circumstances might call for a higher undergraduate limit.

In other areas, TPC committees recommended changes in the College's fund-raising organization, which were in place for the successful carrying out of the $17-million, capital-gifts campaign; a consolidation of all intercollegiate, intramural, and physical education programs under a single administrator, with policy guidance provided by the Dartmouth College Athletic Council; and changes in many phases of the Dartmouth alumni program, looking toward better lines of communication between the College and alumni, improved regional organization to complement the highly successful class organization, and more programs to satisfy the intellectual interests of alumni. One of the recommendations—that the Alumni Council be enlarged from forty to fifty members—was approved by the General Alumni Association at its June 1959 meeting. As a sort of non-TPC offshoot of the studies made of the Thayer and Tuck Schools, an *ad hoc* report recommended to the Trustees a joint Tuck-Thayer program leading to the new degree of Bachelor of Industrial Administration. This received the board's approval, along with the introduction of two new courses: Engineering Analysis and Design, taught by the Thayer faculty, and Scientific Analysis in Industry, taught by members of both faculties.

Monday morning, November 2, 1959, the first working day of Mr. Dickey's fifteenth year as President, was following the regular weekly practice of holding a staff meeting of top administrative officers. Mary Shaw, the President's secretary, broke in to remind Mr. Dickey that it would soon be time for an important noon appointment. He stopped in bewilderment, knowing that his lunch period was free. Before he could say anything, however, the entire remaining administrative staff trooped into his office to extend affectionate greetings to him at the start of his fifteenth year. The meeting came to an abrupt end. A message was read from Mr. Hood, extended on behalf of the Trustees, and also one from Dean McDonald in London. Mr. Hayward, acting for the President's administrative colleagues, presented to him an oversized greeting card signed by all those present, and then read an inter-office memo that saluted him as the senior president in the Ivy Group and said, in part: "There are not enough occasions for us as associates to say to the man so capably filling your job that we admire and respect, and are grateful for, the qualities of leadership and the devotion to the great cause of the liberal arts that distinguish your administration.

"Nor are there enough opportunities—so welcome as this one is—for a group of your friends to greet you warmly in person, to say as one man to another, that we know something of what you go through to do your job; to express our deep appreciation for your friendly interest in each of us; to declare hopefully that the first fourteen years are the hardest; and to say that we would like to be here ten years from today when the College celebrates its 200th year, and you your twenty-fifth."

President Dickey, in his response, was generous in the credit he gave to his associates for the advances Dartmouth had made in the past fourteen years. He mentioned some of these advances, as he had when he reviewed the first decade of his presidency four years earlier, and then he made a very characteristic remark. "I don't think I have made any big mistakes," he said. John Dickey was not given to hasty decisions. He carefully weighed the pros and cons of a matter, and more than once expressed the view that it was a sound policy to take all the time necessary to arrive at the right decision. This caution sometimes caused delays, as was true in launching a capital-gifts campaign, but the end result was no big mistakes and very few little ones.

The tribute to John Dickey from administrative staff was later matched by one from the faculty at their annual meeting on October 19, 1960. The faculty adopted this resolution: "Whereas John Sloan Dickey has completed fifteen distinguished years as President of Dartmouth College: Be it resolved that the Faculty of Dartmouth College congratulate him on his many successes during these years, and wish for him health, vigor, and continuation of his leadership during many years to come."

The faculty had good reason to be supportive of President Dickey. His office was open to any faculty member who wanted to see him, as it was to students and others. He had quickened the pace of intellectual life at the College and he had been mindful, from the very first days of his presidency, of the need to keep striving for increasingly higher levels of compensation for the teaching staff. The College's total of instructional expense when he became President was $1.317-million. For the year preceding the faculty's resolution of congratulation it was $4.269-million.

Shortly after beginning his fifteenth year, President Dickey held a press conference in his office with three U.S. Army generals involved in the establishment of the Army Corps of Engineers' Cold Regions Research and Engineering Laboratory (CRREL) in Hanover. Also present was U.S. Senator Norris Cotton, who along with Senator Styles Bridges and Congressmen Perkins Bass and Chester Merrow had shepherded authorization of the new laboratory through Congress. Lieutenant General Arthur G. Trudeau, chief of Army research and development, explained that research in the physical properties of snow, ice, and permafrost would be combined with the development of engineering techniques applicable to arctic construction. Lieutenant General E. C. Itschner, chief of the Army Corps of Engineers, announced that the new facility, to be ready by 1962, would cost $3.2-million and have a staff of about 170 persons. This meant an influx of about eighty families and the addition of some seventy children to Hanover's school population. Beyond the economic impact on the community, the arrival of a number of eminent polar scientists was anticipated as a stimulus to the College's own educational work about the polar regions.

The Dartmouth Trustees at their January 1960 meeting approved the final stage of the plant expansion made possible by the capital-gifts campaign. In place of the auditorium-arena originally planned, the revised program called for two separate buildings, one an auditorium seating up to three thousand persons, for events that could not be accommodated in Webster Hall; the other a large field house for indoor track and practice facilities for football, baseball, and other sports. The latter would be available for holding Commencement and other large events, in case of bad weather. Also included in the plant program was the remodeling of the west wing of Alumni Gymnasium, to provide a new basketball court and stands, as well as a complete reconstruction of the east wing of the gym to house a swimming pool meeting the highest intercollegiate standards. The cost of the four-part program was estimated at $3.2-million. As things turned out, the idea of a separate auditorium was eventually dropped, but the other plans were successfully carried out.

To coincide with the presence in town of both the Trustees and members of the Alumni Council, holding their annual winter meeting, a celebratory dinner was attended by three hundred persons in Commons on January 22, marking the success of the capital-gifts campaign. National Chairman Zimmerman announced that the final total of the two-year drive was $17,574,794. The dinner was another black-tie event, and with colorful decorations, a student orchestra, and the glee club, it was reminiscent, on a much smaller scale, of the Hopkins dinner held at the Waldorf two years previously. Mr. Hopkins was present as an honored guest, and once again heard the glee club sing "Ernest Martin Hopkins" to the tune of "Eleazar Wheelock." On behalf of the Trustees, Mr. Hood presented Mr. Zimmerman with an inscribed gift "for extraordinary service to the College." As the final speaker, President Dickey chose as his subject "The Mission of Liberal Learning," but preliminary to that he spoke of the new strength the campaign had given to the College. "We are entitled," he said, "to the confidence that goes with knowing that we go forward from a strong situation, that the critical fronts of the College are more strongly held than they were five years ago, that we see more clearly where we need to go, and perhaps above all, that we have learned we have it in us to mount and sustain the kind of total effort that brings reality to great aspirations."

Mr. Dickey stated that there was no mystery about the foundation that must sustain any great institution of higher learning. "It has three parts: primarily, an institution-wide sense of adequate purpose; secondly, teachers who personify that learning which goes higher because it is both broad and deep and which is education because it teaches the self to learn; thirdly, students who are able, ready, and willing to work for a truly higher education. No edifice of educational preeminence can be erected if all those elements are not present and strong." Regarding the maintenance of a first-rate faculty, he declared that compensation was not the whole of the matter, although it was a good place to begin. He was happy to announce, he added, that the Trustees had accepted the challenge of enabling Dartmouth's top teacher-scholars to reach an annual income, including benefits, in the $25,000 range, well before 1969. Vital to the achievement of that goal, he said, would be an Alumni Fund that progressively exceeded $1-million.

On April 1, 1960, the deadline arrived for eliminating all nationally imposed discrimination clauses in the constitutions of Dartmouth fraternities. In the six years since the Trustees had set the deadline, in accordance with the results of an undergraduate referendum, only one fraternity, Phi Gamma Delta, had not met the requirement, but over the summer it also gained local autonomy. The process of bringing all Dartmouth fraternities to the position of being free of outside dictation had been a long one, going back, in fact, to the Larmon report of 1936. That report called for severing all national ties and was particularly critical of the discriminatory membership criteria imposed upon local chapters. After a three-year trial period, the situation was deemed improved enough to permit the tabling of the Larmon report. And so things remained until 1949, when the Northeastern Interfraternity Conference asked the National Fraternity Conference to eliminate all discriminatory clauses. The Dartmouth Interfraternity Council, in turn, endorsed the position of the Northeastern Conference. Of three Dartmouth undergraduate referenda that followed, all overwhelmingly against discrimination, the one of 1954 was the most important, because it led to the setting of the 1960 deadline by the Trustees.

President Dickey had made it clear that he believed fraternities had a place in the social life of the College, if they could conduct themselves in keeping with the educational philosophy of the institution. In a WDCR interview one year before the deadline, he also had made clear his belief that students should be free to choose their social fellows. "I have never taken the position," he said, "that we should have a policy that requires fraternities to take men they do not want. Personally all I want is that every Dartmouth social group may take or reject their members from the Dartmouth undergraduate body on the basis of the preferences and prejudices, if you will, of that group itself, rather than the preferences and prejudices of some very remote national charter written long ago."

The month that brought a completely independent status to Dartmouth fraternities also brought the third annual April Music Festival, which had taken on an established character and enhanced the College's reputation as a place seriously interested in the arts. The festivals, directed by Professor James A. Sykes, were a sort of warm-up for the more ambitious musical programs envisioned for the Hopkins Center. Even so, they were top-level, international events, important in their own right, and they were significant in the Dickey administration as evidence that a fresh emphasis was being given to the arts. The three-day festivals enjoyed the participation of leading composers, conductors, orchestral groups, soloists, musicologists, and critics, and this had the advantage of bringing Dartmouth increasingly to the attention of the art world. A conductor who had a prominent role in the early festivals was Mario di Bonaventura, who in the spring of 1962 became a professor in the Music department and the Director of Music for the Hopkins Center. That appointment was balanced a few months later by the naming of James Clancy of Stanford University to be Professor of English and Director of Theater for the Center.

As the academic year 1959–60 neared its end, on April 30 President Dickey was honored by the Federal Republic of Germany with its Commander's Cross of the Order of Merit. The presentation was made in Hanover by Dr. Guenther Motz, German consul in Boston, acting in behalf of President Heinrich Lubke of West Germany. Mr. Dickey was cited for fostering international understanding between the United States and Germany and for extending hospitality to guests from that nation, including President Theodor Heuss, who had received a Dartmouth honorary degree and addressed the graduating class at the 1958 Commencement.

One other year-end action was the Trustees' approval of an enlargement of Dartmouth's already generous fringe benefits for faculty and staff. Under the plan the College assumed the full cost of a group major-medical insurance program providing protection against the catastrophic expense of severe illness or accident. At the same time, President Dickey announced added coverage in the group life-insurance plan, with $3,000 remaining in force at no cost after retirement.

In mid-summer, a change in the Parkhurst Hall staff occurred with the arrival of Charles F. Dey, a history teacher at Andover Phillips Academy, to be Assistant Dean of the College. He succeeded Eugene Hotchkiss 3rd, Associate Dean, who left to be dean of students at Harvey Mudd College in California. The administrative staff of which Mr. Dey became the newest member numbered ninety men and women in the fall of 1960. This compared with forty-three administrative officers who were on the College roster when John Dickey became President fifteen years earlier. The increase had occurred mainly in the business offices and in the office of development. Creation of the Tucker Foundation and reorganization of the admissions and financial-aid offices also were factors in the doubling of the administrative corps.

With the "refounding" of the Dartmouth Medical School so much to the fore in the College's march toward a new level of excellence prior to the bicentennial, the time was propitious for another Great Issues Convocation. This one, held September 8–10, 1960, was devoted to "The Great Issues of Conscience in Modern Medicine." Like the convocation of three years earlier, it consisted of an opening assembly, several major addresses, panel discussions, and a closing honorary-degree ceremony. And like the 1957 convocation on Great Issues in the Anglo-Canadian-American Community, it had a very distinguished group of participants, headed by Dr. René Dubos, world-famous microbiologist and staff member of the Rockefeller Institute, who was convocation chairman. Twelve others who took part in the assemblies and panel discussions were Aldous Huxley, author; C. P. Snow, author and scientist; Mohamedali Currim Chagla, Indian Ambassador to the United States and Canada; Brock Chisholm, Canadian physician-author and former director-general of the World Health Organization; Ralph Gerard, professor of neurophysiology at the University of Michigan's Mental Health Research Institute; George B. Kistiakowsky, physical chemist and special assistant to President Eisenhower for science and technology; Walsh McDermott, professor of public health and preventive medicine at Cornell Medical College; Hermann J. Muller, professor of zoology at Indiana University and winner of the 1946 Nobel Prize in physiology and medicine; Wilder Penfield, Canadian neurosurgeon and director of the Montreal Neurological Institute; Sir George Pickering, Regius Professor of Medicine at Oxford University; Sandor Rado, dean of the New York School of Psychiatry; and Warren Weaver, vice president of the Alfred P. Sloan Foundation and former Rockefeller Foundation vice president for the natural and medical sciences. Dr. Ward Darley, executive director of the Association of American Medical Colleges, also attended the convocation and was the principal speaker at a ceremony at which President Dickey and Trustee Harvey Hood spread the mortar for setting an inscribed slab in the floor near the main entrance to the new medical sciences building. (After he had performed his part of the masonry, Mr. Dickey asked Leo Wexler, president of the Wexler Construction Company, if he would like to hire him. "I don't think so," Mr. Wexler replied.)

Requests for tickets to the sessions of the convocation totaled more than two thousand and made it necessary to hold the two evening assemblies and three panel discussions in the west wing of the gymnasium. Some of the problems taken up by the panelists were environmental dangers, food additives, increasing longevity, new techniques for human reproduction, overpopulation, birth control, the so-called "statistical morality," and the control of social conduct through the behavioral sciences, drugs, and psychiatric procedures. As C. P. Snow pointed out in a final summing-up, more questions were raised than answers provided, but the discussions made all aware that scientific advances had brought not only benefits but also moral issues that medicine had never faced before.

The convocation aroused considerable interest beyond Hanover and was well covered by newspapers, medical journals, radio, and television. Boston's educational TV station WGBH carried nearly the entire proceedings the week after the convocation, and some months later the national educational television network presented three ninety-minute programs based on the convocation discussions. WBZ Radio of Boston broadcast a series of eleven half-hour programs, and tapes of the Hanover sessions were used by Voice of America and by the British

Broadcasting Corporation. One of the strong points of the convocation was its international character, and in this respect the hand of John Dickey could clearly be detected.

The symbols of the medical convocation were still in place when students and faculty gathered in Alumni Gymnasium for the opening exercises of the College's 191st year. Student sit-ins had begun in the southern states in February 1960 and President Dickey, in his Convocation address, mentioned the part played by students in political upheavals in Hungary, Korea, Japan, and Cuba. While expressing his understanding of youth's urge to storm the barricades of the existing order, and adding that "Dartmouth stands where education has always stood: we're on the side of youth," he nevertheless made clear his aversion to mob action. "Reason alone can lead us to positive answers to such problems," he said. "Mobs, whether composed of students or savages, can only destroy and never create, because they are a mechanism of hate, rather than of mind. There are few things more fundamental to a man who aspires to the power of higher learning than an acquired distaste for mobs. Never doubt that this distaste requires our constant cultivation. This is especially true for the American student, because it is his lot to inherit an appointed task of personal and national leadership that simply cannot be performed in hotheaded self-indulgence." Before the Sixties were over, Mr. Dickey had reason, on his own campus, to sharpen his denunciation of mob action and to lose patience with "those who are more interested in using youth than in their education."

The citation accompanying an honorary degree from Oberlin College several weeks after Convocation called Mr. Dickey "an apostle of 'public-mindedness' and an authority on international relations." He was there to deliver an address at the October 22 inauguration of his Dartmouth classmate, Robert K. Carr, as Oberlin's president. (To take that post Mr. Carr had resigned as Professor of Government at Dartmouth.) President Dickey's relatively short address was one of his best statements concerning the importance of institutional purpose in the undergraduate college. It also provided him with the opportunity to speak again of the undergraduate liberal arts college as the last institutional embodiment of the dual purpose of competence and conscience. In other addresses Mr. Dickey had rarely spoken of religion. To his

Oberlin audience he said, "The dispersed and reduced position of formal religion in secular higher education is the most conspicuous and probably the most powerful negative factor in the progressive weakening we are witnessing in the college's sense of a dual purpose. This negative factor is paralleled on the positive side by the rise of a philosophy of pluralism and relativism that while nurturing the imperatives of specialized scholarship has so far proved a thin and acid soil for any new growth of institutional purpose."

Back in Hanover, President Dickey announced that Dudley Orr had assumed the chairmanship of the Trustees Planning Committee, succeeding Mr. Hood, who had headed it since its formation in October 1954. Mr. Hood continued as a member of the committee and also as chairman of the executive committee of the Board of Trustees.

Mention has been made of the warm welcome given to an increasing number of foreign guests at the College. Late October brought to the campus ten prominent Soviet scholars, writers, artists, and administrators, who met for a week of discussions with a similar group of Americans. President Dickey was a member of the planning committee for the conference, one of a series sponsored by the U.S. State Department and financed by the Ford Foundation. The Americans participating included such distinguished citizens as George F. Kennan, Norman Cousins, Walt Rostow, Grenville Clark, Arthur Larson, Philip Mosely, Stuart Chase, William Benton, Agnes de Mille, Russell Crouse, and Jerome Wiesner. Topics dealt with were the economic development of emerging nations, arms control, the creation of a structured peace, the psychological foundations of peace, and the role of the citizen in the development of foreign policy. The discussions were closed and no news stories were written, but a joint statement released in New York after the Soviet delegation left Hanover said that enough progress had been made in the amicable discussions at Dartmouth to justify another such meeting in the following year, probably in the Soviet Union. The College could take a further bit of credit in the leadership provided by Shepard Stone, Class of 1929, international affairs program director for the Ford Foundation.

The Dickey administration's efforts to develop the faculty took a new form with the adoption of a faculty fellowship program that would allow selected members of the faculty, particularly young assistant professors, to devote a full, uninterrupted year to research or other scholarly activity. The plan, which was separate from regular sabbatical leaves, provided a grant of up to $2,500 in addition to regular compensation, to cover travel and special expenses. To finance the initial faculty fellowships, the Trustees allocated $100,000 from the 1960 Alumni Fund. In announcing the program, President Dickey said that assistant professors would be favored because they usually had to forgo the advancement of their scholarship in order to establish themselves as teachers. He also said that the faculty fellowships were being established as much to attract young teacher-scholars to Dartmouth as they were to advance the careers of those already at the College.

Faculty news of a different kind came out of the winter meeting of the Board of Trustees. President Dickey disclosed that the new dean of Thayer School of Engineering would be Professor Myron Tribus of the University of California at Los Angeles, beginning with the academic year 1961–62. Professor Tribus, an award-winning researcher in heat transfer, thermodynamics, and fluid mechanics, was chosen to succeed Dean Kimball, who asked to be relieved of administrative duties so that he could devote full time to developing a new concept of civil engineering education called "environmental engineering." Dean-elect Tribus was to bring to Hanover an impressive record as developer of thermal ice protection equipment for aircraft in World War II, as chairman of several divisions of American engineering societies and institutes, as visiting director of icing research at the University of Michigan, consultant to NATO in London, and as author and host of a CBS television series on the problems of science and society. A dynamic, hard-driving personality, he was just the man to make things happen at Thayer School.

That Mr. Dickey had been finding some time for non-presidential interests was attested by the publication of *The Secretary of State* (Prentice Hall, 1961), for which he had written the chapter entitled "The Secretary and the American Public." For this contribution he naturally drew on his experience as Director of the U.S. State Department's Office of Public Affairs, the position he held when elected president of Dartmouth. Mr. Dickey's main point was that secrecy in the conduct of foreign affairs is a thing of the past, having given way in the Twentieth

Century to a "public dimension" that is now perhaps the major factor in diplomacy. Four things, he wrote, have brought this about: extension of the democratic process, modern communications, the need of statesmen and nations to woo public opinion on an international scale, and the absolute necessity to have public support for policies of state that involve the commitment of national resources and manpower or the changing of rules governing domestic life. "Leaks are effective only under conditions of secrecy," Mr. Dickey wrote, "and the essential story told in this paper is that a climate of secrecy is no longer compatible with the conduct of the office of the Secretary of State."

President Dickey took a much more substantial break from his Dartmouth duties when, on February 24, he left for Poland as head of a five-man cultural delegation sponsored by the Ford Foundation. The purpose of the mission was to interview and select some sixty Polish scholars, executives, and cultural leaders for awards enabling them to travel to the United States and to Western European nations for study, research, and conferences with their Western counterparts. The assignment took about three weeks, and Mr. Dickey was back in this country by March 19.

Three days later the President was off on a series of alumni dinners in nine major cities from coast to coast, beginning at Philadelphia on March 22 and ending at Los Angeles on April 7. Since the Alumni Fund with its first million-dollar goal was about to begin, the tour was especially important and Mr. Dickey was accompanied by John D. Dodd, fund chairman, and Clifford L. Jordan, executive secretary of the fund. It was the President's own suggestion that his travels on the alumni circuit be more purposefully planned, so he could visit the more populated alumni centers and meet with enrollment workers and other key volunteers, as well as with Alumni Fund class agents. With his tour in the spring of 1961 a pattern was set for the rest of the Sixties: New York and Boston dinners every year, West Coast dinners every other year, and varying schedules of other major cities on a rotating basis. Mr. Dickey found it productive to have daytime meetings as often as he could with secondary-school counselors, as well as with alumni volunteers. He preferred to travel by train, but because of tight scheduling and the distances to be covered, flying became unavoidable. However,

President Dickey never lost his liking for trains. Perhaps he felt, as President Tucker did, that on a train a man had time to think.

Clifford Jordan, in an unpublished memoir called "Travels with John," has described what it was like to be on the alumni circuit with President Dickey. "The President was fun to travel with, and most times it seemed good for him to get away from the constant pressures of the Hanover routine and have a chance to meet many of his alumni friends," writes Jordan, who also gives a picture of a very hard-working President when he was on the road, with press conferences and radio and television interviews added to his full schedule of meetings. At one press conference, in San Francisco, Mr. Dickey was asked if the kind of student protests then happening at Berkeley could ever happen at an Ivy college. "Make no mistake," he replied, "these kinds of protests can, and will, occur on our campuses in the future." Before his administration ended he was to have his own experience with student uprisings, and his handling of them was to be a great credit to his leadership.

While visiting alumni centers, President Dickey was happier in a simple hotel room than in the fancy suites his hosts wanted to arrange for him. Jordan's memoir tells how the President once left his key at the hotel desk before going off to meet someone and then, while taking a taxi back to his hotel, couldn't remember where he was staying. Embarrassed, he asked to be left off in the center of the city so he could walk about a bit. After a half-hour of searching, he found what looked like the right hotel and was relieved to see Cliff Jordan in the lobby when he went in. Walking was not easy for him, because recurrences of his phlebitis sometimes happened on his alumni trips, and when it was particularly bothersome he would rest his knee on a chair beside him at the podium when he stood to speak.

President Dickey's talks to the alumni were invariably serious, about the liberal arts college in general and about Dartmouth's purpose in particular. In the early years of his administration, when fundamental changes were taking place at the College, he had a selling job to do regarding the recruiting of a new breed of faculty, the reformulation of admissions and financial-aid policies, the stiffening of the academic pace, the desirability of more graduate programs, and the urgent need to find funds for faculty compensation and financial aid. The alumni in time acquired an understanding of John Dickey's goals, and they supported them. Although their backing did not take the form of the unquestioned support and affection that had been showered upon President Hopkins during his latter years in office, they found in John Dickey a man to their liking and a leader whose judgment they trusted and whose integrity and wholehearted commitment to his job they admired. Over the years Mr. Dickey developed deep friendships with many alumni, and one of his professed pleasures when he was on tour was the chance to get together with these friends in a relaxed way.

Among the things President Dickey reported to the alumni was the College's intention to make fuller use of its plant by increasing the number of programs attracted to the campus during the summer. To direct that effort, Waldo Chamberlin of New York University was named to the position of Dean of Summer Programs. An important responsibility assigned to him was developing plans for a proposed summer term, expected to be introduced in 1963. Existing programs coming under his supervision when he took over were the Dartmouth College Conference in Liberal Arts for business executives, the Graduate School of Credit and Financial Management at Tuck School, the Russian Language Institute for secondary-school teachers, and a course in computing for mathematics instructors. At New York University, Professor Chamberlin taught both undergraduate and graduate courses in international relations. During World War II he served with the U.S. State Department and the War Shipping Administration. After the war, he was documents officer at the San Francisco conference that established the United Nations, and he then became deputy director of the documents division of the United Nations Secretariat.

Exciting news came out of the April 1961 meeting of the Board of Trustees. Not only was construction to begin on a new field house, key unit in the athletic plant expansion financed by the capital-gifts campaign, but the architect was Pier Luigi Nervi, the internationally famous Italian engineer-designer, whose use of precast, reinforced-concrete units in his practical, yet aesthetically beautiful, buildings made architectural history. Dartmouth was honored to be the location of Nervi's first complete structure in this country. The field house, requiring a huge unobstructed ground area, was to be a rectangular adaptation of the circular *Palazzetto della Sport*, one of three buildings Nervi designed and built in Rome for the 1960 Olympic Games. His Dartmouth "sports palace" was to be located at the southeast corner of Memorial Field, with a main entrance on South Park Street. Enclosing an area nearly the size of two football fields, it was to have as its most dramatic feature a vaulted ceiling, sixty-two feet high at the center, constructed in a diamond pattern of reinforced-concrete blocks. The new kind of reinforced concrete, given the name *ferro-cemento* when Nervi invented it, had the virtue of being flexible, strong, and light. Since the units were precast on the ground and then hoisted into place, the construction process was both economical and fast. Nervi had used his *ferro-cemento* process when he built his stunning main exhibition hall at Turin, in the late 1940's, and had only eight months in which to do the job. Dartmouth's field house was built in a comparatively short time and was ready in the fall of 1962.

How Nervi came to design the Dartmouth field house, and later the ice arena, is a story that began in the spring of 1960, when Mr. Olmsted, the College's Business Manager, was in Rome on a trip that was partly an administrative sabbatical. As a Thayer School graduate, he knew about the innovative work of Nervi and was anxious to see it and learn more about it. He went to the Nervi office in Rome, explained his interest, and was given a warm welcome and a tour of Nervi buildings by an English-speaking member of the staff. Olmsted returned to Hanover with photographs and a burning desire that Nervi should design the field house the College was ready to build. John Dickey and the Trustees were equally enthusiastic about the idea, and before long Olmsted was back in Rome—the first of several trips—to close the deal and to begin work on the details of construction. When public announcement was made, after the Trustees' April 1961 meeting, the field house design was already in hand and a model had been made in Rome.

Fortunately, early in April, Nervi came to the United States to take part in the centennial of M.I.T. On April 9 he made a special trip from Boston to Hanover, in order to see the site of the field house and to discuss design and construction matters with College officers and with the American architects and engineers working with him on the project. Among the latter were Phillip R. Jackson, general manager of the Wexler Construction Company, the builders, and Professors John H.

Minnich and Russell Stearns of Thayer School, in charge of the foundation engineering. After business was attended to, the College gave a reception and supper party for Nervi at the Outing Club House, attended by officers of the College and Athletic Council, faculty members from Thayer School and the art department, and some area architects.

The field house was dedicated November 18, 1962, as the closing event of a Convocation on the Arts, during which Nervi participated as lecturer and panelist. That event proved that the new structure could easily accommodate large College gatherings such as convocations and Commencement, if needed. From that point on, little was heard of the separate auditorium that had been included in TPC plant planning.

That the field house would bear the name of Nathaniel Leverone of Chicago was announced by President Dickey at the dinner of January 18, 1963, honoring the 1962 football team, which was undefeated in nine major games. Mr. Leverone, Class of 1906, who was founder and chairman of the Automatic Canteen Company of America, had made a gift of $1.5-million for the field house, as part of the capital-gifts campaign. He was present at the dinner and on the following day attended the Dartmouth-Maine track meet, the first athletic event held in the field house. A more formal dedication of the facility, with its name properly in place, was held several months later, on May 4, 1963, with the U.S. Navy Band there for a concert.

Along with the news about the field house, the spring meeting of the Trustees also produced an announcement that the College's study programs in public affairs would be consolidated in a new Public Affairs Center located in Baker Library. Professor Gene M. Lyons of the government department, with the title of Associate Professor of Public Affairs, was named director of the center. He and his staff were assigned responsibility for the Great Issues Course on a continuing basis. During the fourteen years of the course the job of director had been rotated among senior professors from a variety of departments. The Public Affairs Center was also expected to initiate faculty seminars and research projects that would lead to an interdepartmental tackling of public policy problems. A third responsibility was the supervising of student activities, such as internships, in the field of public service.

While developments such as the Public Affairs Center received special attention, other changes in the educational program were going on routinely and without fanfare. For example, three new majors were being readied for the fall of 1961 and a fourth major was being substantially revised. The English department, in a break from the standard literature major, was offering a major in drama, consisting of courses not only in dramatic literature, but also in the history of the theater, playwriting, acting, directing, stage design, and criticism. Professor Henry B. Williams, who was in charge of the Experimental Theater, was named director of the eight-course curriculum. Students electing the new major were to have in the Hopkins Center ideal facilities for their studies. A second major being introduced in the fall was a single major in biology, replacing the separate botany, zoology, and biology majors. (This consolidation carried one step further a process that began with an interdepartmental course in life science. A third and final step, shortly after, was the merging of Departments of Botany and Zoology into the Department of Biological Sciences.) The third new major was offered by the Department of Classics and was called Greek and Roman Studies, designed for the student planning a career in any of the three areas of the humanities, the social sciences, or the sciences. Added to the three new majors mentioned, the history department announced a revision of its major program, in order to give it better balance. At the same time it added five senior seminars to the six already being offered.

Although the curriculum changes described happened to be bunched for the fall of 1961, they were the sort of thing that went on regularly as the faculty sought to diversify and strengthen the College's educational program. These efforts were usually undertaken department by department, but sometimes the changes came about through interdepartmental collaboration—which was more and more the case as the interrelatedness of fields of study became apparent.

Work in the field of human relations was also strengthened with an endowment grant of $250,000 from the Lincoln and Theresa Filene Foundation. The grant gave permanent support to activities that had been financed for three years on an experimental basis. These activities included faculty and student research, an interdepartmental course in human relations, and the Lincoln Filene Lectureship. Mr. Filene, a Boston merchant and philanthropist, was not a college graduate, but primarily through his close friendship with President Hopkins he had shown a special interest in Dartmouth. The College in 1916 awarded him an honorary Master's degree, and the Class of 1916 made him an honorary member. The 200-seat auditorium connecting the Bradley Mathematics Center and the new psychology building was named the Lincoln Filene Auditorium in his honor.

Before the busy 1960–61 year ended a few more noteworthy events occurred. President Dickey went to Bowdoin College's commencement to receive an honorary Doctorate of Laws and heard himself described as "this blithe spirit of academia." The citation went on to say: "Now the puissant and seasoned president of a peerless liberal college grown to university function, he is foresightedly concerned that the able leaders of tomorrow graduating from our colleges of today be men of commitment and dedication, as well as men of knowledge, skill, understanding, and wisdom."

On June 15, while the Dartmouth Alumni Council was meeting in town in conjunction with class reunions, President Dickey and President-Emeritus Hopkins were the principal participants in a Hopkins Center cornerstone ceremony. The cornerstone itself was out of the ordinary, because Wallace Harrison, the architect, who was also present, had designed it in the shape of a pine tree. With silver-plated trowels presented to them by Governor Volpe of Massachusetts, the Messrs. Dickey and Hopkins spread the mortar for the cornerstone and doubtless remembered the day when, in hard hats, they had ridden the bulldozer that started it all.

Alumni Fund history was made when the 1961 fund became the first to pass the million-dollar mark. The official totals were $1,015,545 in dollars and 20,936 in number of contributors, both records for the annual fund. John D. Dodd had the distinction of being chairman of this historic achievement. From that point on, $1-million became the base on which to build. The height to which future funds were destined to soar was probably no more in mind then than a million-dollar fund was conceived by President Tucker who, after the very first Alumni Fund, predicted that it would grow to $25,000.

The high point of another busy summer was the celebration of Hanover's bicentennial on July 4. The College and town collaborated in an all-day program. For the parade and other events, including the inevitable speeches, Colonial dress was worn by those who could find it.

President Dickey, depicting a somewhat indefinite period in the 200-year history of the town, appeared in a long frock coat and a stovepipe hat. Dean-Emeritus McDonald went him one better, by appearing as the hornsman atop an old Concord Coach entered in the parade by the Hanover Historical Society. It was a day of fun and good cheer, beginning with a children's costume parade in the morning, followed by the grand parade, a picnic on the green, field day events, a band concert, community singing and fireworks in the stadium, and a street dance to wind things up. To commemorate its 200th birthday, Hanover published a bicentennial book, edited by Professor Francis Lane Childs, which contained twenty-two chapters written by as many Hanover authors. Dartmouth College figures prominently in the story it tells from prehistoric times to the anniversary year 1961.

President Dickey's Convocation addresses, which for years had dealt mainly with an examination of higher education and liberal learning, were becoming more and more attuned to national and international events. Student uprisings had been discussed in 1960, and for 1961, following the Bay of Pigs fiasco in April, the President titled his address "The Cold War and Liberal Learning." The United States would be grievously wrong to emulate the policies and methods of the Soviet Union, he declared, and in the failure of the invasion of Cuba he saw a salutary result for this country, which had not thrown away its character as the world's leader in the ways of freedom and honor. The Cold War would be a severe test of this country's historic character, he said, but "No men ought to welcome such a challenge more gladly and more confidently than those who are committed to the work of liberal learning."

At its regular October meeting the Board of Trustees brought its membership closer to the new maximum authorized by the New Hampshire legislature. Elected as Alumni Trustees were John D. Dodd, Class of 1922, of Montclair, N.J., vice president of the New York Telephone Company; William E. Buchanan, Class of 1924, of Menasha, Wis., president of the Appleton Wire Works Corporation; and Robert S. Oelman, Class of 1931, of Dayton, Ohio, president of the National Cash Register Company. At the same time, the board elevated Congressman Thomas B. Curtis from Alumni Trustee to Life Trustee. By these actions the board grew to fourteen members, with two more places to be filled to reach the maximum of sixteen. At its winter meeting the board completed its enlargement by electing Frank L. Harrington, Class of 1924, of Worcester, Mass., a Life Trustee and Roswell F. Magill, Class of 1916, of New York City an Alumni Trustee to fill the unexpired term of Mr. Curtis. Mr. Harrington was president of The Massachusetts Protective Association and the Paul Revere Life Insurance Company. Mr. Magill, former Under Secretary of the U.S. Treasury, was a partner in the New York law firm of Cravath, Swaine and Moore, and had been a law professor at both Chicago and Columbia.

The Dartmouth faculty, also meeting in October, voted approval of its executive committee's recommendation that an honors system be adopted for all academic work. The faculty called upon the Undergraduate Council to draw up a plan that could be approved in time to take effect with the academic year 1962–63. An honors system managed by the students themselves had been a subject of campus debate for some time, but the stumbling block to any agreement was the question whether mandatory reporting of cheating should be part of the system. A spate of letters to *The Dartmouth* denounced "ratting" on fellow students, which would be involved in a mandatory plan. Despite such misgivings, the Undergraduate Council persevered, and it succeeded in having an honors system for academics in place for 1962–63, thus substituting personal honor for faculty policing.

On the academic front, a special event early in the college year was a gathering of some of the country's leading mathematicians for a conference on "New Directions in Mathematics," marking the formal opening of the Albert Bradley Center for Mathematics. On the first evening of the two-day event, November 3–4, a dedication ceremony featured remarks by President Dickey, Professor Kemeny, department chairman, and Alfred P. Sloan Jr., representing the Alfred P. Sloan Foundation, which had provided most of the funds to build the center. Mr. Sloan paid tribute to Mr. Bradley, his friend and business associate of many years, and also had kind things to say about Dartmouth's mathematics department, which, quoting an outside report, he described as "the most energetic, imaginative, and effective one in any American liberal arts college today." A separate dedication, within the center, honored John Brown Cook, Class of 1929, donor of the Wallace Cook Memorial Library in honor of his father.

Dr. Albert W. Tucker, chairman of Princeton's mathematics department and president of the Mathematical Association of America, headed a group of ten visiting scholars who took part in panel discussions dealing with research and teaching in secondary-school and college mathematics. The others came from the University of California, Chicago, Columbia, Harvard, New York University, Wisconsin, St. Paul's School, Bell Telephone Laboratories, and the Rockefeller Institute. Under the dynamic chairmanship of Professor Kemeny, Dartmouth's mathematics department had earned both its new home and the plaudits bestowed upon it. Of all the undergraduate departments, mathematics had grown the most in scholastic distinction during the Dickey presidency. The new psychology building, joined to the Bradley Center, was scheduled to have its own dedication and conference some months later.

Two steps of historic significance, taken in December, exemplified the extent to which Dartmouth College, despite its name, was increasingly fulfilling the function of a small university. One was the announcement by President Dickey that the coming fall would see the introduction of a graduate program in molecular biology, leading to the doctoral degree. The other was the faculty's unanimous adoption of a resolution proposing to the Trustees that other Ph.D. programs be introduced in selected areas as a means of enhancing the educational position of the College and the recruiting and maintaining of faculty. Shortly after these events, the Trustees gave approval to the inauguration of a doctoral program in mathematics, also to begin in the fall of 1962.

Immediately the question arose: What does this mean for the primacy of undergraduate, liberal arts education to which the College had adhered so strongly, even proudly, throughout its history? President Dickey took pains to explain that the graduate programs were being adopted on a limited basis and, aside from their own intrinsic merits, were intended to strengthen the undergraduate college by attracting the sort of teacher-scholars Dartmouth wanted for its faculty. Although the molecular biology program was primarily a Medical School program, the Trustees in approving it stipulated that faculty members from the College's science division should have a collaborative role. The mathematics Ph.D. was the more significant of the two programs, in that it was being offered by a department of the College without participation by an associated school. In both cases, introduction of the Ph.D. amounted to a further recognition that Dartmouth was in fact a small university—falling into a category of its own between the undergraduate college and the full-fledged university. President Dickey in his remarks, made as part of the College's oral-history project, asserted that Dartmouth had to get over being afraid of the word *university*, but at the same time he was second to none in believing liberal arts learning for undergraduates to be at the heart of Dartmouth's purpose.

The Ph.D. was not something brand new for Dartmouth. The degree went back to 1885, when the first one was awarded in the Classics, followed by two more in 1887. From that point on, however, only seven earned doctorates were awarded by the College, all in the sciences. The last three, from 1926 to 1939, were for work in physiological optics at the Dartmouth Eye Institute. So, the College decided to revive in 1962 doctoral-level studies that had come to a halt two decades ago. Two years after that revival, the Trustees asked the Council on Graduate Studies to report on how the programs were doing. On being informed that progress was satisfactory, the board authorized the faculty to proceed with graduate education "on the assumption that it is the policy of the College to move forward in this area with the adoption of selectively conceived programs." By that time the Ph.D. was already being offered not only in molecular biology and mathematics, but also in physics, engineering, and physiology-pharmacology. A total of seventy doctoral candidates were enrolled, with the largest number, twenty-five, in mathematics. Support for the mathematics Ph.D. had been provided by the Carnegie Corporation, with a four-year grant of $250,000. Also extremely helpful to the various doctoral programs was fellowship support from the National Science Foundation, the U.S. Office of Education, the National Institutes of Health, NASA, and the Department of Defense. The College was able to divert to Ph.D. candidates some of the teaching assistantships that were available to graduate students working for the M.A. degree.

Before the college year ended, President Dickey had a chance to get away from the office for a month's holiday in Europe. He and Mrs. Dickey flew to London on April 27 and, then, visited Edinburgh before going to Athens, where they joined Mr. and Mrs. Andres and Mr. and Mrs. Stanley for a two-week cruise of the Greek islands. On the way home, Mr. Dickey met with the Dartmouth Club of Paris, and he was back in New York on May 30, in time to prepare for Commencement.

While the Dickeys were away, Provost Masland represented the President at the dedication of the new psychology building, May 18–19. By Trustee action during the winter, the building was named Gerry Hall in memory of Edwin Peabody Gerry, a prominent medical figure in Boston. Both Dr. Gerry and his wife created trust funds with Dartmouth College as the residuary legatee, stipulating that their combined bequests be used for a building bearing the Gerry name and serving either as a center for an academic department or as a dormitory. The two-day dedication and conference program was the occasion also for dedicating the Filene Auditorium, where the psychology conference sessions were held. President-Emeritus Hopkins, a lifelong friend of Lincoln Filene, and George E. Ladd Jr., Mr. Filene's son-in-law and a trustee of the Filene Foundation, were the principal speakers at the auditorium dedication.

To mark the formal addition of Gerry Hall to its academic facilities, the College held a conference on The Role of Psychology in the Resolution of International Conflict. Dr. Ralph J. Bunche, Undersecretary of the United Nations for Special Political Affairs and a winner of the Nobel Peace Prize, was chairman of the conference, in which nine other public officials and educators took part. Five of the participants were Dartmouth graduates: Hadley Cantril, public opinion expert at Princeton and chairman of the Insititute for International Social Research; Leonard Doob, propaganda expert and professor at Yale; Leonard C. Mead, vice president and provost of Tufts University; Charles E. Osgood, director of communications research at the University of Illinois and president-elect of the American Psychological Association; and Howland Sargeant, president of the American Committee for Liberation and director of Free World broadcasts to the Soviet Union. Also participating in the panel discussions were Professor B. F. Skinner of Harvard; Gerald Sykes, author; Dore Schary, playwright, director, and movie producer; and Wolfgang Kohler, Visiting Research Professor of Psychology at Dartmouth and internationally celebrated as one of the founders of Gestalt psychology. Once again, as with the conferences previously held on mathematics, the arts, polar research, moral education, modern medicine, and the Anglo-Canadian-American community, participants of the highest distinction came to Dartmouth and by doing so betokened the growing academic stature of the College under President Dickey's stimulus.

The pursuit of academic excellence was especially pronounced in the sciences, and for the undergraduate departments this was enhanced by the opportunity to collaborate with the Medical School and the Thayer School of Engineering, both of which were pushing ahead to new levels of their own in research and educational programs. Two major gifts, announced late in the college year, gave a tremendous boost to the biological sciences. The Charles A. Dana Foundation gave $400,000 to help build a library linked to the Medical School, and shortly after, the Gilman Foundation gave $1-million for the Charles Gilman Life Sciences Laboratory. The Gilman Laboratory was to house the College's department of biological sciences and, like the Charles Dana Library, was seen as a means of strengthening the close working relationship between the medical scientists of the Medical School and the life scientists of the College.

Growth was taking a variety of forms, and one of them, especially noticeable in June of 1962, was the start of a summer schedule that brought eleven study groups to the College, compared with only three or four in previous years. Dean Waldo Chamberlin, who had been on the job one year as Director of Summer Programs, announced that groups would be on campus for periods varying from two days to eight weeks and would be comprised of foreign students, scientists, social scientists, business executives, bankers, engineers, Russian language teachers, and secondary-school teachers. The largest program involved two hundred foreign students meeting for an international seminar under the sponsorship of the National Student Association. Almost as large was the Graduate School of Credit and Finance at Tuck School, in its twelfth year and attended by 180 men. The Russian Language Institute was back, also the Management Objectives Conference for executives, and the liberal arts study group from the National Association of Mutual Savings Banks. Two new Thayer School programs dealt with information theory and the properties of materials, the latter conference sponsored by the National Science Foundation.

Summer for several years running had witnessed a great deal of plant expansion, and 1962 saw a start on one more facility, when ground was broken in the east wing of Alumni Gymnasium for an eight-lane swimming pool. The designer was R. Jackson Smith, Dartmouth's former AAU diving champion, who naturally enough gave special attention to the three diving platforms. In the west wing of the gymnasium, work was progressing on the remodeling of the basketball court, which was to have permanent spectator stands.

Hopkins Center

A MONG the notable accomplishments of the Dickey administration the addition of Hopkins Center to Dartmouth's facilities holds a very high place. No construction project at the College had such a long gestation period as did the Center, nor did any undergo so many revisions in design and function. From the appointment of a planning committee by President Hopkins in 1929 to the formal opening of Hopkins Center on November 8, 1962, thirty-three years elapsed. And long-suffering through all those years was Warner Bentley, the Center's first director, who had come to Dartmouth from the Yale Drama Department in 1928 with the promise that he would be provided with a new theater.

The first of three abortive attempts to build either a student union or an auditorium-theater began in 1929 when President Hopkins named Robert C. Strong, his Executive Assistant, to be chairman of a committee to make a study of student unions at other institutions and to determine what sort of center would best serve the social needs of the College. This happened at a time when Mr. Hopkins had thought of adopting something like the Harvard house plan, but had decided that the College could best function as a single unit, if it had a central student union. The Trustees had every intention of building such a center in the early Thirties, but the Great Depression intervened and made any major expenditure for plant out of the question. The planning committee, however, went ahead with its work and submitted a report in 1931. The initial idea of razing College Hall in order to provide a central location was dropped in favor of tearing down the old Thayer School of Engineering and filling the southern end of the Green with the new structure. The committee's proposals were very ambitious and called for moving the Hanover Inn to an outlying location, if its site were needed. The student center was tentatively called Dartmouth

174

House and was to be a huge structure, including an auditorium seating 2500, a theater for 500, a Freshman Commons with adjoining lounge, a cafeteria and grill, nine private dining rooms, a billiard and card room, four basement bowling alleys, a second-floor music room, offices for student organizations, a Graduate Club for the faculty, and living quarters for bachelor faculty on the second and third floors. The estimated price tag of $4-million in 1931 dollars gives some idea of the magnitude of the project. Baker Library had been built only a few years earlier for $1-million.

In December 1937, when the financial woes of the Depression were almost over, President Hopkins named a second planning committee, headed by Sidney C. Hayward, Secretary of the College. Since Thayer Hall, with its dining facilities for upperclassmen, had opened that fall, the assignment was to plan a smaller and less expensive center that would primarily meet the College's needs for an auditorium and a theater. The Thayer School site was still the first choice for the location of the million-dollar structure. The planning committee's initial idea was to erect a new Webster Hall, duplicating the facade of old Webster at the north end of the campus. J. Fredrick Larson, the College Architect, who was a member of the committee, drew plans for such a building, containing an auditorium-theater seating 2700, a little theater seating 400, music and drama rooms, and offices for student organizations. Revised plans dropped the Webster name (in favor of Dartmouth Center), as well as the exterior look of old Webster Hall. Once again the trustees were ready to move ahead with construction, and a campaign headed by Basil O'Connor was being readied to raise $2-million, half for construction and half for operation. This time World War II intervened, and Warner Bentley's theater was again postponed.

President Dickey inherited the auditorium-theater project when he took over the Dartmouth presidency in November 1945. Five months later, in March, he appointed another planning committee, this one headed by Professor Russell R. Larmon, and including Mr. Hayward, Mr. Bentley, and Mr. Larson, and others from the previous planning group. The committee went back to some of the ideas of the 1929 planners and gave more attention than before to alumni needs, adding an alumni lounge and an alumni promenade leading to the Hanover Inn. The revised plans called for the Inn to connect with the center at all four levels and to add thirty bedrooms on the upper floors of the connecting unit. The main features continued to be a 2700-seat auditorium, large enough to hold the entire student body, and a theater for 500 adjoining it and sharing a backstage workshop. The new exterior design was quite different from the Webster Hall idea. As described by Mr. Hayward in an *Alumni Magazine* article, "The structure will balance Baker Library at the opposite end of the campus, in architectural harmony with the dominant Colonial exterior of the Dartmouth plant. But liberal use of glass will achieve a concept, which originated with President Dickey, for expanding the opportunity to view the passing scene of life on the campus, the tower of Baker Library, the white stretch of Dartmouth Row."

When President Dickey named the third planning committee, the Trustees had already approved the recommendation of the Alumni Council that the new auditorium-theater be named in honor of President-Emeritus Hopkins, who began the string of studies that eventually produced the edifice of 1962. The center was intended to be the major component of a three-part Hopkins War Memorial Program, which included the Hopkins Scholarships, for the sons of Dartmouth men who had lost their lives in the war, and the enlargement and modernization of Wilder Hall, the physics building. Once again the Trustees, at their October 1946 meeting, gave final endorsement to revised plans for the center, and preparations began for mounting a special fund campaign, this time under the leadership of John W. Hubbell as national chairman and Charles J. Zimmerman as vice chairman. Robert K. Hage was named executive secretary of the Hopkins Center Project. The $3.5-million campaign was handicapped from the start by a limited solicitation of alumni, lest the annual alumni fund be jeopardized. Lack of progress in raising the needed funds, plus more urgent needs related to faculty and curriculum, resulted in putting the Center project on hold for a third time. President Dickey was not unhappy with this turn of events. He was not entirely convinced that either the architecture or the purpose of the projected building was exactly right, and his natural inclination to go slow in making a major commitment was thus brought into play.

It was not until 1955 that the Trustees authorized a reactivation of the Hopkins Center project. The assignment was given to the Advisory

Dictating to secretary Mary Shaw, with Rusty on daily duty, in the President's Office in Parkhurst Hall.

With classmates at the Dartmouth 1929 reunion, June 1960.

J.S.D. with architect Wallace K. Harrison and Nelson Rockefeller, Building Committee Chairman, at the Hopkins Center dedication, November 1962.

John and Christina Dickey in Japan in the spring of 1964.

J.S.D. in the press box with coach Doggie Julian, at the Princeton football game in Hanover, 1964.

The President confers with Dean of the Faculty Leonard Rieser in April 1966.

J.S.D. receiving an honorary LL.D. from Chancellor Omond Solandt of the University of Toronto, May 1968.

IN 1769 KING GEORGE III OF HIS SPECIAL GRACE CERTAIN
KNOWLEDGE AND MEER MOTION CHARTERED DARTMOUTH
COLLEGE FOR THE EDUCATION & INSTRUCTION OF YOUTH OF
THE INDIAN TRIBES IN THIS LAND IN READING, WRITING & ALL
PARTS OF LEARNING WHICH SHALL APPEAR NECESSARY AND
EXPEDIENT FOR CIVILIZING & CHRISTIANIZING CHILDREN OF
PAGANS AS WELL AS IN ALL LIBERAL ARTS AND SCIENCES; AND
ALSO OF ENGLISH YOUTH AND ANY OTHERS.

THE COLLEGE, FOUNDED BY THE REVEREND ELEAZAR
WHEELOCK WITH THE SUPPORT OF GOVERNOR JOHN WENT-
WORTH, BEARS THE NAME OF ONE OF ITS EARLIEST BENEFAC-
TORS, THE SECOND EARL OF DARTMOUTH.

IN 1969 THE NINTH EARL OF DARTMOUTH UNVEILED
THIS PLAQUE TO INAUGURATE THE TWO-HUNDREDTH ANNI-
VERSARY OF THE COLLEGE. THE BICENTENNIAL MEDALLIONS
ABOVE SHOW THE "OLD PINE", LONG A SYMBOL OF THE COL-
LEGE AND THE ARMS AND MOTTOES OF THE SECOND EARL OF
DARTMOUTH AND OF THE COLLEGE.

Lord and Lady Dartmouth unveiling the Bicentennial Plaque in front of Hopkins Center,
June 1969.

President Dickey in serious mood at the all-College assembly after the seizure of Parkhurst Hall, May 1969.

J.S.D. speaking at his final Convocation.

John Dickey welcomed to the faculty as Bicentennial Professor of Public Affairs. With him are Errol Hill, Douglas Bowen, and Walter Stockmayer.

Mrs. Dickey receiving an honorary degree at the inauguration of President Kemeny, as
.S.D., similarly honored, watches, March 1, 1970.

Shown at the unveiling of an oil painting of John Dickey in 1981 are (from left) President David T. McLaughlin, Mr. and Mrs. Dickey, Judy McLaughlin, and Peter Gish '49, the artist.

Committee on Plant Planning, headed by Professor John P. Amsden as part of the board's comprehensive review of the College in anticipation of its bicentennial. The Amsden committee began its work with the belief that a fresh approach was called for, one that would address educational needs more fully than before, and one that would insure daily and multiple use by students. In its report to the Trustees' committee on buildings and grounds the study committee spelled out six alternative plans for the Center: (1) the plan proposed by the Larmon committee, featuring a 2700-seat auditorium; (2) a small theater and large auditorium-theater; (3) a theater alone; (4) a building that would be essentially a student union serving as a focus of student social and recreational activity; (5) an educational building with a 900-seat lecture hall, two or more 450-seat lecture halls, seminar rooms, faculty offices, and headquarters for the Great Issues Course; and (6) a creative arts center to enhance Dartmouth's aims as a liberal arts college. The committee unanimously recommended to the Trustees the adoption of Plan No. 6.

Mr. Olmsted, then Business Manager of the College and a member of the Amsden committee, recalled that it was Adelbert Ames Jr., former director for the Dartmouth Eye Institute and a man personally involved in the arts, who put forward the idea of the arts center. He also recalled that President Dickey, when informed of Plan No. 6, "picked up the ball and ran with it." Here was a purpose that Mr. Dickey felt to be right for the building, in contrast to his doubts about previous plans; and from that point on, his enthusiasm and his caring about every detail were the driving force in moving the project to completion. In the main lobby of Hopkins Center today a plaque, balancing the one about President Hopkins, states that the Center owes its existence to John Sloan Dickey. Among the contributions he quickly made to the arts-center concept was the idea that the performing arts be given as much attention as the creative arts, also that display of the arts be a major consideration.

After the Trustees had approved the new concept, responsibility for bringing the Center into being was given to a building committee, which Mr. Dickey headed at the outset. At the committee's first meeting, on September 23, 1955, Nelson Aldrich of Boston met with the group as consulting architect. Mr. Larson, the College Architect, had left to establish an office in New York City and it was decided that the College would follow a new policy of having consulting architects from outside. Mr. Aldrich had previously been associated with Harrison and Abramovitz of New York, and it was he who proposed that Wallace K. Harrison, architect of Rockefeller Center and the United Nations headquarters, be brought into the planning of Hopkins Center. Early on, Harrison became the chief architect of the Center. As planning progressed, more members were added to the building committee, and Nelson A. Rockefeller became its chairman. One constant throughout the thirty years of sporadic planning was the presence of Warner Bentley on all the building committees, and another was the inclusion of his long-awaited theater in the approved plans, whether for a student union, an auditorium-theater, or an arts center. That the scheme now being worked on was almost certain to be realized was an assurance given to the newest planning group in June 1956, when John D. Rockefeller Jr., in token of his great admiration for Mr. Hopkins, contributed a million dollars toward constructing the Hopkins Center. That fall the Trustees announced that Dartmouth would launch its first capital-gifts campaign, and the largest part of the money raised would, of course, be allocated to constructing the Hopkins Center. The project was on its way at last.

A detailed description of the new concept of the Center was presented to the Trustees by President Dickey in a memorandum dated January 5, 1956. In that memo he stated that the Center "will provide at the crossroads of the Dartmouth community a campus gathering point where the fellowship of the College may be enjoyed in creation, in recreation, in learning, and in contemplation." The major needs it would fill, he said, were central social facilities, a theater, a public place for the doing and the viewing of the creative arts, and lecture-hall facilities that would permit greater teaching flexibility. The Center's "crossroads" site and "cross-fertilization" of the arts were points that Mr. Dickey liked to make, and after a trip to Greece he spoke of Hopkins Center as Dartmouth's version of the Agora, the marketplace of ancient Athens where people gathered daily for social discourse as well as business. To insure the daily influx of students, it was decided to locate their mailboxes in the Center. This accomplished its aim and served to put students in touch, even if only fleetingly, with some of the artistic offerings of the Center. To the same end, the "sidewalk superintendent" principle was adopted for some of the student workshops, studios, and backstage areas, so passers-by could see the activities going on within and perhaps become interested in doing creative work themselves.

President Dickey's memorandum to the Trustees also dealt at some length with the architectural design of the Center. Not only was the purpose of the building greatly transformed from earlier concepts, but with Mr. Harrison as architect the way was clear for a structure contemporary in design but still in harmony with older campus buildings. That was what John Dickey wanted from the outset of his involvement with the project. Harrison's first design, depicted in a painting by Paul Sample, appeared on the cover of the *Dartmouth Alumni Magazine* of May 1957. It was definitely contemporary, with a great deal of glass on its north front facing the campus, but its exterior was disappointing to some, who did not like the flat lines above the main entrance or the excessive use of glass at the west end of the front, next to the Inn, and at the south end, on Lebanon Street. The revised design was a vast improvement. Some of the glass areas were bricked in, particularly at the south end, and Harrison came up with the vaulted roof (using thin-shell concrete) that makes Hopkins Center so distinctive. The vaulted treatment was repeated in the five large windows looking out on the campus, which harmonized with the facing windows of Baker Library. (Behind McKenzie Hall, off Lebanon Street, a row of four garages with vaulted roofs can be seen today. Mr. Olmsted had the roofs built after Harrison changed his design, in order to see how they would weather.) Another of the architect's successful moves was to set the Center back from the street, with a plaza in front, so the large structure, with its appearance of openness, was kept in scale with other campus buildings. Many alumni, wedded to Dartmouth's Georgian architecture and the simplicity of Dartmouth Row, were harshly critical of the Center's contemporary intrusion, but in time its "rightness" for the inner workings of the Center was appreciated and even applauded. (Mr. Harrison apparently was pleased with the barrel-vaulted treatment of Hopkins Center; he subsequently repeated it in his design of the opera house at Lincoln Center in New York City. The two buildings have a striking similarity.)

In his memorandum to the Trustees, President Dickey also dealt at some length with the thinking that went into the interior design of the Center. As with the exterior, some fundamental changes were made before final working plans were approved. Unchanged from the start, however, was the concept of the Center as a composite of four main units: (1) the theater and Top-of-the-Hop lounge at the front; (2) the Alumni Hall unit next to the Hanover Inn; (3) the studio and workshop unit extending along two levels on the west side of the building; and (4) the 900-seat auditorium unit at the southern end, with its own entrance on Lebanon Street. Major revisions made after the first Harrison design involved Alumni Hall and the auditorium unit. The former was enlarged by shifting the projected Drake Room (originally viewed as a replacement of the Hanover Inn's ski hut) to the main floor. Above the main art gallery, also relocated, a large roof terrace was added, connecting with both the Top of the Hop and a newly created faculty lounge. At the southern end of the Center, the decision to move the Music Department into the music area, beneath the auditorium, necessitated the provision of more floor space. Out of this revision came seven offices instead of three; twelve practice rooms instead of eight; three group listening rooms and nine smaller ones not previously planned; and a larger library.

Gone from all the planning, once the changed concept for Hopkins Center had been accepted, was the idea of an auditorium large enough to seat the entire student body. No one would have argued for anything that large in the Center, but Warner Bentley did try to get the seating capacity of the auditorium increased from 900 to 1,500, with full stage facilities. His proposal was one of the sacrifices that had to be made in order to keep costs within the $5.5-million construction budget — beyond which some $2-million in other costs had to be met. The lobby of what came to be named the Spaulding Auditorium was, in Mr. Bentley's opinion, also too small, but the property line did not permit its being extended any farther to the west. In President Dickey's Trustee memorandum he spoke of an auditorium-arena. That was one of the earliest indications of new thinking about the way to solve the problem of having a place in which to assemble the entire college.

On October 24, 1958, a ground-clearing ceremony took place at the Bissell Hall site, attended by the Dartmouth Trustees, who were in town for their regular fall meeting. While not much was cleared—only one end of a frame building—the occasion was jovial and mostly symbolic. Wearing crash helmets, President Dickey and President-Emeritus Hopkins rode together on a huge bulldozer, painted green and white and bearing the Latin inscription *Initium rapidissimum in tertium saeculum Dartmuthiense*: a running start into Dartmouth's third century. In addition to the Trustees, the capital-gifts campaign steering committee, which was meeting in Hanover that weekend, also attended the ceremony. Those who took part in a brief speaking program were Mr. Dickey, Warner Bentley for the building committee, Edward W. Gude '59 for the students, architect Wallace Harrison, and Mr. Hopkins, who had a one-day permit to operate the bulldozer but left that privilege to someone else. Mr. Bentley expressed the fear that another national calamity would abort plans to build the Center and provide him with his theater, but President Dickey assured him that this time it was for real. It was announced that clearing the site would continue and that working drawings would be completed later that fall and sent out for bids, so that construction might begin in the summer. Since South College Street was being closed off for the Center, by agreement with the town, the College during the summer had paid for the widening and resurfacing of Crosby Street, which became the main traffic artery from Wheelock Street to Lebanon Street.

Construction of the Center began with excavating in the spring of 1959, and for the next three years the College watched as the greatest addition to the campus since Baker Library, inched its way into existence. While construction was going on, much thought was being given to the cultural, educational, and social activities that would have their home within the building. To have the benefit of professional advice of the highest order, the College invited notables of the theater, art, music, and crafts worlds to be members of Hopkins Center advisory groups. The first of these groups, formed in April 1960, consisted of fourteen distinguished personages of the American theater. The chairman was Arthur Hornblow Jr., Hollywood and Broadway producer, and the other members were Luise Sillcox, executive secretary of The Dramatists Guild; actress Jessica Tandy and her husband, actor Hume Cronyn; Harry Ackerman, production head of Screen Gems; Moss Hart, Pulitzer Prize playwright; Leland Hayward, Broadway producer;

William Inge, also a Pulitzer Prize dramatist; Lawrence Langner, founder of The Theater Guild; Sidney Lumet, stage and film director; Jo
Mielziner, set designer; Robert Ryan, actor; Sylvester Weaver Jr., former
president of National Broadcasting Company; and Fred Zinnemann,
film director.

The Music Advisory Group was equally distinguished and had as its
chairman Goddard Lieberson, president of Columbia Records. Other
members were Leonard Bernstein, David Brubeck, E. Power Biggs,
Aaron Copland, Igor Stravinsky, Eugene Ormandy, William Schuman,
and Erich Leinsdorf; plus five alumni: Richard Leach of Lincoln Center,
orchestra leader Paul Weston, music patron Arthur Virgin, music publisher Charles Griffith, and Metropolitan Opera stage director Nathaniel Merrill.

The Hopkins Center Art Advisory Group was chaired by William B.
Jaffee, New York attorney and art collector. Serving with him were
Alfred H. Barr Jr. of the Museum of Modern Art; D. Herbert Beskind,
Fellow of the Metropolitan Museum of Art; Russell Cowles, painter;
William Bright Jones, art historian; Modie Spiegel, art patron; and
James J. Rorimer, director of the Metropolitan Museum of Art; also three
art dealers: Frank Caro, Leo Castelli, and Daniel Wildenstein; and four
art collectors: Mrs. John De Menil of Houston, Mrs. Albert Greenfield
of Philadelphia, and Joseph H. Hazen and Alex L. Hillman of New York
City.

The Crafts Advisory Group was headed by Mrs. Vanderbilt Webb,
founder of the New Hampshire League of Arts and Crafts and the
American Craftsmen's Council. Others in the group of fifteen were
David Campbell, president of the American Craftsmen's Council; Roger
H. Hallowell, president of Reed & Barton, silversmiths; Rene d'Harnon-
court, director of the Museum of Modern Art; Mrs. Dorothy Liebes,
New York textile designer; Francis S. Merritt, director of the Haystack
Mountain School of Crafts; and Dana P. Vaughn, dean of the Cooper
Union School of Arts and Architecture.

The construction period gave the College an opportunity to settle
upon the top management staff for Hopkins Center. In April of 1960,
President Dickey announced that Warner Bentley, at that time Graduate
Manager of the Council on Student Organizations and director of theatrical productions, would be Director, with responsibility for developing

a comprehensive program for the Center. At the same time, it was announced that his chief assistant would be John Scotford, who since 1956 had been serving as special assistant on the Hopkins Center project. His main assignment was to look after educational exhibits and the promotion of special events. Later, in January 1962, Professor John L. Stewart of the English department was named Associate Director, to be in charge of coordinating Center programs with those of the instructional departments of the College. That summer Thomas E. Byrne 3rd was made Business Manager.

Directors of the arts programs to be offered by Hopkins Center also were needed, and the first of these positions was filled, in the spring of 1962, with the naming of Mario di Bonaventura to be Director of Music. A gifted composer and conductor, he had been a member of Dartmouth's music faculty for the spring terms of 1959 and 1960, and at the time of his Hopkins Center appointment he was music director and conductor of the Fort Lauderdale Symphony Orchestra. The position of Director of Theater was filled in the summer of 1962, when James Clancy, a member of the Department of Speech and Drama at Stanford University, was chosen. With the opening of Hopkins Center, Professor Churchill P. Lathrop of the Dartmouth art department, who was director of the Carpenter art galleries, took over the expanded position of Director of Art Galleries at the Center. In the crafts area, Virgil Poling continued as Director of the Student Workshop, but with far better facilities than he had in Bissell Hall.

The date chosen for the formal opening of Hopkins Center was November 8, 1962. To make it on schedule, a small army of volunteers joined the regular workers, and even the Dean of the Faculty was laying carpet until the small hours of the morning of the 8th. Thanks to this extra help, all was ready—or ready enough—for opening day. That afternoon, a fanfare written especially for the occasion by Darius Milhaud launched not only the dedication but an eleven-day inaugural program. The formal ceremonies took place in Spaulding Auditorium before an audience that occupied the stage as well as all 900 seats. Dudley Orr, chairman of the Trustees Planning Committee, presided over a program that included short addresses by principals in the planning and building of the Center and culminated in remarks by President-Emeritus Hopkins.

Architect Harrison, in his remarks, paid tribute to President Dickey and to the Trustees "who put up with the ideas we put forward in times when nobody wanted anything but Colonial architecture." He concluded by saying, "A building is either clean and straightforward or it is a mess. This building will never have any conspicuous marks like pimples on the outside because it is a clean building." Harrison was followed by Governor John Volpe of Massachusetts, chairman of the board of the Volpe Construction Company, the builders. He declared that no building, in twenty-nine years of construction work, had given his company so much satisfaction as the Center had; and with an expression of special appreciation of John Dickey's role presented to the President the key to the building.

In his remarks of thanks, President Dickey said he wanted to include the critics of Hopkins Center, because they were needed to keep one's nerve up. Among the choice items he kept under the glass top of his desk, he added, was a card that simply said, "Dear Sir, I was wrong, you were right. It's great." Becoming serious about the purpose and potential of the Center, Mr. Dickey concluded by saying: "Used well, these facilities will be what great facilities have always been to man— multipliers of his efforts and a witness of his aspirations. Here the spirit of liberal learning as it came to us from Greek society can be kept vital and meaningful as the essential friend rather than the uneasy conscience of a professionally strong society. Here the skill and the discipline of the professional can inform the enthusiasm, yea, I say unashamedly, the love of the amateur in that mission to man's humanity which at its best has always needed both the skill of the professional and the enthusiasm and love of the amateur."

Warner Bentley, the man who was perhaps the most emotionally touched by the opening of Hopkins Center, spoke next and pledged that the staff of the facility he now took over would be untiring in its efforts to make the life of the Center live up to the excellence of the building provided for it. "I never thought I would live long enough to be present on my own two feet on an occasion such as this. I have sometimes speculated that I might possibly be wheeled in, but I never dreamed of being wheeled into a building as magnificent as the one we are now in."

Governor Nelson Rockefeller of New York, chairman of the building committee, closed the scheduled speaking program with praise for the architectural achievement of Mr. Harrison and the vision of President Dickey. He spoke of his great affection for President-Emeritus Hopkins, and asked him if he wouldn't like to say something about the Center that now bore his name and about his feelings on the occasion of its opening.

Mr. Hopkins, who had reached his 85th birthday just two days earlier, jokingly recalled the promise of a new theater he had made to Warner Bentley in 1928 and the succession of unforeseen events that had made him a liar. "A man very seldom exults in his own failures," he said. "Twice in association with faculty and Trustees and undergraduates we formulated plans for a Center, but we did not have the ability to carry them out. In other words, accomplishment was not within us. And it has been for years a disappointment. But I am happy today that we did not carry out the plans, because without the vision and imagination and persistence of John Dickey we would never have had a structure of this scope and this significance."

Mr. Hopkins spoke mostly of the importance of the Center in the years ahead, and added that he did not think the magnitude of its influence could be appraised for many years. "I am happy to see Dartmouth a pioneer in a project of this sort," he said. "If one believes, as I do, that education is not education if it's simply an education of the specialist; if one believes, as I do, that something more is necessary than to become technically expert in the sciences; if one believes that beauty and art and all that microcosm we call culture are as essential to man as anything else, then the significance of this occasion begins to be apparent. This is something more than the addition to the campus of a structure of dignity and grandeur. It is something more than a meeting place for undergraduates. It is something more than an exhibit of what a college plant can be made. It will in the course of events, I am certain, become the heart and soul of Dartmouth. Man is something more than a chemical compound enclosed in a skin, the mind is something more than a computer, and the soul of man—nobody knows what it is, but it exists. And this Center stands for all those things."

In the evening of opening day, the Center's main theater was inaugurated with the presentation of Georg Buechner's *Danton's Death*, a 19th-century drama about the French Revolution, directed by James Clancy.

Spaulding Auditorium had a similar baptism that evening with a concert by the Dartmouth Glee Club. Every facility within Hopkins Center was put to use during the next ten days, as the College carried out an inaugural program arranged by Nichol M. Sandoe Jr. Spaulding had its formal, separate dedication on November 12, in connection with the first meeting of the Great Issues Course in Hopkins Center. The visiting speaker was August Heckscher, President Kennedy's White House adviser on the arts, who addressed the seniors on "The Arts and the National Life." Nine art shows and exhibitions throughout the Center were headed by an exhibition of "Impressionism 1865–1885" in the main Jaffe-Friede Gallery and a showing of paintings by Hans Hofmann in the Beaumont-May Gallery.

The inaugural program had its culmination in a four-day "Convocation on the Arts," which began November 15. Music came to the fore with two Dartmouth Community Symphony Orchestra concerts conducted by Mario di Bonaventura, a chamber music concert, and a concert by the combined glee clubs of Dartmouth and Mount Holyoke College. The significance of film as an art form was recognized with two world premieres: *Arctic Circle*, covering Vilhjalmur Stefansson's early journeys, was shown in the Studio Theater (later named the Warner Bentley Theater) located on the ground floor beneath the Center's main theater; and Spaulding Auditorium was used for the premiere preview of *Freud*, attended by producer-director John Huston, actress Susan Kohner, and officials of Universal Films.

Four distinguished men who participated as speakers and panelists in the Convocation on the Arts were Hans Hofmann, American abstract artist; Pier Luigi Nervi, Italian architect of Dartmouth's new field house; Michel St. Denis, French theater director; and Meyric Rogers, curator of the Garvan Collection of American Decorative Arts at Yale. Their presentations provided the daytime highlights of the Friday and Saturday programs, and on Saturday evening a black-tie dinner for 500 was held in Alumni Hall, the first big event of the kind in the new facility. Trustee Zimmerman presided and President Dickey was the main speaker.

The Convocation on the Arts reached its climax Sunday morning with the dedication of the Nervi-designed field house and the conferring of honorary degrees upon six notable figures in the world of the arts. Besides Hofmann, Nervi and St. Denis, recipients of the honorary Doctorate of Humane Letters were film producer Arthur Hornblow, artist Paul Sample, and William Schuman, composer and president of New York City's Lincoln Center, who gave the Convocation Address. The ceremonies were attended by an audience of 2,500, and at the conclusion President Dickey was more convinced than ever that Dartmouth no longer had need for a separate auditorium that could seat that many persons. Warner Bentley recalled that he tried to deflate Mr. Dickey's conviction by telling him that the acoustics were terrible, even when curtains were hung and the audience area was reduced.

With the eleven-day inaugural program Hopkins Center was impressively launched, and the Hanover community began to get some idea of what great new things had come into its life. Throughout the opening days, the hordes of students in the Center were one of the greatest satisfactions for those who had created it. Ever since, "the Hop" has been at the heart of campus life, bringing with it a cultural richness enjoyed by few colleges and universities in the nation and giving to Dartmouth, in the world of the arts, a singular prestige that would never have been imagined in any of the years prior to the Dickey presidency.

A Period of Fulfillment

WHEN the academic year 1962–63 was all over and President Dickey was speaking about it to his Convocation audience in September, he called it "an historic Dartmouth year" and said it was "one of those years whose mark will endure in the life of this institution, because it was a year great with fulfillment."

"It began," he said, "in the summer of '62 with a one-million-dollar grant from the Sloan Foundation for graduate engineering in the Thayer School, and it closed last month with Dartmouth's first regular fourth term and the most wonderful summer of music, theater, and the fine arts this North Country had yet known. In between were such other headlines as a second in the nation for the mathematics team; a grant of $675,000 from the Ford Foundation for a program of comparative studies in the humanities and social sciences; championships in football, skiing, debating, and baseball; the Nathaniel Leverone Field House, with its demonstrated potential for multiple use; the fulfilled promise of the Hopkins Center, for both College and community; a record Alumni Fund, with recognition to match in the Grand Award of the American Alumni Council for sustained alumni support; the largest peacetime graduating Class, nearly seven hundred strong, eighty percent of whom plan advanced study—all this and a Commencement address which, by any standard, was historic for both nation and College."

It was, indeed, an exceptional year, and the crowning event, nearly everyone would agree, was the formal opening of the Hopkins Center. But before that happened, the Trustees had taken an historic step in approving a fourth term, to be introduced in the summer of 1963. This had been seen as a likely, almost inevitable, development ever since the three-term, three-course program began in 1958. While course work was to be up to the standard of the other three terms, students enrolled

188

in the summer were required to carry only two courses during the eight-week term, but classes would meet five or six times a week, compared with the four or five times during a regular, ten-week term. The summer term was open to men and women from other colleges, and the College hoped to attract most of the four hundred or more Dartmouth undergraduates who had been attending summer sessions at other institutions. Dean Waldo Chamberlin estimated that close to one thousand students might be enrolled for the summer, but this proved to be overly optimistic. The actual enrollment was 153 men and 138 women from eighty-one colleges. Although the numbers were a disappointment, Dean Chamberlin was pleased with the quality of the term. Most important, the College had made a start on year-round operation, and with four terms it was now making more effective use of its educational facilities.

The Alfred P. Sloan Foundation grant of $1-million mentioned by President Dickey was one of five of the same amount made to engineering schools whose educational programs were strongly related to the basic sciences. Besides Dartmouth, the universities singled out for support were Brown, Johns Hopkins, Princeton, and Rochester. The grant came at an opportune time for Thayer School. Dean Myron Tribus had outlined ambitious plans, and the Sloan Foundation money now made possible more faculty, more research, a larger enrollment, new laboratory equipment, and the expansion of graduate programs. The Trustees at their June meeting had approved the Bachelor of Engineering degree, to be awarded after one year of graduate study following the major in engineering science. At their winter meeting they added approval of programs leading to the Master of Engineering and Doctor of Engineering degrees. Dean Tribus stated that it was his aim to make Thayer School "a pilot plant for modern engineering education" by adding to the professional approach the requirement that each candidate for a graduate degree demonstrate the creative ability to design engineering works, with attention paid to managerial and economic considerations. To help carry out this program Thayer School, in the fall of 1962, had added five new faculty members, who brought with them distinguished records in teaching and research.

Another of the international conferences for which Dartmouth was becoming a favorite site took place October 1–7, 1962, with forty prominent citizens of Japan and the United States participating. President Dickey, who delighted in such events, was co-chairman with Shigeharu Matsumoto of Tokyo, managing director of International House of Japan. The conference, sponsored by the College and International House of Japan, with support from the Ford Foundation, was similar to the gathering of Russian and American leaders in Hanover two years earlier. Problems in the relations between this country and Japan were examined by men and women from the political, academic, cultural, communications, and business life of the two countries. Delegates from the United States included Hanson Baldwin, Saul Bellow, Philip Mosely, David Riesman, Eugene Rostow, Walt Rostow, Arthur Schlesinger Jr., James Tobin, and Lionel Trilling. At the end of the conference, Mr. Matsumoto attached great value to its frank and vigorous exchange of ideas, and he expressed the hope that a second symposium could be held in Japan. Such a follow-up meeting did take place, and in March of 1964 Mr. Dickey headed a nineteen-man delegation to Japan, for the second half of what came to be known as the Dartmouth Conference on Japanese-American Relations. Mrs. Dickey accompanied him, and after the week-long conference in Kurashiki they remained in Japan for an additional week. They were guests of honor at a dinner given by the Dartmouth Club of Tokyo, and on the way home they stopped off in Honolulu for an alumni luncheon there.

When President Dickey called 1962–63 "an historic Dartmouth year" and ticked off some of the things that made it so, he did not forget the 1962 football team, one of the year's three unbeaten, untied major teams in the nation, and the finest Dartmouth team since the national championship team of 1925. Led by quarterback Bill King and All-American center Don McKinnon, the Big Green brought to a peak the coaching era of Bob Blackman, who in seven seasons of formal Ivy League play had a record of thirty-six wins, two ties, and eleven losses. In a hard-fought final game, Dartmouth defeated Princeton 31–27, to maintain its undefeated record; and the following year it overcame Princeton's 21–7 fourth-quarter lead, to win 22–21 and tie Princeton for the Ivy League title. It was the heyday of postwar Dartmouth football, and this was certainly a positive factor in the mounting dollar and contributor totals for the Alumni Fund and in all-around satisfaction with the Dickey administration.

John Dickey was a genuine football fan, as evidenced by his faithful attendance at home games, sometimes sitting in the press box, and by his frequent appearance at practice sessions. At the conclusion of the historic 1962 season, he took time from his busy schedule to write a personal letter to each senior on the team. The honors paid to the championship team were numerous, but the climax came in mid-January, when the Dartmouth Alumni Council and the Dartmouth Athletic Council jointly hosted a football dinner for some five hundred persons in Alumni Hall of the brand-new Hopkins Center. A special feature was the return of most members of the famous undefeated team of 1925, headed by Captain Nate Parker. Once again, such famous names as Swede Oberlander, Dutch Diehl, George Tully, Myles Lane, Hooker Horton, and Josh Davis were heard on campus. The dinner was the occasion also for honoring Nathaniel Leverone, identified that evening as donor of the Nervi-designed field house.

Dedication ceremonies had become almost a way of life for Dartmouth, as its building boom went on. On December 1 another dedication took place at the Kellogg Medical Auditorium, the newest completed unit of the Gilman Biomedical Center. The one-day program, attended by two hundred members of the medical profession, consisted of two symposia and a dinner. It was the occasion also for the first meeting of the Nathan Smith Medical Society, the new alumni organization of the Medical School. Dean Gilbert Mudge expressed Dartmouth's thanks to the W. K. Kellogg Foundation for the $500,000 grant that made the auditorium possible and praised the foundation's diversified support of medical education, particularly its interest in developing the two-year medical school. President Dickey, in his address at the closing dinner, spoke of the modern man of medicine and observed that growing specialization was eroding the physician's historic role as community leader. This, he said, "is not just a problem to be solved but a condition of life to be understood." The medical school, and particularly one like Dartmouth's, allied with the liberal arts, can make a contribution both to understanding and to solving the problem, he concluded.

Along with the remarkable development of the College's physical plant, a distinct characteristic of the Dickey administration was the foundation support being given to Dartmouth with greater frequency and in major amounts. This was a decided change from the Hopkins administration, when most of the large gifts to the College came from individuals. The largest portion of foundation support was going to engineering and the medical sciences, but in December 1962 the Ford Foundation made a grant of $675,000 for the purpose of establishing a Comparative Studies Center that would give the faculty the training needed to develop the international, non-Western content of the undergraduate curriculum. Dartmouth's grant was the largest of the six made by the Ford Foundation for that purpose, and it is fairly safe to surmise that a factor in Dartmouth's being chosen was the marked success with which the College had conducted the Russian-American and Japanese-American conferences held in Hanover with Ford Foundation support. Somewhat later, in February, it was announced that the co-directors of the Center for Comparative Studies would be Professors Francis W. Gramlich and Laurence I. Radway. It was also disclosed that it was the plan of the center to free selected faculty members from one-half of their teaching loads, so they could engage in activities and studies that would give them a better understanding of the values, philosophies, cultures, and institutions of non-Western societies.

Another mark of the Dickey administration was the steady upward march in the tuition fee in order to obtain funds needed for the steady upward march in faculty compensation. The Trustees at their January 1963 meeting voted an increase of $125 for 1963–64 and another $125 for 1964–65. This meant a rise from $1,550 to $1,800 over the two-year period, and a total cost of approximately $2,700 for tuition, board, and room rent. Some months after the Trustee action, the Dartmouth chapter of the American Association of University Professors released the fourth of its faculty compensation reports, begun in 1959. The report stated that "substantial progress" had been made and gave the average figures (salary and fringe benefits) of $14,000 for professors, $11,780 for associate professors, $9,470 for assistant professors, and $7,280 for instructors. Since 1959, the average gains were $2,928 for professors, $2,423 for associate professors, $1,962 for assistant professors, and $1,748 for instructors. On the basis of the national AAUP rating scale of AA to F for high and low in each rank, Dartmouth in the first report had two A's, four B's, and two C's. In this newest report, the College had six A's, one B, and one C. The efforts of John Dickey to make Dartmouth more competitive with the country's top institutions in faculty compensation obviously were showing results.

More foundation support for the biological sciences at Dartmouth was forthcoming in April 1963 when the National Science Foundation announced a grant of $740,000 for research, laboratory facilities, and graduate fellowships. All but $6,000 of the grant was applied toward construction of the Charles Gilman Life Sciences Laboratory, for which the Gilman Foundation had made the major gift a year earlier. The NSF grant was given specifically to provide research and graduate training facilities for a biological-sciences faculty of twenty members, ten postdoctoral fellows, and fifteen graduate students.

The death of Orvil E. Dryfoos, publisher and president of *The New York Times*, created a vacancy on the Dartmouth Board of Trustees, and at its June meeting the board elected F. William Andres to serve out the Dryfoos term. Andres, a partner in one of Boston's leading law firms, was President Dickey's classmate at Dartmouth and Harvard Law School and over the years he had become perhaps his closest friend, sharing his interests in hunting and fishing and in education. Most of all, he was the sort of public-minded citizen upon whom John Dickey placed such high value, and his addition to the board was something to which the President gave his wholehearted endorsement. Andres continued on the board until 1977 and became its chairman.

June regularly brought the Dartmouth Alumni Council to town for its annual meeting, but the 1963 gathering was special because it marked the fiftieth anniversary of the College's alumni senate. President-Emeritus Hopkins, who had been chiefly responsible for bringing the Council into being in the fall of 1913 and had been its first president, was the central figure in the anniversary observance. He spoke at the Council dinner, as did President Dickey and Sidney Hayward, Secretary of the College, who up to that point had been the Council's secretary for thirty-three of its fifty years. President Dickey chose to speak to the Council about the principal factors that, in his estimation, went into making the Dartmouth spirit unique. This, he explained, was something he liked to share with each senior class on the eve of graduation. The factors he listed were place, an adventurous founding, a struggle for independence in the Dartmouth College Case, a rededication to the College's historic purpose under President Tucker, and the achievement of a unique unity of College and alumni under President Hopkins. Addressing Mr. Hopkins directly, he said: "The last factor I speak of is one which I credit to you. This College, far above all others, not only by our own admission but by the assertion of others, has achieved a sense of identity on the part of its products with the institution—a unique unity of the alumnus and his College in the sense that the individual is fulfilled only as the institution is fulfilled through its alumni. This identification, this unity between College and product, is your work as that of no other man. And on this foundation Dartmouth will remain the unique College she is. And for that, sir, we thank you."

With a fourth term added, one now had to think of the academic year as extending from September through August. Although the pace was still slower, the summer transformation of Hanover into a quiet New England village was gone forever, just a memory. Aside from the academic program—fifty-nine courses offered by twenty-one different departments and a faculty of sixty-five—the summer term had its noteworthy extracurricular features, such as a Congregation of the Arts, and a nearly even division between men and women in the student body (which brought three directors of dormitories at Wellesley College to Hanover to serve in a similar capacity for the summer). With women housed in the Wigwam and Choate Road dormitories, better street lighting and increased patrolling by campus police were necessary. Fortunately for Dean Chamberlin and Assistant Dean Robert W. MacMillen, Mrs. Margaret Ward had joined the staff as director of women's activities, to look after the myriad of details with which Dartmouth's male administrators had little or no experience.

Note should be made of another important first for the 1963 summer term. Dartmouth was asked by the Peace Corps to provide seven weeks of intensive language instruction, cultural indoctrination, and physical training for a group of thirty-three young men and women volunteers, who were going to the African Republic of Guinea to teach English to French-speaking students. The Peace Corps group was the first to be trained at Dartmouth, as well as the first to be going to Guinea. The language training devised at Dartmouth had remarkable success; on their final tests, the young volunteers who went through the seven weeks of study scored, on average, three points higher than the U.S. high school teachers of French taking the same test.

This first Peace Corps experience for Dartmouth was the beginning of a long and successful association between the College and the Peace Corps, with larger and larger groups coming to the campus during succeeding summer terms, and the College's reputation as an ideal training ground growing all the while. For the summer of 1964, the Peace Corps contingent was quadrupled in size and was special in that the trainees were college students who were about to begin the senior year and were planning on enlistment in the Peace Corps after gradua- tion. The language coordinator for the second summer was John Ras- sias, whose dramatic method of intensive language learning was to become nationally, even internationally, celebrated.

The summer term was notable also for the beginning of a series of summer Congregations of the Arts, characterized as "a coming to- gether of students and teachers in the arts." The newly established Summer Repertory Theater, using both professionals and students, gave twenty-one performances of Shakespeare, Wycherley, and Shaw. Three noted composers—Elliott Carter, Vincent Persichetti, and Walter Piston—were in residence for two-week periods and participated in the music program directed by Mario di Bonaventura. Both faculty and students from the Juilliard School of Music were involved in the Congre- gation's music program. Frank Stella, painter, and Tal Streeter, sculp- tor, were artists-in-residence and worked with advanced students. At- tendance in the art galleries and at the plays and concerts was very high, and in its first summer the Hopkins Center showed what a super- lative dimension it was adding to the life of the College and to that of the whole surrounding region. As the Congregations grew in fame, leading figures from this country and abroad came to participate; but the expense also grew, requiring the College to draw on general funds, and ultimately it became necessary to continue the summer programs on a more modest scale.

As Dartmouth began its 195th year in the fall of 1963, protests about the treatment of blacks in this country were taking a more active form, and this was especially true on the campuses of colleges across the country. Only the month before, some 200,000 blacks and their white supporters had demonstrated in Washington, D.C., and there Martin Luther King had made his famous "I have a dream" speech. Earlier, in October 1962, James Meredith became the first black to enroll at the University of Mississippi, where three thousand troops had to be called out to put down the ensuing riots. President Dickey, in preparing his Convocation address, was not only mindful of the changing situation in racial relations, but he was still deeply affected by the previous June's Commencement address at Dartmouth, given by the Rev. James H. Robinson, director of Operation Crossroads Africa—an address "which, by any standard, was historic for both nation and College." The President described the racial problem as one that "presses on our national life with an urgency that now requires 'all deliberate speed' be measured in hours and days, rather than years and generations. . . . All of these are on my mind, but the overriding reason for speaking of this matter on this occasion is that it is immensely relevant to the annual joint venture of higher education on which we today embark in this College's one hundred and ninety-fifth year."

Participating in the Convocation exercises for the first time was the Rev. Richard P. Unsworth, newly appointed Dean of the William Jewett Tucker Foundation. Dean Unsworth, the chaplain of Smith College, came to Dartmouth as successor to Professor Fred Berthold, who after six years on the job was returning to full-time teaching.

Yet another dedication took place October 11, to mark the completion of the Dana Biomedical Library and its being put to use at the start of the new academic year. Charles A. Dana, chairman of the Dana Corporation of Toledo, Ohio, and founder of the foundation that gave $400,000 toward building the library, was present at the ceremony and spoke briefly of his interest in education and of the pleasure he had experienced in making trips to Hanover to watch the Dana Library come into being. Mr. Dickey presided at the dedication and also was a speaker, along with College Librarian Richard Morin.

One month after the Dana dedication, College officials and faculty members participated in the offical dedication and opening of the U.S. Army's Cold Regions Research and Engineering Laboratory. The College's scientific neighbor on Lyme Road was finally ensconced in its new home after a construction delay caused by a January 1961 fire in the basement area where cold storage rooms were located. Colonel William L. Nungesser took command of the laboratory and a staff of two hundred civilians, mostly scientists and researchers with graduate degrees, and forty-five enlisted personnel, the majority of whom were college-trained technicians. Relations between CRREL and the College were in the formative stage, but on both sides there was anticipation of the academic and scientific advantages to be realized, and Thayer School was already doing some contract work for the Army installation.

Like every other city, town, and hamlet in America, Hanover was shocked into speechless grief on Friday, November 22, when it learned of the assassination of President John F. Kennedy. The College came to a virtual standstill. All scheduled events were cancelled, and although thousands of students were in residence, the campus had a deserted look. President Dickey and President Goheen of Princeton quickly agreed that the football game scheduled to be played the day following the national tragedy should be called off and played instead on November 30. Rollins Chapel was filled for a special memorial service on Sunday. In his brief address, Mr. Dickey said, "Let us at this moment only ask for ourselves that out of this awful thing we and other men who presume to be called civilized may be made a little more aware of where our own hatreds and hostilities may lead not merely us but others as well.

"I shall not presume to speak to you of the President whose life has been taken as the price of his leadership of our Nation. May we not simply say here in unmeasured tribute that he was a man of his time who as a leader of men brought to his duty and to his death the timeless virtue of bravery."

On Monday, the official day of national mourning, all classes were cancelled and all offices closed. Palaeopitus, representing all Dartmouth students, sent a letter of condolence to President Kennedy's widow and, in his memory, made a contribution to The National Association of Mental Health, a charity in which he had a special interest.

The Dartmouth Alumni Fund reached its fiftieth anniversary year with the 1963–64 campaign, and at the biennial joint meeting of the Board of Trustees and the Alumni Council, in January, the anniversary was celebrated at a dinner held in Alumni Hall of Hopkins Center and attended by three hundred members of the Dartmouth family. Head fund agents and their wives were invited to the special event and heard Alumni Fund Chairman Charles F. Moore Jr. announce that a goal of $1.5 million had been set for the anniversary year. (The final total was a record-breaking $1.6 million.) In recognition of alumni who had been loyal supporters of the fund, Mr. Moore also announced the founding of The Ancient and Honorable Society of Latter Day Letter Men of Dartmouth College, in token of which some fourteen thousand regular contributors would receive a certificate bearing a small "D" in green felt. The first two certificates were presented to President Dickey and President-Emeritus Hopkins, who were at the head table.

Shortly before the Alumni Fund dinner, Ford Whelden of the Development Office released a report on alumni financial support of the College, showing a remarkably accelerated rate of giving in the vintage years of the Dickey administration. His initial report, ten years earlier, had shown a total of $13,809,250 in gifts of all kinds from all the living classes, from 1884 through 1952. His similar report a decade later showed a total of $44,180,240 from the classes of 1894 through 1962, an increase of more than $30-million in the past ten years alone. The capital-gifts campaign and the steady rise of the annual Alumni Fund were major factors in the previous decade's record, but the growth of the bequests and estate planning program also deserved a large measure of credit. Over all, the development program that was reshaped and expanded in the early Dickey years had taken hold and given the College new strength, but funds in much greater amounts were needed if progress was to continue. In the remaining half-dozen years of John Dickey's presidency the biggest financial push of all was to be mounted—and brought to a resounding bicentennial success.

The Alumni Fund, with a fiftieth anniversary, was a mere youngster to the Dartmouth Alumni Association of Boston, which in the same month celebrated its one-hundredth birthday. A gala dinner at the Statler Hilton was attended by twelve hundred persons, and Governor Rockefeller of New York came to give the main address. President Dickey also spoke and President-Emeritus Hopkins was present as guest of honor. For Mr. Hopkins, in his 87th year, it was the last large alumni event he attended. Some months later, on August 13, 1964, he died at his summer home in Manset, Maine.

With a variety of milestones being passed in the College's forward march, financial aid reached one of its own by granting for the first time more than $1-million in scholarships. To this annual sum was added $375,000 in student loans, the bulk of them made possible by funds from the National Defense Student Loan Program. College employment, consisting usually of jobs for meals at Thayer dining hall, was the third main component of financial aid at Dartmouth, providing help to approximately three hundred men. In order not only to maintain, but to increase, the level of scholarship aid, President Dickey and the Trustees were willing to use more of the College's general funds for that purpose. For 1963–64, for example, the College used $400,000 of general operating funds to supplement the $600,000 derived from endowment income and from gifts earmarked for scholarship aid.

A great expansion of the computer's place in Dartmouth's life was assured by the February announcement that a new computation center would be constructed. As planned by Professors Kemeny and Kurtz, with the help of General Electric, the central computer was to have a unique "time-sharing" capability that would permit virtually simultaneous use by faculty and students at twenty input-output stations located about campus. It was claimed that no other college in the country could provide such a large percentage of its students with immediate access to a high-speed computer. Toward the estimated $800,000 cost of the computation center the National Science Foundation made a grant of $300,000, and it also gave Professor Kemeny $84,150 for the first year of a two-year program of experimental undergraduate instruction. During the first year he and his colleagues invented the widely used computer language known as BASIC. Several months later, at the June meeting of the Alumni Council, President Dickey announced that Peter Kiewit of Omaha, Nebraska, had given the remaining $500,000 needed to build the computation center and that the center, to be located next to the Bradley Mathematics Center, would be named for him. Mr. Kiewit, Class of 1922, was at the time president of one of the world's largest construction firms—builder of dams, tunnels, power plants, and airports. Among the company's biggest projects were the Atomic Energy Commission's $1.2-billion gaseous diffusion plant in Ohio, the Thule Air Force Base in Greenland, and the Titan and Minutemen missile facilities in several western states.

As a memorial to Orvil E. Dryfoos, who was a Dartmouth Trustee at the time of his death, the College established the Orvil E. Dryfoos Conference on Public Affairs. The first conference, sponsored by Dartmouth's Public Affairs Center, was held on campus on March 7 and 8 and had as its theme Congressional Reorganization: Problems and Prospects. Eight members of the U.S. Congress took part, along with educators and members of the press, one of whom was John B. Oakes of *The New York Times*, the newspaper that Orvil Dryfoos headed as publisher and president. President Dickey presided at a conference dinner and took part in all three of the panel discussions held in Sanborn English House.

John Dickey's interest in public and international affairs continued unabated, and when he engaged in non-Dartmouth activities, more likely than not they were in those two areas. In the month following the Dryfoos conference, the President's name was among those appearing on a printed report on "The College and World Affairs," which was a summary of a two-year study in which Dartmouth's Provost John Masland also took part. Mr. Dickey was one of six college presidents in the ten-man study group. The conclusions of the report were certainly in line with ideas that Mr. Dickey had expressed many times in his addresses and writings. The central proposition was that U.S. colleges were failing to prepare Americans for the responsibilities of world leadership and that they needed to make a much stronger institutional commitment to "the international studies dimension of liberal learning." In discussing the development of educational programs to that end, the report cited Dartmouth's new Comparative Studies Center as one of the significant efforts to encourage more non-Western content in liberal arts curricula.

Early in June, before giving his attention to Dartmouth's own Commencement, President Dickey went to Bucknell University to receive the honorary degree of Doctor of Civil Law and to address the graduating class. The address he gave on that occasion was one of the most engaging he ever delivered. Serious in a light-hearted way, it reflected perhaps "the happiness of coming home." Mr. Dickey spoke of his boyhood in central Pennsylvania, near Bucknell, and of how he had attended that university in the summer of 1925 before going to Dartmouth. For the benefit of his young audience, about to take on the responsibilities of citizenship, he recounted some "selected examples from the public record of my time that give me confidence in the capacity of our democracy both to teach and to learn." He was not going to be one of those commencement speakers, he said, who assert that their generation had made a mess of things, which the new graduates would have to clean up. In fact, he said, Bucknell's graduating class was inheriting a world that could have been much worse. In reviewing the events that led him to such an optimistic view, Mr. Dickey threw light on how he felt about a number of national and international happenings of his time.

Referring to this country's rejection of the League of Nations after World War I and its leading role in establishing the United Nations after World War II, Mr. Dickey said, "The changing of a great nation's mind on anything so fundamental within one generation is something worth your understanding and your remembering." He mentioned also "the most creative and positive postwar period the world had ever known," and urged the Bucknell graduates "to remember that you and the family you are raising are the stuff of a nation that had the maturity and the vision to put its wartime enemies back on their feet with two of the most enlightened enemy occupations ever recorded in the affairs of nations. Beyond this wisdom and this magnanimity toward vanquished foes, your country has been generous to a fault toward its friends. . . . I will offer the judgment that few foreign policies have done as much to keep the future open for your generation as the Marshall Plan."

Mr. Dickey closed out the record of national behavior with mention of the fact that for the first time in one hundred years America was facing the problems of civil rights and racial relations rather than evading them. All in all, he told his youthful audience, it was not a bad inheritance they were getting from his generation. "On this occasion of your going forth from college to buckle on the sword of full-fledged citizenship," he said, "I do want to urge on you the less obvious truth that whatever else democracy has in common with other systems, at its best it is uniquely the great teacher of the community. . . . So far as I can see, democracy is the only form of human discourse and decision that can conceivably give a community the experience of learning its own way into the paths of fairness, wisdom, and fulfillment."

Upon his return to Hanover from Bucknell, President Dickey became the bestower of honorary degrees rather than a recipient. Among those honored at the 1964 graduation exercises was Jean LeSage, the Premier of Quebec, who joined other Canadian statesmen upon whom Mr. Dickey had conferred degrees with special pleasure because of his interest in that nation. Canadians honored earlier were Louis Stephen St. Laurent, Secretary of State for External Affairs; Lester B. Pearson, who held the same position and also served in Washington and at the United Nations; and Prime Minister John G. Diefenbaker. Three other Canadians received honorary degrees at the Anglo-Canadian-American convocation of 1957 and two more at the medical convocation in 1960. Dartmouth's long and friendly relations with Canadian institutions and personages were certainly deepened during the Dickey presidency, and Canada in turn held him in great respect, as evidenced by honorary degrees from McGill and Toronto and by the serious attention given to his writings about Canada. The latest of John Dickey's publications about Canada was a book, *The United States and Canada*, which he edited and Prentice-Hall published in 1964. Under the auspices of the American Assembly, six essays were prepared by Canadian and American scholars, dealing with relations between the two countries and with the political, economic, and cultural problems that sometimes strain that relationship.

With the opening of the summer term, a reorganization of the academic administration of the College went into effect. It was largely a change in nomenclature. Leonard Rieser, Deputy Provost and Director of Graduate Study, became Dean of the Faculty for Arts and Sciences, a newly created position. Under him the chairmen of the three divisions of the faculty became Associate Deans of the Faculty—for the humanities, the social sciences, and the sciences. The object of the reorganization was to bring together in one office all administrative responsibilities for the faculty of arts and sciences, at both the undergraduate and graduate levels. Top responsibility for all academic affairs of the College remained with Provost John Masland, under whom Dean Rieser operated.

The summer program in 1964 had two important firsts: the two-year Peace Corps Training Program, which some 150 college students began between junior and senior years, and the Dartmouth Alumni College, attended for eleven days by 180 alumni, wives, and family members. But the summer newcomer that attracted most attention was Project ABC (A Better Chance), designed for the educational uplift of economically and scholastically disadvantaged high-school students. The idea of the project, allying Dartmouth with thirty independent preparatory schools, was to bring some fifty selected blacks and others from low-income families to the College for eight weeks of intensive tutorial instruction, as a bridge to their entering the participating independent schools in the fall. There their education would continue, in the hope that they would eventually be ready to go on to the college of their choice. In support of the collaborative program, the Rockefeller Foundation provided a three-year grant of $150,000.

Charles F. Dey, Associate Dean of the College, was named Director of Project ABC. The teaching staff for intensive instruction in English and mathematics was assembled from the College and secondary schools, and eight Dartmouth undergraduates were recruited to be resident tutors. Before Dartmouth and the schools joined forces in Project ABC, each had in mind some form of program that would give promising but deprived high-school students a better chance to get a college education. Dartmouth had the problem of finding the right prospects to tutor and, then, of devising the necessary follow-through after their summer study. The schools, by means of the Independent Schools Talent Search, had identified the good prospects, but they had the problem of too great a cultural and scholastic shock for students going from a poor neighborhood school to a resident preparatory school. The summer session at Dartmouth, after which the participating schools took over, seemed to be an ideal solution for both. The joint program proved to be not only workable but successful. Of the fifty-five boys who came to Hanover, fifty-four completed the full program, and all but seven were recommended to prep schools committed to their admission with full scholarships.

Off to an equally successful start in the summer of 1964 was Alumni College, which took firm root and ever since has been the star event in Dartmouth's varied program of continuing education. President Hopkins in his inaugural address of 1916 is credited with sounding higher education's first call for continuing education for alumni. A beginning was made in the thirties with Hanover Holiday, immediately after Commencement and reunions, but it was in the Dickey administration that continuing education took hold and was purposefully developed not only for alumni but for other groups encouraged to come to the campus, mainly in the summer when facilities were available. The growth of continuing education programs, not only on campus but also in alumni regions, was another of the distinctive hallmarks of the Dickey years. President Dickey himself participated in some of these programs and was willing to add the staff personnel needed to direct and develop them.

Conscious of the fact that Dartmouth had only five years to go to its bicentennial, President Dickey entitled his 1964 Convocation address "Prelude to a Third Century" and said, "Let us look for a few minutes at this wonderful living thing we call 'the College' — venerable in years and service, and yet, as young as the youngest here today, and as full of fresh promise as the best among us." Recalling the establishment of the Trustees Planning Committee ten years before, and its commitment to fifteen years of sustained rededication and refounding, he repeated from his 1955 address the goal of "bringing this institution to a running start of preeminent performance when it enters its third century." As he had on one or two previous occasions, President Dickey recapitulated what he considered the important advances already made, advances that set the stage for the final five years of the TPC agenda. He began his list with the Tucker Foundation, the elimination of fraternity discrimination, the academic honor system, and the three-three educational plan. He continued by citing interdisciplinary programs in public affairs and human relations, the overseas study program for language majors, faculty fellowships, the refounding of the Dartmouth Medical School, new instructional and faculty facilities for all three divisions of the curriculum, new student housing, a recasting of engineering education, the Gilman Biomedical Center, Hopkins Center, Leverone Field House, the comparative studies program, the Kiewit computer center, three doctoral programs, a vital and expanded summer term, and, making it all possible, a new level of financial support from alumni, foundations, and others.

It was not in any boastful fashion that President Dickey reviewed the accomplishments of the past decade. Because of these things, he said, it was his opinion that ". . . the essential educational foundations of rededication—purpose, faculty, student body, facilities, and standards—are now largely laid. The immediate future will be built on these foundations." He added that he did not foresee any significant increase in the size of the faculty and student body in the next five years, but that some limited growth in graduate enrollment was likely. Finally, he revealed what must have been a restricted topic of Trustee consideration, when he added that major new financial resources must be found to compensate the kind of faculty the College wanted and to continue having a student body admitted solely on merit. This was perhaps the first inkling that the Third Century Fund was then in the making.

At the October meeting of the Board of Trustees, Thomas W. Braden, Class of 1940, editor and publisher of *The Daily Blade-Tribune* of Oceanside, California, was elected a Trustee to fill the vacancy created by the death of Roswell Magill. Braden, who was also president of the California State Board of Education, had been a member of the Dartmouth administrative staff, as assistant to President Dickey in 1947–48 and as executive secretary of the Great Issues Course in its first year. With Stewart Alsop he was the author of *Sub-Rosa* (1946), a history of the wartime O.S.S., and from 1951 to 1954 he was assistant to Allen W. Dulles, director of the Central Intelligence Agency. Not only the youngest member of the board, he also was the only one from the West Coast.

The 1964–65 college year opened with one of the largest foundation grants the College was to receive during the Dickey presidency. It was $2-million from the James Foundation of New York, in support of the Dartmouth Medical School. A few months later the Medical School received $1-million from the Irene Heinz Given and John LaPorte Given Foundation of New York to establish two endowed chairs, in the departments of cytology and pharmacology. This latter grant carried the School past its capital-gifts goal of $10-million, but $750,000 of that total had been given for purposes not included in the original objectives of the campaign, and it was decided to withhold an "over the top" announcement until another $750,000 had been raised to fulfill the original objectives.

Within a year the James Foundation gave Dartmouth another

$500,000, when it distributed its remaining assets, as required by the charter drawn up when the foundation was established twenty-five years earlier. This final grant "for general corporate purposes" brought to $2.7-million the total of gifts from the foundation, making it one of Dartmouth's greatest benefactors.

Tuck School also came in for a share of foundation support at the start of the 1964 fall term. It received $250,000 from the Alfred P. Sloan Foundation, for the purpose of expanding the School's research and its M.B.A. curriculum. Since 1953 the Sloan Foundation had shown its interest in Tuck School by making annual grants of $35,000 to finance the publication of a series of economic bulletins and to help faculty members in the writing of books and articles. Tuck School at the time of the large grant had increased its enrollment to 205 and its faculty commensurately. The Medical School had 150 students and Thayer School forty-five. The total of other graduate students was ninety-one.

Dartmouth's predilection for international conferences and programs surfaced again with an extended program on classical and contemporary Japan, held throughout the winter and spring terms of 1965. Jointly directed by the Comparative Studies Center and the Hopkins Center, the program brought together academic and artistic efforts to make Japan better understood and appreciated in this country. Faculty seminars on modern Japan and five undergraduate courses were the major parts of Dartmouth's academic contribution, which was bolstered by a long string of visiting scholars. Hopkins Center staged presentations of Japanese drama, fine arts, music, films, and crafts, in connection with all of which artists from Japan were in residence for varying periods of time. An especially attractive feature at Hopkins Center was the Japanese garden created in the outdoor sculpture court. It was designed by landscape artist Kaneji Domoto, and among those who enjoyed it was Ryuji Takeuchi, the Japanese Ambassador to the United States, who came to Hanover for the American premiere of a Mishima play, directed by Takeo Matsuura of Tokyo. The Japanese events were the third program with a general theme that Hopkins Center had put on since its opening in November 1962. The first dealt with Religion and the Contemporary Arts and the second with The World of William Shakespeare.

Amidst all the public programs on campus, providing a liberal arts education for undergraduates remained the central business of the College. The faculty was steadily engaged in efforts to improve the curriculum, and after a year-long study by the Committee on Educational Policy the faculty approved changes for the freshman and sophomore years, to go into effect with the coming 1965–66 academic year. The basic revisions had to do with the distributive requirement and the time of choosing a major, and they were adopted because of advances in secondary-school education and the improved intellectual competence of Dartmouth's entering classes. Under the revised curriculum, the student no longer had to fulfill the distributive requirement of courses in the humanities, social sciences, and sciences by the end of sophomore year, but could spread out over four years the meeting of that requirement, if he chose to. The requirement that a major had to be elected by the end of the third term of sophomore year still stood, but the student was now given the option of choosing his major at any time after the first term of freshman year. Most students entering the College were planning to go on to graduate study in a known field and were capable of handling some courses in the major department or division before junior year. Spreading the distributive requirement over four years gave them the freedom to make an earlier start on advanced courses and to set their own pace toward reaching their academic goals.

It was also faculty thinking that cramming a lot of "sample courses" into the first two years was too much of an extension of secondary-school education. The new curriculum lessened the importance of these so-called introductory courses, elected mainly by freshmen and sophomores, but the professionally oriented faculty welcomed this and was ready to work earlier with the brighter and better prepared students entering the College. In the report of the Committee on Educational Policy, it was disclosed that over the past decade the average verbal and mathematical aptitude scores for Dartmouth freshmen had risen 120 points—verbal from 530 to 650 and mathematical from 580 to 700.

Also on the academic front, it was announced at the beginning of the winter term that the Trustees had approved two more Ph.D. programs, bringing the number to five. The Department of Physics and

Astronomy, which was offering an M.A. degree, was permitted to extend its graduate program to a Ph.D. in physics. The Medical School, already offering the doctoral degree in molecular biology, was permitted to add the Ph.D. in physiology and pharmacology. The two new programs were expected to involve about fifty graduate students when fully in operation. In both cases the fields of doctoral study were to be those in which members of the faculty had research interests. The extent to which faculty research at Dartmouth was growing is partly indicated by the fact that at that time twenty-three faculty members were engaged in research in the physiology-pharmacology area, and fourteen were doing research projects in physics and astronomy, plus five more in radio-physics.

President Dickey was never involved in New Hampshire state affairs to the extent that Mr. Hopkins was, but on February 24, 1965, he went to Concord to add his voice to those testifying against the Feldman Bill, which would ban Communist and alleged subversive speakers from state institutions. In the name of academic freedom, there was a chorus of protest against the bill. Dartmouth faculty members joined their colleagues at the University of New Hampshire and other state colleges in defending the right of public institutions, as well as private, to establish their own policies regarding speakers. In the statement he made to the Education Committee of the New Hampshire House of Representatives, Mr. Dickey said that despite the differences between public and private institutions of learning, the day was long past when there could be a double standard in the fundamental matter of academic freedom. "From coast to coast," he stated, "public education is now the dominant educational experience of American youth. If those who enjoy this education have a bad experience with academic freedom and free speech during their learning days, I am sure the day is not far off when every sector of American life, private as well as public, will in some measure be less free." He spoke of the importance of a good educational climate at a university or college and said that open discussion was the most fundamental factor in creating a good climate. "Any attempt," he added, "however well-intentioned, to restrict or regulate that open discussion from outside the institution itself is bound to be regarded as, and therefore in fact to be, a distorting and distracting influence that in spite of all else will pervade the educational experience of the place. Many other things may be arguable, but I hardly think it can be doubted that this must be the inevitable outcome of any effort by legislation to remove these matters from the responsibility of an institution's trustees, faculty, and academic officials."

The appearance of radical speakers at Dartmouth was not to the liking of everyone, on the campus or off, but the administration followed a hands-off policy and accepted the plan of having the Undergraduate Council extend invitations on behalf of the student body. About three weeks before President Dickey's appearance in Concord, Malcolm X had addressed a standing-room-only crowd in Spaulding Auditorium of Hopkins Center, and one month previously Moral Rearmament leader Peter Howard had done the same. A third speaker, Levi Laub of the Student Committee for Travel to Cuba, was unable to keep his Dartmouth date, when a federal court forbade him to leave New York City while under indictment for violating a State Department ban on travel to Cuba. Not all speakers invited to Dartmouth by the UGC were controversial figures, but the freedom granted by the administration was well known and the "good educational climate" described to the legislators by President Dickey was a reality under his leadership.

The consideration that the faculty had been giving to the freshman and sophomore curriculum was carried one step further with a close decision at its March meeting to drop the compulsory English 2 course and to require, in its place, a freshman seminar. The seminar could be chosen from a variety of topics, offered by more than the English department, but the development of writing skills remained the primary purpose of this course, offered in the second term of freshman year. There was advantage, the faculty felt, in having the student learn to write clearly and correctly in a discipline that interested him more than English. The Committee on Educational Policy, which proposed the change, made it clear that one of its objectives was to emphasize that good writing should be demanded by every department, not by the English faculty alone.

Nineteen sixty-five was a year for Mr. Dickey to include the West Coast in his spring alumni tour. Early April found him speaking in San Francisco and Los Angeles and, then, he went on to Honolulu for an April 11 engagement. From there he and Mrs. Dickey flew to New

Zealand to spend some time with their son John Jr., who was a graduate student at Otaga University in Dunedin. Their itinerary thereafter took them to Bangkok, by way of Sydney, and to New Delhi, which they reached on April 30. After a week in India they moved on to Greece for a rather lengthy stay and then headed north to London on May 24. Three days later they were back in the States, again just in time for winding up the academic year.

While the Dickeys were away, the Undergraduate Council was host on April 23–24 to the Northeast Colleges Conference on the Civil Rights Movement, attended by two hundred delegates from colleges and universities in the Northeast. The theme was The New Direction of the Civil Rights Movement, and in Hanover as guest speakers were some of the leading figures in the movement, including Lawrence Guyot, chairman of the Mississippi Freedom Democratic Party; John Leins, chairman of the Student Non-Violent Coordinating Committee; Hosea Williams, chief assistant to the Rev. Martin Luther King Jr.; and Thomas Hayden, chairman of the Newark Project of Students for a Democratic Society. A Dartmouth faculty debate on Vietnam also sponsored by the UGC about the same time, was a sign that civil rights and the war in Vietnam were becoming lively issues, after a period in which the Dartmouth campus was quiescent compared with the student activism at other colleges and universities.

Dartmouth's efforts to broaden its educational interests to more non-Western areas of the world got a boost with a $25,000 grant under the National Defense Education Act, enabling the College to establish a Language and Area Center for East Asia. The new program was coordinated with that of the Comparative Studies Center, which since 1963 had been supporting faculty study and research in non-Western cultures and history. Its content, according to the May announcement, was to consist of undergraduate courses in literature, philosophy, religion, history, and the Chinese language. Bit by bit, since the early postwar years, when Russian Civilization was added to the curriculum, the College was increasing the opportunities for students to learn about areas of the world that had never before figured in the College's educational program. And added to that were all the conferences and special programs that were, in the words of Dean Rieser, making Hanover an "international crossroads."

Only a few days after the Dickeys returned from their trip around the world, the College administration suffered a great loss in the death of Sidney Hayward, who had for thirty-five years been Secretary of the College and the central figure in Dartmouth's very successful alumni program. His death on May 29, 1965, ended a Dartmouth career that began, immediately after graduation in 1926, as assistant to President Hopkins. Mr. Hayward was one of President Dickey's hunting and fishing companions, and a Paul Sample painting of him, in the field with his dog, hangs in the Hayward Lounge of the Hanover Inn. He headed innumerable committees and study groups for the College, the most important of which had to do with the Hopkins Center, undergraduate social life, public relations, the Outing Club, and alumni relations (which report won the American Alumni Council's 1958 alumni service award). While editing the *Dartmouth Alumni Magazine* for thirteen years, Mr. Hayward in 1943 won the Robert Sibley Award for the best alumni magazine in the country.

Commencement for the first time was held in Leverone Field House, when heavy rain washed out the traditional outdoor exercises for the Class of 1965. The field house easily accommodated the five thousand persons attending graduation, while five thousand wet and empty chairs remained in front of Baker Library. This expensive duplication led to the proposal that Commencement henceforth be held in Leverone, thus eliminating the double set-up. But the Class of 1966 was strongly in favor of keeping the exercises out of doors, and so matters have remained ever since.

The summer term that began soon after had a notably excellent music program, highlighted by the presence of Hungarian composer Zoltan Kodaly, who as Composer in Residence conducted some of his own works. Ernst Krenek, another celebrated composer, also spent two weeks at Dartmouth and conducted three concerts, one of which was the world premiere of a chamber composition of his. Project ABC was back, this time with eighty-two disadvantaged boys, eighty of whom finished the course and seventy-five of whom went on to prep schools. (Mt. Holyoke had inaugurated a similar program for girls, and during the summer their student group came to Hanover for a social weekend with Dartmouth's boys.) Although enrollment in the regular academic summer term was still disappointing, it was growing—from

291 to 377 to 440. Sixteen different institutes and projects also represented a significant growth in summer activities, and at the end of the three-year trial period set by the Trustees there was no doubt that the multi-faceted summer term would be continued.

Over that summer, a grant of $100,000 from the Richard King Mellon Charitable Trusts of Pittsburgh made it possible to reactivate the Dartmouth-MIT Urban Studies Project, which had lapsed after being in operation from 1960 to 1963. During that three-year period twenty Dartmouth undergraduates had spent one term each in Boston's South End, engaged in various urban study projects. Nine of the twenty went on to city-planning careers.

The Trustees at their October meeting elected J. Michael McGean to be Secretary of the College, filling the vacancy created by the death of Mr. Hayward, whom he had assisted for several years. They also created the new post of Director of Public Programs and elected Nichol M. Sandoe Jr. to fill it. Mr. Sandoe's previous administrative positions had been Executive Secretary of the Alumni Fund and Associate Director of Development. He had borne a large share of the responsibility for the several convocations Dartmouth had staged, as well as for its summer congregations of the arts. His new position gave him responsibility for coordinating the planning for Dartmouth's bicentennial. One other Trustee action was to approve razing the old corner section of the Hanover Inn and rebuilding it with more guest rooms and new meeting rooms. This section dated from 1902 and was distinctly antiquated. The newer wing, added in 1923, was to be retained with improvements.

John Dickey reached the twentieth anniversary of his presidency on November 1, 1965, and three days later observed his fifty-eighth birthday. As was the case when he completed his first decade as head of the College, congratulations flowed in from all segments of the Dartmouth family and the temptation to review what had happened so far in the Dickey administration was too great to be resisted. Speaking for thousands of alumni, the *Dartmouth Alumni Magazine* editorialized: "John Dickey is not inclined to make much of his own anniversaries, but the editors are certain that Dartmouth men everywhere will look upon his completion of twenty years in office as an important event and as a fitting occasion to let him know of the warmth of their personal regard

for him, the admiration they have for the remarkable quality and accomplishment of his leadership, and the deep appreciation they feel
for the unsparing way in which he has thought and planned and
worked to bring Dartmouth to a new level of excellence and educational
effectiveness. The rich bounty of this twenty years of leadership is
evident on all sides."

A summary of the major achievements of President Dickey's first ten
years in office was given earlier in this account of his administration,
and he himself, in his 1964 Convocation address, reviewed the advances that he thought had been made in the decade since the Alumni
Planning Committee began its intensified pursuit of excellence leading
up to the College's bicentennial. That review covered just about all the
actions and developments of real significance, but one area not mentioned in any detail was the growth of the College in financial terms.
When the Dickey administration began in 1945, Dartmouth's total assets were $31-million; twenty years later they were more than $140-
million, at book value. Endowment had grown from $22-million to
more than $114-million, at market value. Instructional expense had
increased nearly fivefold, from $1.2-million to $5.6-million, and library
expenditures from $163,000 to $760,000. The College's annual operating
budget for educational and general purposes, as distinct from so-called
auxiliary activities, had grown from $2.25-million to $15-million, including $3.2-million for sponsored research and $545,000 for the Hopkins Center, both of which were items added to the budget during the
Dickey administration. Accompanying the impressive growth in assets
and in the annual operating budget was a planned expansion of the
plant that added some twenty new buildings, plus additions to Thayer
School, Steele Hall, Baker Library, and Thayer Dining Hall, and such
new facilities as the Dartmouth Skiway, the swimming pool, and the
basketball court.

The citation accompanying Mr. Dickey's fourteenth honorary degree,
an LL.D. from Notre Dame in 1964, depicted him as "a college president
who, oddly enough, devotes almost all of his time to education." To
make that true he firmly restricted his outside activities and his writings
to those things in which he was genuinely interested, mainly education
and foreign affairs. At the time of his twentieth anniversary he was
involved with a half-dozen organizations—nowhere near the number

that would have liked to enlist his active participation. He was a trustee of the Rockefeller Foundation, a director of the Atlantic Council of the United States, a governor of the Arctic Institute of North America, a member of the Committee on Studies of the Council on Foreign Relations, a member of the Public Policy Committee of The Advertising Council, and a member of the Visiting Committee of the Johns Hopkins Medical School.

If the Trustees Planning Committee had included a winning football team among the desiderata for the years leading up to the College's bicentennial, it could have claimed one more great success. For the second time in four seasons, Dartmouth had an undefeated, Ivy League championship team, and this time the 1965 eleven also won the Lambert Trophy, as the outstanding team in the East. Two of only three Dartmouth teams with perfect records happened during the Dickey years, and the football history made in the fall of 1965 was, in one sense, a fitting undergraduate contribution to the celebration of Mr. Dickey's twentieth anniversary on the job.

There was, however, one alarming development for Dartmouth football fans. Coach Bob Blackman, at the peak of his Ivy League success, was invited by the University of Iowa to come and talk about transferring his talents to that Big Ten university. There had been other offers during Blackman's eleven years at Dartmouth, but he had not been interested. This time the possibility existed of advancing his career in the toughest of all football conferences, and the choice was that much harder. Hundreds of letters and telegrams flooded in from alumni, asking him to remain in Hanover, and 1,500 students signed a petition urging him to stay. Coach Blackman went to see President Dickey and said that perhaps he ought not to make the trip to Iowa. But Mr. Dickey told him that he wanted him to go, because only in that way could he look into the situation at firsthand and make a decision that would give him peace of mind. The President's concern for Coach Blackman, as much as for the College, certainly was an important factor in Blackman's remaining in Hanover.

Planning for the observance of Dartmouth's bicentennial during the academic year 1969–70 entered its initial phase in January 1966, with the naming of two key committees to devise a schedule of events and to take responsibility for carrying it out. Trustee Harvey Hood was designated chairman of the bicentennial executive committee, with overall responsibility for the observance. Professor Smallwood of the government department, former assistant to President Dickey, was named chairman of a faculty and staff planning committee. Mr. Sandoe, head of the office of public programs, served as executive secretary of the main committee and was a member of the faculty and staff group. Trustees Dudley Orr and Charles Zimmerman also were named to the executive committee by Mr. Dickey, who announced that the sesquicentennial of the U.S. Supreme Court's 1819 decision in the Dartmouth College Case would be marked in conjunction with the bicentennial of the granting of the Dartmouth College Charter.

At the same time that the bicentennial planning committees were established, the Trustees disclosed that the College would undertake a major capital-gifts campaign as part of its 200th anniversary observance and that this would be a three-year effort beginning in 1968. Rupert C. Thompson Jr. of Providence, Rhode Island, chairman and chief executive officer of Textron, Incorporated, was chosen by the Trustees to be national chairman of the campaign. At the time he was serving as chairman of the 1966 Alumni Fund. The capital campaign, only the second in Dartmouth's history, was later designated as the Third Century Fund and was assigned a goal three times as large as the amount of the successful $17-million campaign conducted earlier in the Dickey administration.

Student Dissent in the Sixties

PRIOR to the academic year 1965–66, Dartmouth students in general gave little evidence of being seriously concerned with the issues that were creating tumult on other campuses from Berkeley to Columbia. Such activism as existed in Hanover was related to civil rights and was promoted by a group of approximately forty undergraduates forming the Political Action Committee of the Dartmouth Christian Union. The PAC in the fall of 1962 had raised funds for the Student Non-Violent Coordinating Committee, the national organization then working for voter registration of blacks in Mississippi and in other southern states. At that same time, *The Dartmouth* began printing front-page stories about student protests elsewhere and about the efforts, mainly by college students, to put a stop to racial injustice. Without these activities by the PAC and the student newspaper, the Dartmouth campus would have been even more isolated from the unrest and activism that were building in colleges across the land. But Dartmouth was not so different from other northeastern universities in that respect. Spring riots at Princeton and Brown in 1963 were nothing more than panty raids.

After sending two delegates to the annual summer conference of the National Student Association, the Dartmouth Undergraduate Council withdrew as a member, stating that the association was overemphasizing political issues and was of no value to the College. This action by the UGC occurred about the same time that Governor George Wallace made his first visit to Dartmouth and was received without incident, leading *The Dartmouth* to print the headline, "More Cheer Than Jeer Wallace." However, to offset the Wallace visit, Paul Zuber, black leader of the school integration drive, was invited to Hanover to speak on civil rights. The Political Action Committee, noting that only three blacks were in the entering Class of 1967, began its agitation for more blacks

216

at Dartmouth, and during the Christmas vacation four members went south to see if they could set up a student exchange with black colleges. In April, three events indicated that Dartmouth undergraduates were slowly moving away from their passive attitude. Three Dartmouth students were jailed for taking part in a civil rights demonstration in St. Augustine, Florida; a chapter of the National Association for the Advancement of Colored People was formed; and six students went to Washington to lobby for Senate passage of the civil rights bill. These actions were mild enough, but they were straws in the wind. It would take another year before student activism became a definite part of campus life.

During that year, Dartmouth students were jailed while working for the Mississippi Freedom Democratic Party in Jackson and while participating in the black registration drive in Selma, Alabama. Equal opportunity and justice for blacks continued to be the main purpose of student activism at the College, and this was underscored by the fund drives conducted by PAC and the visit to the campus, at the invitation of the Undergraduate Council, by Malcolm X, who spoke on "The Black Revolution in America" and predicted a bloody summer. The racial riots in Watts in August 1965, similar to those in Harlem the summer before, proved him to be right. Urban riots from 1964 on were numerous, even though Congress in June of that year had passed the civil rights bill outlawing discrimination in voting, jobs, and public accommodations. Among colleges in the Northeast, Dartmouth became the center of the civil rights fight for two days in April 1965, when it sponsored a conference of students from many institutions to discuss ways to coordinate their activities. Lawrence Guyot, chairman of the Mississippi Freedom Democratic Party, was the keynote speaker, and other black leaders present included John Lewis, national chairman of SNCC.

The conference was the last major case of activism on campus that devoted itself entirely to civil rights. Vietnam came into the picture in April 1965, when a dozen students went to Washington to be part of the 25,000 students who marched against the war, in a demonstration organized by Students for a Democratic Society. In May the Undergraduate Council kept the Vietnam pot boiling by sponsoring a debate among five faculty members on the pros and cons of the U.S. presence in Vietnam. Before long the feelings of both students and faculty against

U.S. involvement were to focus on ROTC, an innocent victim, but up to that point Armed Forces Day had been held successfully each May and the ROTC units had paraded without incident. In fact, a straw vote taken by *The Dartmouth* showed students and faculty supporting U.S. Vietnam policy by a margin of three to one. This margin may have been wider than at most colleges, but other polls showed that students nationally supported the war.

What made the year 1965–66 the starting point for a sharper spirit of dissent at Dartmouth was the formation of a chapter of Students for a Democratic Society (SDS) by the Political Action Committee of the Dartmouth Christian Union, which recognized that militant protest against the Vietnam war was less its forte than civil rights. SDS now became the central force in campus protests, just as it had taken on that role in the national student movement. An offshoot of the League for Industrial Democracy, SDS got its start at the University of Michigan about 1960, with Al Huber and Tom Hayden, editor of the Michigan student newspaper, as the prime organizers. The organization took more precise form in June 1962, when students from a number of colleges and universities drew up the celebrated Port Huron Statement, which proclaimed the "New Left" and laid out an agenda of social and political reforms, calling for radical confrontation if necessary. At its first national convention in 1963, SDS adopted the theme, "America and the New Era," with civil rights a top concern. Before it went into decline in the seventies, SDS had 350 to 400 chapters throughout the educational world and gave to each chapter a firmer sense of direction and of protest procedures than any had before becoming part of the national alliance. Dartmouth lost a lot of its lassitude and acquired a confrontational mindset, although not in any radical way.

Dean Thaddeus Seymour, recalling the change in campus atmosphere, stated in one of his oral-history interviews that even before the period of overt dissent there had developed among the students a spirit of ugly belligerence, "of young people turning on their world." Discontent with their environment, he thought, produced rebellion against authority and thus a turning against President Dickey and the Trustees—indeed against all officers of the College who were seen as figures of authority and dictators of how students should conduct themselves. *The Dartmouth* complained that President Dickey had become a remote figure who no longer took into account what students thought about College affairs. Mr. Dickey was aware of this new atmosphere on campus, and it distressed him, but it was not until his Convocation address of September 1968 that he tackled the subject head on and spoke of "a mounting—although, often, unarticulated—rejection throughout all human affairs of the role of authority."

As Dartmouth entered the latter half of the Sixties, with the lines of confrontation more sharply drawn, the spirit of dissent on campus was three-pronged. The Afro-American Society was one group, quick to protest statements and actions it interpreted as racist, and persistent in its proposals to improve the status of blacks at Dartmouth. The second major group was the newly arrived Students for a Democratic Society, which took control of organized protest about the Vietnam war and civil rights. The third force, underlying the two protest groups, was the push for student power, which came to the fore in the Sixties and was most strongly manifested in demands for self-regulation of social life and in sharp disagreement with the disciplinary actions of the Committee on Administration. The Afro-American Society wanted its own judiciary committee to handle the cases of black students—a form of separatism which the College was not willing to grant. In a case involving an obscene fraternity publication, the Interfraternity Council Judiciary Committee clashed with the administration over who had the disciplinary authority. Students fighting for the divestiture of all College investments in companies doing business in South Africa wanted, as a matter of "community morality," a voice in the formulation of College investment policy, a proposal that got no support from the Board of Trustees. Although the Afro-American Society and SDS had their separate agendas and rarely joined forces, it was in the push for more student power in College affairs that they found common ground. (Later, when coeducation came to Dartmouth, feminist organizations, involving students, faculty, and staff, became a fourth prong of campus dissent, but that is not part of the story of the Sixties or of the Dickey presidency.)

On April 14, 1966, General Lewis B. Hershey, director of Selective Service, came to Dartmouth to give an address and to answer questions about the draft, which was a topic of intense student interest, since rumors persisted concerning changes in student deferments, along with fears that anti-war activity would be penalized by a call to military duty. SDS was busy the whole week before General Hershey's appearance, and on the day of his address the demonstrations for peace were the largest and most visible that Dartmouth had witnessed up to that time. Afternoon rallies were staged in front of Dartmouth Hall and Hopkins Center, and the evening address was picketed. But General Hershey proved to be an affable expositor of Selective Service policies, answered questions for an hour, and was judged to be, in the words of the *Alumni Magazine*'s undergraduate editor, "a nice old man." In that same issue of the magazine, the vice president of the Dartmouth Christian Union wrote about student activism at Dartmouth and found it wanting. He was critical of the Undergraduate Council for cutting its ties with the National Student Association, and also critical of President Dickey for not stating his views on Vietnam and other controversial issues. The seminars sponsored by SDS were called the most hopeful sign of a new concern on campus.

Incidents of student protest continued to be sporadic throughout the academic year 1966–67, but angry feelings broke through the surface of non-violence in one instance, a sit-in in the President's office took place, and the annual May parade of the ROTC units on Armed Forces Day came in for heckling and picketing for the first time. The intensity of dissent was on the rise. To lead off the year's activities, Stokely Carmichael spoke about black power to an audience of 1,400 in Webster Hall. His appearance in November was a rare case of joint sponsorship by the Afro-American Society and SDS, along with the Undergraduate Council and the Dartmouth Christian Union. January saw the introduction of a Vigil for Peace, held on the Green for one hour each Wednesday noon. This eventually led to a counter-vigil by those supporting U.S. involvement in Vietnam, just as the arrival of SDS, now given official status by the Council on Student Organizations, had produced an opposing Dartmouth Conservative Society.

The so-called Kodak Controversy began in late April, when the College refused to accede to the demand that it revoke a proxy it had given to the Eastman Kodak Company, supporting a company decision involving blacks in the Rochester community. Dartmouth at the time held about $400,000 of Kodak stock. Student denunciation arose because the company had abrogated an agreement with FIGHT, a black community organization, to train 600 unemployed blacks for Kodak jobs. To press their point, students occupied President Dickey's outer office, but they did so in a non-disruptive way and only for a short period of time. A rally against Kodak was scheduled to be held in front of Parkhurst Hall on May 3, but it was called off, perhaps because a more pressing concern was the speech to be given in Webster Hall that night by Governor Wallace of Alabama. Wallace, who had spoken at Dartmouth in November 1963, was invited back by *The Dartmouth*. The difference in the receptions given to him on these two occasions provided dramatic proof that in three and a half years the atmosphere on campus had swung from backwater calm to antagonism and overt protest.

What happened during the Wallace speech and afterwards provided the press with another story of college students on the rampage. Almost as soon as Wallace began to speak there was heckling and waving of signs. Then, six black students, acting on their own and not as AAS members, arose and began to chant "Wallace is a racist." The rest of the audience grew impatient with their actions and told them to leave, whereupon the six and some of their supporters walked out. Outside there was a small crowd of those who had not been able to get into overcrowded Webster Hall, among them a young instructor from Colby Junior College. He rallied a student group to rush into the hall, and as they marched up the center aisle toward the stage, Wallace's bodyguards got him away from the podium. Ushers and other students blocked the intruders, and after a wild few minutes the storming group turned and left the hall. Order was restored and the Governor was able to finish his speech without further disruption.

The Webster proceedings were being carried live by the campus radio, and the report of the excitement there attracted more students to the crowd outside the hall. All would have been well if Wallace had made a quick departure, but his car was tightly parked between two others, and as flash bulbs popped and pinpointed his location, the crowd surrounded him. Some students began rocking his car and pounding on the roof, which was dented, and things were on the verge of getting out of control. College Proctor John O'Connor and the police moved in to save the situation, and after ten or fifteen hectic minutes the Wallace car was freed and driven off. In the melee the police had not swung clubs or drawn their guns, as overblown press reports stated.

The College was genuinely shocked that any such thing could have happened, so greatly at variance with what Dartmouth had always been like. Later that night Dean Seymour sent a telegram of apology to Governor Wallace in Concord, New Hampshire, saying, "I sincerely apologize that certain Dartmouth undergraduates so flagrantly abused the cardinal principle of an academic community by infringing on your rights as a guest on our campus. There can be no justification for their abusive behavior. I speak for the overwhelming majority when I assure you that this College stands on the principle that a man's opinions, however unpopular or controversial, deserve a free and unobstructed platform. As Dean of Dartmouth College I am ashamed and I convey my apologies to you."

The next day President Dickey also made a statement: "It's an old story. A few silly people got the trouble they apparently wanted and a few irresponsibles demonstrated that they neither know nor care about democracy." *The Dartmouth*, as a student voice, printed an emphatic editorial against "a horrible ugliness we hope this campus will never experience again." The post-mortem to the Wallace Affair went on for days, with a public forum, a flood of letters, and much give and take among students and faculty. Later in May, at a regular meeting of the full faculty it was voted that the Undergraduate Council be requested to name a student-faculty committee to draw up "some general guidelines for conduct which are consistent with free expression and active participation in issues confronting Dartmouth and our society." On the disciplinary side, the judiciary committee of the Undergraduate Council and the Committee on Administration jointly voted conditional suspension for students who admitted overt participation. Conditional suspension would have granted them automatic readmission upon application, but no students came forward to confess.

After the tumult of the Wallace visit, the anti-war demonstration on Armed Forces Day was mild, but the College was taking no chances. It moved the ROTC review from the Green to the football stadium, and police, reinforced by a few state troopers, were visible as a deterrent to those who might want to cause trouble. Protesters had planned a silent vigil encircling the green while the ROTC units paraded, but when the ceremonies were transferred to the stadium they marched there with placards and watched from a distance, as the review went off without disturbance. This was the last demonstration of any consequence before the academic year came to its close. At year's end, *The Dartmouth* editorialized: ". . . the College community has left the easy chair from which it once viewed life and become an active participant in the world around it." Students demanded, the paper declared, that the College face the social, political, and moral issues of the times.

In contrast to the very small group of students who had previously taken part in anti-war demonstrations beyond Hanover, nearly one hundred Dartmouth undergraduates went to Washington to be in the peace march of 100,000 in late October. The protesters rallied at the Lincoln Memorial and then marched on the Pentagon. Three Dartmouth students and one faculty member, history instructor David Kubrin, were arrested, and Kubrin elected to be jailed for a short period rather than pay his fine. Kubrin and Jonathan Mirsky, Assistant Professor of Chinese, were faculty mentors of the student activists and participated in most of the forums and demonstrations. The student leader of SDS was John Spritzler '68.

In November the student-faculty committee delegated to produce guidelines for dissent released an interim statement, pending its more formal report. "As an institution committed to fostering the free and critical mind," the interim statement said, "Dartmouth College seeks to encourage the expression of controversial views—and the freedom to dissent and protest against such views. In the light of this commitment, the College should not forbid the appearance of individuals or groups holding controversial opinions. Neither should it permit expressions of dissent which employ means, such as the threat or use of physical force, which hamper the rights of expression of others. To the extent that the College cannot maintain an orderly exchange of ideas, it forfeits its mandate in the community to protect freedom of inquiry, and so gives up its right to self-discipline.

"The Committee holds that recruitment interviews of students by business firms, academic institutions, government agencies, etc., are in the interests of students seeking to advance their education or careers, and fall within the general principles the Committee has outlined. Representatives of all legitimate organizations should be permitted to recruit at the College, and all students should be able to meet with them unhampered. At the same time, protest against the views the recruiter represents should not be discouraged, so long as the recruiter and those wishing to see him are not restrained. For example, speeches, pickets, or the use of the right to meet with the recruiter by appointment would constitute legitimate, tolerable dissent, while the blocking of access to a building or the threat or use of force against a recruiter would not."

The portion of the interim report dealing with recruiting was timely, because this had become a bigger issue on campus. Military recruitment was the main object of protest, but when in January a recruiter from the Dow Chemical Company came to Hanover, he was picketed— but not obstructed—because the company was a manufacturer of napalm used in Vietnam.

Columbia University was brought to a standstill in late April when SDS members instigated a week-long rebellion, occupied five buildings, and seized a dean. The university finally called in the police, and hundreds of them cleared the buildings by force and arrested seven hundred student protesters. It was an extreme example of the radical action that SDS and other protest groups threatened to use if their demands were not met. Moreover, it gave ideas to SDS chapters at colleges throughout the country, and it alerted college administrators to be prepared to handle this new development in the student protest movement. At Dartmouth, President Dickey turned his legal mind to what the College would do if faced with a situation similar to the Columbia outburst, and a year later, when the College reached the peak of its problem with radical activism, it was ready to handle it promptly, firmly, and humanely.

After the Columbia affair and a national student strike on April 26, SDS at Dartmouth stepped up its push for student power. On May 6 it demanded that among ROTC changes an enrolled student should have the freedom to drop out and that the College should agree to cover the trainee's loss of financial aid from the services. If these reforms were not made by May 15, SDS action was threatened. May 15 happened to be the day for the annual ROTC review, and the campus wondered what SDS might be planning to do. The ROTC ceremonies were moved once again, from the stadium to Chase Field, and the only police present were the College's own, with instructions to let any demonstration take place, so long as its leaders maintained order. Three hundred students and faculty members marched to Chase Field, and there the anti-war protest was the most vociferous to date, but still peaceful.

As the college year neared its end, the build-up of student dissent undoubtedly had its effect on two actions, one by the faculty and one by the Trustees. The Executive Committee of the Faculty voted to request of the Committee on Organization and Policy a report on ROTC's compatibility with the educational objectives of the College. The Trustees voted to refer a student petition to the Trustees Planning Committee "with the recommendation that the committee consider sponsoring and organizing a comprehensive study of campus life and opportunities for student participation in the responsible government of the College."

The climax of student dissent made the final full year of John Dickey's presidency an extremely trying one. Dissent became more persistent and more militant, culminating in the May 6 seizure of Parkhurst Hall, which of all the turbulent events of the Sixties was the greatest shock to the College community. The academic year 1968–69 had scarcely begun when SDS resumed its anti-ROTC activity, joined in some instances by the Dartmouth Christian Union. Student power won a round in October, when undergraduates were added to the Committee on Standing and Conduct, which replaced the Committee on Administration and was made up of four students, four faculty members, and two deans. But SDS was turned down on its request that there be an open meeting with the College Trustees. On November 25, SDS organized the picketing of two Army recruiters visiting the College, but the peaceful intent got twisted into a physical barring of the two officers when after lunch they returned to Fairbanks Hall. SDS members linked arms in front of the building, and when one of the recruiters went to the side of the front porch and started to climb over the railing, he was pulled back. One of the two men restraining him was John Spritzler '68, who after graduating had remained in town to be regional coordinator for SDS. The officer filed charges of simple assault against the two men who had kept him from entering the building, and when tried in the

Hanover court on December 10, they were fined $75 each and given suspended 30-day jail sentences. Four other students who had been identified by Proctor O'Connor as he attempted to escort the officers through the picket line were charged as violators of the College policy on dissent. Thirty-eight other students protested that they were equally guilty and signed affidavits to that effect. While hearing the cases, the new Committee on Standing and Conduct ran into criticism for its procedures and finally agreed to hold an open hearing—one more slight gain for student power. The end result was varying terms of social probation for the men identified as participants. As for the other thirty-eight, the committee ruled that they had only "intended" to violate the policy on dissent.

Student antagonism toward authority did not spare their own governing bodies. In late November, the Undergraduate Council and Palaeopitus both came to an end. Both were under fire as useless and as wielding no real power in decision-making, and a student referendum, instigated by Palaeopitus, resulted in the required two-thirds vote for abolition. The campus was left to come up with some new form of student government, if it wanted one.

On January 21, the Dartmouth faculty voted to endorse in principle the recommendation of its Committee on Organization and Policy that all degree credits for courses given by the three ROTC programs be phased out over a three-year period. The vote for a three-year phase-out of credits, rather than a quick termination of ROTC as proposed by some faculty members, did not satisfy the anti-ROTC forces at the College. This continued to be a festering issue throughout the winter term and into the spring. On April 13, SDS issued a demand for the complete abolition of ROTC at Dartmouth and announced a sit-in in all the offices of Parkhurst Hall on April 22. Its belligerent attitude was no doubt reinforced by reports from beyond Hanover of violent confrontations at Harvard, Wisconsin, Massachusetts, Duke, and Berkeley, plus the occupation of Willard Straight Hall at Cornell by armed black militants. Opposition to the announced Parkhurst Hall sit-in led to the formation of SBD (Students Behind Dartmouth). On the scheduled day, April 22, some 250 students filled Parkhurst Hall and SDS made three demands: complete abolition of ROTC by September 1969, scholarships for all ROTC men, and the discontinuation of all military recruiting on campus. On the same day, the executive committee of the faculty offered to reopen the question of ROTC at Dartmouth, if a student referendum wanted it. The referendum, held six days later, resulted in 75 percent wanting the question reopened, but there was considerable student support for letting ROTC men graduate with their commissions before abolishing the service units entirely.

Another Parkhurst sit-in was staged on April 29, and this time May 12 was set as the deadline for faculty and Trustee decisions to abolish ROTC. The faculty a week before that date met to reconsider the ROTC question, in accordance with the student referendum, and came up with a resolution that ROTC should be abolished "as soon as possible," with a June 1973 deadline, which would permit students to fulfill their service contracts. This was a bitter disappointment to SDS, which had expected its pressure to bring about a vote for quick abolition. It now turned its wrath on the proposed continuation until June 1973, and it promised militant action—something toward which the anti-war campaign had been building ever since SDS took control of campus dissent in 1965.

During that stretch of nearly four years from 1965 onward, ROTC, in President Dickey's opinion, was not treated as an educational issue, but as a way of getting at the government on Vietnam. It would have been more honest, he believed, to have tackled the issue of Vietnam head on rather than indirectly. He was one of the Ivy Group presidents who went to the Pentagon to discuss the improvement of ROTC as an educational program. He saw a positive value in ROTC in non-nuclear collective security under the United Nations, and he advocated the benefit of a liberal arts input in the military services. Dartmouth had no government contracts related to arms development, and ROTC was its most direct contribution to national security. Mr. Dickey was not in tune with the faculty members, mostly in the younger ranks, pushing for the immediate end of ROTC at Dartmouth. Furthermore, he was determined that the College would meet its contractual obligations to the government.

The threat of militant action by SDS was viewed as something likely to be carried out, and President Dickey by means of a telephone conference call informed the Trustees of an impending crisis. He explained to them, as he did to the faculty at two meetings, that he intended to resort to a court injunction if college buildings were seized. Earlier, at an April 26 Focus sponsored by the Senior Symposia, he told the students that it would be naive to think that being on a college campus provided immunity from the laws that govern everyone else or that they would be given some sort of amnesty after the laws had been broken. The President was determined that any building occupation would not be a long, drawn-out affair, as had happened at Columbia, and it was his strategy that the confrontation, if an injunction were granted, would be shifted from the College to the courts.

SDS, since it had promised to disrupt the College in some fashion, met on the afternoon of May 6 to decide upon its tactics. Its leaders incited the group to act without delay, and approximately seventy-five students moved to occupy Parkhurst Hall. Everyone in the building was ordered to get out. President Dickey left on his own after saying "Get out of my way" to Spritzler, who tried to manhandle him. Dean Seymour and Dean Dickerson were forced out, and the heavy front doors of Parkhurst were nailed shut. Students sat in the windows and hung a large banner above the main entrance, saying, "Join Us. Abolish ROTC and military recruiting." The number of persons inside fluctuated, since the rear entrance was guarded but not barricaded. At least two faculty members were among the occupiers. SDS thought it would have a lot more adherents than it got. Two hundred or more students massed in front of the building, giving uncertain support, but hundreds more were there merely as onlookers, most of them against what SDS was doing. Some interpreted the seizure of Parkhurst Hall as an effort to polarize the College, but this did not happen, and twelve hours after the occupation began it was over, thanks to a court injunction and the removal of defiant occupiers by the state police.

Soon after Parkhurst Hall was occupied, a petition for a court injunction went off to Superior Court Judge Martin F. Loughlin in Woodsville. About 8 p.m. the Grafton County Sheriff, Herbert W. Ash, read the injunction over a bullhorn and gave those in the building one hour to vacate it. At 9 p.m. he read the injunction again and extended the vacating time to 10:45 p.m. A few students left Parkhurst, but the rest ignored his warning. Judge Loughlin declared the occupants in contempt and ordered their removal and arrest. Governor Walter Peterson meanwhile had arrived from Concord and gone to Lebanon to address the state troopers assembled there, urging them to carry out the court order with restraint.

At 3 a.m. the New Hampshire troopers, with a contingent of Vermont state police in reserve, forced open the front doors of Parkhurst Hall and without the use of clubs or weapons removed the occupants one by one. They met with little or no resistance. The group arrested included forty students, two faculty members, two staff employees, and twelve others, including two juveniles who were turned over to their parents. After being taken by National Guard buses to Lebanon Armory, those arrested were transferred to the Grafton County jail in North Haverhill and then released on $200 bail each. Judge Loughlin heard the cases in the Woodsville court on May 9. Nine defendants were granted continuances; the other forty-five charged with contempt of court received sentences of thirty days in jail and fines of $100 each. A series of appeals and legal maneuvers by defense attorneys, involving both the state and federal judiciaries, resulted in new trials for five students who claimed they had not taken part in the seizure of Parkhurst and the acquittal of a student photographer, but nothing more was changed before the thirty-day jail sentences were finished.

Later during the morning of the arrests, the anti-ROTC forces gathered on the campus and talked about a strike. What actually happened was picketing in front of Dartmouth Hall for a day or two, but with small participation and no campus support, the idea of a strike faded away. One proposal put forward was the holding of an all-College conference to discuss the Parkhurst seizure and the College's ROTC policy. The Executive Committee of the Faculty gave its backing to this idea, and on the afternoon of May 14 more than 1,500 persons gathered in Alumni Gymnasium. President Dickey and seven members of the Board of Trustees took part in two hours of discussion, which did not mollify everyone, but did clear the air and reduce the tension. College discipline remained to be meted out, but it had to be delayed until jail sentences were completed and each student could appear in person. The hearings by the Committee on Standing and Conduct continued into early September and resulted in one permanent separation, two suspensions, five acquittals, and thirty-nine disciplinary penalties. Most felt that the committee's verdicts were more lenient than expected. The two faculty members involved in the Parkhurst Hall take-over—Dona Strauss, Assistant Professor of Mathematics, and Paul Knapp, Visiting Assistant Professor of Chemistry—were both suspended for two years by the Faculty Committee Advisory to the President. Both, however, had contracts expiring on June 30, 1969, and their connection with the College was allowed to lapse.

The handling of the Parkhurst occupation was mainly a Dickey operation. The President said later that he had the advantage of being on the eve of retirement and therefore not inclined to worry about personal repercussions. He wasn't, as he put it, going to let anyone push him around. Although the faculty was kept fully informed about what he was prepared to do, and its advice was welcome, President Dickey did not look upon the faculty as being able to make quick decisions or to handle the situation. Advance planning, a firm and prompt carrying out of the plan, and a certain amount of luck, compared with what other institutions had to contend with, combined to produce a favorable outcome for the College. The institution continued to function throughout the Parkhurst Hall seizure and its aftermath, which was the best indication that the situation was under control.

Six days after the occupation of Parkhurst, the executive committee of the Board of Trustees gave its approval to the faculty resolution of May 5 calling for the termination of ROTC at Dartmouth by June 1973. This was later approved by the full board. There is no doubt that the Trustees' decision, supported by Mr. Dickey, was influenced by the crisis the College had just gone through and by the fear that other militant actions might follow. One member of the board later expressed the opinion that the Trustees had perhaps acted too hastily. On the other hand, the Trustees had to deal with the resolution submitted to them by the faculty.

During the remaining months of the Dickey presidency, student protests were sporadic and loosely organized. The campus had refused to be polarized or radicalized, which had been the basic objective of the leaders of SDS, now in decline since the College had undercut its Parkhurst ploy. The disruption by black students of Dr. William Shockley's address on October 15 was one more incident that required disciplinary action by the Committee on Standing and Conduct, as reported elsewhere in this review of the Dickey years, but the end of the Sixties marked the end also of strident and militant dissent. Dartmouth in the course of this turbulent period had caught up with the outside world in awareness of critical issues and in willingness to do something about them. Dartmouth students, by comparison, had conducted themselves with restraint, even in the one big instance of radical action. The police had never been required to swing their clubs, and in this and other respects the College had been fortunate. Student power had won some skirmishes, but not the war, and this perhaps was the one definite outcome of all the unrest. Opinions were gradually coalescing into agreement that students were entitled to a greater voice in College affairs.

Two Decades Completed

IN his Convocation address opening the 1965–66 academic year, President Dickey mentioned a planned review of the curriculum for the junior and senior years, particularly with regard to the Great Issues Course. Was there an opportunity, he asked, to "serve our concern for the public-mindedness of our graduates and advance significantly the ideal of independence in learning here at Dartmouth" by turning over to a student steering committee the responsibility for planning and administering the course, leaving to a faculty advisory committee the setting of examinations and oversight of the experiment? The plain truth was that Great Issues was running out of steam. The course had lost the excitement and stimulation of its earlier years, and had become more and more academic, as those running the course turned to professors from other institutions as lecturers rather than to leaders from the outside world. The seniors resented compulsory attendance and indulged themselves in blatant discourtesies toward the guest speakers. Clearly, an overhaul was called for, and a student steering committee, as mentioned by President Dickey, was thought to be a possible solution. Student committees did work with faculty members in planning topics, speakers, and readings for the winter and spring terms. Mr. Dickey opened the winter-term series with a lecture on "Law and Individual Conscience."

The hoped-for improvement did not materialize, and the faculty at an agitated, three-hour meeting in May ended up by approving the recommendation of the Committee on Educational Policy that the Great Issues Course be suspended for the coming academic year. In place of the course, the faculty asked President Dickey to organize and direct a reduced program of lectures and panel discussions for seniors, keeping the modified "course" as a requirement for the degree. Mr. Dickey assumed direction of what came to be called Senior Symposia, and with the help of Professor Larry King of the government department and a committee of six seniors he had ready for the fall term a series of three guest speakers of great distinction. They were poet and playwright Archibald MacLeish, former Secretary of State Dean Acheson, and the noted British author and economist Barbara Ward (Lady Jackson). The first symposium took the form of a conversation between President Dickey and Mr. MacLeish, followed the next day by a discussion of issues brought up by a student panel. The new Senior Symposia called for no examinations, grades, or papers. Required attendance was also dropped, but all members of the senior class were expected to participate, not only for the intrinsic merit of the revised program, but also for the common educational experience provided by Great Issues when it was at its best.

The administrative staff is one of the least settled elements of a college. Deans, vice presidents, and chief financial officers might serve for reasonably long periods of time, but around them swirl promotions, additions, resignations, and revised duties. Assistants to the President especially come and go, because that is a prime training ground for advancement, either within or outside the College. Another batch of Dartmouth administrative changes occurred as the academic year 1965–66 neared its end. Mr. Colton, Director of Development, was named Vice President of the College, to succeed Orton H. Hicks when he reached retirement on June 30. To fill the position of Director of Development, Addison L. Winship moved up from the job of Special Assistant to the President in charge of relations with corporations. James W. Stevens, Director of Planning and Project Administration on the financial staff, was named Comptroller of the College, succeeding Robert D. Funkhouser, who had asked to be relieved of his duties for reasons of health. As a fourth change, Clifford L. Jordan became Associate Director of Development, while continuing to be Executive Secretary of the Alumni Fund. Mr. Colton as Vice President assumed responsibility, under President Dickey, for fund-raising, alumni affairs, and public relations, all areas in which he had been extensively involved during his twenty-one years with the College.

For those concerned with maintaining Dartmouth's preeminence in using the computer as part of undergraduate education, there was the exciting year-end news that the College and the General Electric Company would collaborate in setting up, in the new Kiewit Computation Center, a high-speed system that would greatly multiply the time-sharing capability that Dartmouth had pioneered. A large-scale GE-635 computer and supporting equipment, worth $2.5-million, was promised for the fall. Where the College's existing GE-625 medium-range computer was capable of simultaneously handling forty stations scattered about the campus, the larger system was expected to provide access for two hundred persons at the same time. It also would have ten times the memory capacity of the GE-625, raising the number of stored characters to 180 million. As part of the agreement with General Electric, the staff of the Kiewit Center looked forward to collaborative work with a G.E. technical team to develop new applications of the time-sharing principle. With so much user capacity in its new computer system, the College had plans to make some of its lines available to outside users, particularly New England colleges, universities, and secondary schools.

Summer term 1966 in Hanover experienced a continuation of growth in the number of programs and the number of persons attending them. But the coeducational academic term still failed to attract a sizable enrollment, even though 470 students in attendance were a twelve percent gain over 1965. Alumni College, the Peace Corps, Project ABC, and the Congregation of the Arts continued their robust existence, as the base for all other things. Davis Jackson, Associate Director of Admissions, was now Dartmouth's Director of Project ABC, which had five colleges participating and one hundred schools offering places to recommended boys and girls. The scope of the program had been greatly aided by a grant to the Independent Schools Talent Search of $1.5-million from the U.S. Office of Equal Opportunity. Dartmouth added a new wrinkle to the program by sending eight boys to Hanover High School in the fall of 1966, as an experiment to see if topnotch public high schools, with community support, couldn't provide some places for the swelling number of ABC applicants. While all the varied summer programs were going on, the biggest attraction in town was the demolishing of the Hanover Inn's main structure, preparatory to building a new and bigger one. Workmen never lacked an audience and were cheered on to greater destructive deeds as good-sized chunks of the ancient edifice came crashing down. Getting a Hanover Inn brick as a memento was the thing to do, and thanks to one generous alumnus every member of his Class received a green-and-white stenciled brick as a doorstop.

With twenty Convocation addresses behind him, President Dickey faced up to yet another in good spirits, at the opening of the 1966–67 academic year. Almost playfully he began by saying, "Normally, this is not the time for lugubrious meditation. And yet, today's academic community cannot be unmindful that in addition to the terribly real troubles of a world of men at war with themselves on many fronts, we are being asked by some to face bereavements for which, I fear, we are poorly prepared. I have in mind that during the past year or so several notable obituary notices have appeared on the fashion page of American campus life. First came the death of God, then the demise of liberal learning in our colleges, and now, so help us Satan, one death-dealing pundit tells us that sex is dead!" He advised against hasty memorial services and thought that the reports, like that of Mark Twain's death, were premature.

Although very much alive, liberal learning was endangered, Mr. Dickey said, by the fact that the contemporary college "is increasingly hard put to combine, in four undergraduate years, the rigorous pre-professional study now required by all major disciplines, with that kind of wide-ranging awareness of all the varieties of learning—curricular and extracurricular—a modern young man needs to prepare him for a lifetime of self-liberation from the twin provincialisms of ignorance and arrogance." There is no easy solution to the tendency to downgrade the amateur student of the liberal arts, but he suggested "that it would be a useful thing, on many counts, for us of the faculty, individually and collectively, to be alert to the possibility that some of our arts-and-science offerings, at all levels, have become unnecessarily professional in content and spirit both, to the disadvantage of the course itself and the very purpose of the institution." And as a final comment on the matter, he added, ". . . the time has come, I think, both in these remarks and in the larger forum of the higher-education community, to say straight out that the future of liberal learning in the American college will increasingly rest more with the individual teacher and student than with the committee on curriculum."

Because of its proximity to Canada and the special associations it had long maintained with that nation, Dartmouth joined Canada in cele-brating its centennial, by scheduling a year-long series of events enti-tled "The Canadian Year." Under the direction of the Comparative Studies Center, the program called for seminars, conferences, lectures, and cultural events, including gallery exhibitions, concerts, and plays, all by Canadian artists. Canada's independence was gained in 1867 by passage of the British North America Act, which established the Cana-dian Constitution.

President Dickey had a prominent role in the year-long program, speaking twice during the fall term and chairing a March conference on Canadian studies in the United States, attended by scholars from a dozen other colleges and universities. Three other conferences during the spring term dealt with language and the formation of national consciousness, industrial development of southeastern Canada and northern New England, and the politics and economics of Canadian-U.S. relations. Participants in the April conference on industrial de-velopment included Premier Louis Robichaud of New Brunswick and Governor John W. King of New Hampshire, along with government officials, economists, geographers, and engineers from the two coun-tries. Hopkins Center contributed its bit by presenting three plays, nine concerts, eleven art shows, and five films. Various government offices and private organizations in Canada provided materials for an overwhelming total of fifty-five exhibits about the campus from De-cember to June.

Dartmouth's tribute to Canada attracted wide and complimentary coverage in the Canadian press. And most pleased of all, on Dart-mouth's side, was undoubtedly John Dickey, whose special interest in Canada was now firmly fixed and whose reputation as an authority on U.S.-Canadian relations was well established on both sides of the bor-der. To cap the Canadian Year, five of the six honorary degrees awarded at Commencement went to Canadians, including Trade Minister Robert H. Winters, who gave the Commencement address.

The Dartmouth Trustees at their October 1966 meeting gave final approval to the faculty recommendations that three more doctoral-level programs be offered by departments of the College. The additions were in biology, chemistry, and earth sciences, bringing to five the number of Ph.D. programs in the College proper. The other two, established earlier, were in mathematics and physics. Graduate study leading to the Ph.D. was also taking place in engineering at Thayer School and in molecular biology and physiology-pharmacology at the Medical School. All eight doctoral programs were in the natural sciences, and the special faculty committee dealing with post-baccalaureate education pointed out the danger of a serious imbalance in the College, if graduate work were not introduced also in the social sciences and humanities. The committee recommended that graduate enrollment within the next decade should approximate ten percent of undergraduate enrollment and that when that level was reached, the combined post-baccalaureate enrollment in the social sciences and humanities should be roughly equal to that in the natural sciences. The committee stated that it was deliberately using the term "post-baccalaureate" rather than "graduate" education to emphasize that departments might choose any number of ways to engage in education beyond the undergraduate level. It added that the social sciences and the humanities especially had an opportunity to introduce programs "which are not bound by conventional disciplinary or departmental custom." Definitely not bound by custom was Dartmouth's decision to add some sartorial elegance to the Ph.D. degree by having its own doctoral gown. Dark green in color, it had black velvet facing and three sleeve bars, with encircled green pine trees embroidered on the front facing. A trencher hat, also dark green, had gold metallic braid on the brim. The outfit made its bow at the 1967 Commencement and was worn by six men.

Before the fall term ended, Dartmouth engaged once more in a dedication ceremony, this one for the Kiewit Computation Center. In addition to a formal ceremony, at which Mr. Kiewit spoke, there was a two-day conference on the future impact of computers. Panelists for three sessions came from M.I.T., Yale, Princeton, Pennsylvania, Mt. Holyoke, Hebrew University of Israel, and Bell Telephone Laboratories, and they were joined by four members of the Dartmouth faculty. At a general meeting on the first evening, the speaker was Francis Keppel, former U.S. Commissioner of Education. Vice President Louis T. Rader of the General Electric Company, which installed the $2.5-million GE-635 computer system for Kiewit, was kept from attending by illness, but his address was read by a company associate. Among

Dartmouth's delegation at the dedication and conference was Thomas E. Byrne, newly appointed Assistant Director of the computation center, under Professor Thomas E. Kurtz, Director. Byrne's appointment, at the start of the fall term, was made at the same time that Clarence M. Burrill of Laconia, New Hampshire, was named the College's Director of Employee Relations, and Colonel Philip G. Krueger, retired commanding officer of the Army's Cold Regions Research and Engineering Laboratory in Hanover, was named administrative officer for the science departments.

The winter term saw an unusual number of administrative changes, with six major announcements in January and February. In a move as bold as the choice of Donald Morrison to be Dean of the Faculty and Richard W. Morin to be Librarian of the College, President Dickey named Charles F. Dey, Associate Dean of the College and first director of Project ABC, to be Dean of the William Jewett Tucker Foundation. Dey, a layman rather than a religious educator, succeeded the Rev. Richard P. Unsworth, who returned to Smith College as chaplain, the position he held before coming to Dartmouth. In announcing his appointment of Dean Dey, Mr. Dickey stated that in choosing a lay educator he wished to emphasize the Tucker Foundation's institution-wide educational opportunities and to extend its religious role by bringing to the campus visiting ministers and theologians from a wide range of religious backgrounds.

On February 1, the position of Provost was taken over by Leonard Rieser, Dean of the Faculty of Arts and Sciences, in a move that combined the two jobs. This promotion filled the vacancy created in the top administrative staff when Provost John Masland took a leave of absence in order to accept a two-year assignment as educational adviser to the Ford Foundation in India. A further action by President Dickey was the creation of a new position of Associate Provost and the appointment of Professor William P. Davis of the physics department to fill it. The oversight responsibilities assigned to Professor Davis included sponsored research, summer operations, the libraries, and the offices of the Dean of the College and the Dean of Freshmen, admissions, financial aid, and the Registrar. For his Ford Foundation work, Professor Masland established headquarters in New Delhi, where he worked with native educators to identify ways in which the foundation could be helpful to Indian education.

Two more appointments rounded out the flurry of administrative changes that winter. Seaver Peters, Associate Director, was named Director of Athletics, to succeed "Red" Rolfe upon his retirement in June. And A. Alexander Fanelli, cultural affairs adviser in the U.S. Information Agency in Washington, returned to the College to be Special Assistant to the President. Peters, who had captained the Dartmouth hockey team, was Acting Associate Director of Athletics and Assistant Comptroller of the College before becoming Associate Director of Athletics in 1963, in charge of budgeting and financial affairs. Fanelli, after wartime service with the Army Air Force, taught sociology at Dartmouth, Mississippi State, and the University of Michigan. He began ten years with the U.S. State Department as a staff member at the U.S. embassy in Rome and then became chief of West Coast operations for the Office of Inter-American Programs, handling educational exchanges and Fulbright grants for five Latin American nations. Rolfe was only 58 at the time he left the Athletic Council, but he chose early retirement in order to have more time for personal affairs. President Dickey praised him warmly for his integrity and gentlemanly character and for his contributions not only to Dartmouth, but to the Ivy League and intercollegiate athletics.

Dartmouth's cooperation with the Peace Corps was described by its national headquarters as "unsurpassed." In four summers the College had trained 725 volunteers in Hanover and elsewhere, and had been picked as the site of innovations such as the two-year training program beginning between junior and senior years. In February, Peace Corps training was made a year-round integral part of the College's educational program, under the Tucker Foundation and with Phillip Bosserman continuing to serve as the first full-time director assigned to a single college. The participation of Dartmouth graduates also was exceptional. Sixty-six seniors in the Class of 1966 applied for Peace Corps service. This was nearly ten percent of the class, compared with one percent, on average, of other colleges. Federal support of Dartmouth's Peace Corps programs amounted to $495,532 in 1965–66, the second largest sum among the nine categories of government support given to the College. By far the largest part of the grand total of $5-million of federal funding went to research and training, nearly all in the sciences. The growth in government support, from $208 in 1962–63 to more than a half-million dollars in 1966–67, was a striking indication of the way in which the Peace Corps relied on Dartmouth as a training base.

The addition of buildings to the College plant, which had stopped briefly for a breathing spell, was resumed when the Trustees at their winter meeting approved plans for a three-story dormitory to house seventy-eight students of the Tuck School. Sited on Tuck Mall just east of the other Tuck School buildings, the new residence hall was needed to remedy the lack of adequate housing for the School's growing enrollment. Not only were the two existing dormitories, Chase and Woodbury, overcrowded, but some of Tuck's graduate students were placed in Hinman Hall, an undergraduate dorm, and others were living off-campus. The architect's plan for sixty-eight single rooms and five suites was designed to permit the joining of two singles into a double with private bath, thus making the dormitory desirable for people coming to Hanover for summer conferences, institutes, and programs such as Alumni College. Along with the Tuck School dormitory, the Trustees also approved the addition of twenty-four units at Sachem Village, the College-owned cluster in West Lebanon, where married students were housed.

One of the extraordinary developments of the 1966–67 academic year was the winter-term inauguration of the Dartmouth Experimental College, a supplement to the regular curriculum, fully created, organized, and operated by the undergraduates themselves. The driving force of the experiment was Robert B. Reich '68, described as "an intellectual and extracurricular dynamo who has been making things happen on campus ever since he arrived as a freshman." The Experimental College was Dartmouth's answer to the Free University movement, then existent on a dozen or more campuses. Where that movement was largely a critical reaction to established higher education, the Dartmouth venture had a more positive character and aimed to provide informal seminars dealing with contemporary subjects in an experimental and less structured way than could be done in an educational program planned and taught by a professional faculty. Student leaders for eighteen courses were chosen and primed for the winter-term session. Five thousand catalogues were printed, listing courses, for example, in the works of scientist-philosopher Immanuel Velikovsky (who made a two-day visit to Hanover to participate in the course), the fiction of J.R.R. Tolkien, law and the individual conscience, modern jazz, conservative thought, and the stock market.

The great difficulty for the Experimental College was that all twelve hundred of its applicants, from the student body, the faculty and administration, and the community, could not be accommodated. Enrollment had to be arbitrarily restricted to seven hundred. The curriculum was expanded to twenty-one courses for the next term, and enthusiasm continued unabated. In an article about his brainchild, Bob Reich wrote: "It has become more obvious than ever that education must go beyond the classroom lecture and assigned readings, that the Dartmouth experience must come to mean more than 36 courses and twelve big weekends, that our undergraduate learning must transcend the superficialities of grades, credits, and exams. A program of informal, community-oriented seminars, conducted by undergraduates in their own dormitories and fraternities, and centered upon provocative and relevant topics, has provided part of the answer." (Reich subsequently won Rhodes and Marshall Scholarships, studied at Oxford and at Yale Law School, became a teacher at the Kennedy School of Government, and wrote four influential books. In 1988 he was elected to the Dartmouth Board of Trustees.)

The faculty was impressed with student enthusiasm and accomplishment in carrying out the idea of the Dartmouth Experimental College, but it was not about to think any less highly of its own curriculum and degree requirements. The Committee on Educational Policy continued to fine-tune things, and in March its recommendation that students be allowed to major in comparative literature was approved by the faculty's executive committee. Courses in that field had long been offered, but this was the first time that a major was possible. The faculty also voted to split the Department of Sociology and Anthropology and give the anthropologists a department of their own. One further action was the adoption of a resolution, sent to the Trustees, that comprehensive examinations no longer be a requirement for the Bachelor's degree, but that they be left to the wishes of the separate departments. The feeling for keeping them appeared to be strongest in the humanities and social sciences and weakest in the sciences. The faculty proposal called for final examinations in all senior-year courses. Under the old system of required comprehensives, seniors did not take spring-term finals in their major courses.

President Dickey's outside activities were increased somewhat in late winter, when he accepted appointment by the Secretary of the Navy to be a member of the twelve-man board of advisers to the U.S. Naval War College in Newport, Rhode Island. It was the board's duty to review the broad educational policies of the college, which gave mid-career naval officers advanced instruction in the science of naval warfare. Another appointment accepted by Mr. Dickey was membership on the U.S. National Committee for Montreal's World's Fair, EXPO '67.

June brought to a close twenty-five years of Trustee service by Harvey P. Hood, who as chairman of the executive committee, chairman of the Trustees Planning Committee, and chairman of the bicentennial executive committee was one of the dominant members of the board. A resolution adopted by his fellow Trustees paid tribute to Mr. Hood's work for the College and to the quiet generosity with which he had supported it financially. The board elected him honorary chairman of the observance of Dartmouth's 200th anniversary. To fill the Life-Trustee vacancy left by Mr. Hood's retirement at the age of seventy, the board elected Rupert C. Thompson Jr., who at the time was national chairman of the capital-gifts campaign being organized in conjunction with the bicentennial. Both Hood and Thompson are memorialized today in major structures on the Dartmouth campus, the Hood Museum of Art and the Thompson Arena.

Alumni Fund history was made at year's end when the 1967 campaign topped $2-million for the first time. Six years earlier the fund, in its fifty-seventh year, had passed the $1-million mark. Doubling that in such a short time was a notable achievement for the successive Alumni Council leaders who brought it about. The chairman of the 1967 fund was Ralph Lazarus, who had a record total of four thousand class agents and assistant agents helping to lift the annual fund to its new level.

Dartmouth's summer term had a mini-anniversary by reaching its fifth year, with more programs and more students and participants than ever before. College enrollment of 471 undergraduates and ninety-seven graduate students was still well below the enrollment projected when the summer term was established, but the grand total of two thousand persons in town for long or short periods of time kept the campus well populated. The Peace Corps contingent of 327 men and women and the ABC class of eighty-seven boys were two of the groups that stayed the full eight weeks. Before the summer began, Dartmouth's ABC program received a Rockefeller Foundation grant of $130,000 to expand the plan of sending boys to public high schools, as well as independent schools. The success of enrolling eight boys in Hanover High School in the fall of 1966 prompted the three-year grant for sending ten ABC students to a second high school and for supporting Thomas Mikula, who was named the College's first full-time Director of ABC. Mr. Mikula, a member of the mathematics faculty at Phillips Andover Academy, had been mathematics coordinator for the Dartmouth ABC program for three summers. In his new position he taught at Hanover High School and lived with his family and ABC boys in the ABC residence provided by the College.

The extent to which John Dickey abhorred street violence and student protest that went beyond the bounds of civilized disagreement was evident in the address with which he opened the College's 198th year in September 1967. He entitled it "The Betrayal of Idealism." The President singled out an action taken at the annual congress of the National Student Association, where, after debate about the place of violence in public affairs, a majority was won for a resolution endorsing "black power" defined as "the unification of all black peoples in America for their liberation by any means necessary." The crucial issue of the debate was an unsuccessful effort to delete the words "by any means necessary."

"Having begun my service in the cause of Negro 'liberation' twenty years ago as a member of President Truman's historic Committee on Civil Rights," Mr. Dickey said, "and having won a few battle stars since then, I have no reason to be hesitant about saying that this kind of 'provocative bluster' is a tragically ill-advised disservice to the cause of righting the worst wrong of America's proud history."

Trying to justify violent action by calling it idealism leads only to the swamp of human folly, the President told the assembled students. "This swampland," he said, "embraces every form of unworthiness, from the unkindness of bad manners to the arrogance of justifying unprincipled behavior by one's ideals. 'By any means necessary' is the swampland into which some of the nation's finest youthful talent was drawn and tragically lost during the decade of the Thirties. It is the great folly of good intentions en route to their proverbial destiny. It is the betrayal of idealism."

One other speaker at Convocation was Bob Reich, president of the Undergraduate Council and chairman of Palaeopitus, who has been mentioned earlier as the driving force of the Dartmouth Experimental College. His call to the undergraduate body and the College itself to "meet the revolutions of desperation with a revolution in awareness" may have been a turning point in the campus attitude toward activism. Although critical of the College's comparatively placid response to the turmoil of "our very sad society," he noted signs of a new and more widespread involvement on campus. The undergraduate editor of the *Dartmouth Alumni Magazine* wrote about the same accelerating concern in his first fall column. That column also reported the first stirrings of a student action about coeducation at Dartmouth through the formation of an impromptu student committee to study the pros and cons of such a change in undergraduate enrollment. In January, as an experiment to see what coeducation might be like, the Dartmouth Committee on Coeducation invited nearly two hundred Mount Holyoke women to come to Hanover for five days of their intersession. The guests attended regular classes and student-faculty discussions, and also had a full program of social and athletic events. Although the five days were a pleasant success, the consensus was that such a short time could not give a very realistic idea of coeducation. The general idea of coeducation, however, won more advocates. At a closing forum, Dean Seymour expressed a prevalent view when he said, "The question is no longer whether Dartmouth should go coeducational, but when and how."

With the start of the college year, President Dickey announced that Dartmouth was launching a capital-gifts campaign to raise $51-million, for the purpose of strengthening the College on all fronts as it celebrated its bicentennial. The three-year effort, designated the Third Century Fund, was planned to reach its climax in 1969–70. Mr. Dickey reported that, unlike the procedure of the first campaign, the Alumni Fund would continue as a separate fund-raising effort and would seek at least $6-million during the three-year period. Already pledged to the Third Century Fund, he announced, was $5.1-million from present and former members of the Board of Trustees.

Under the national chairmanship of Trustee Rupert Thompson, the organization for the campaign was headed by Mr. Hood as chairman of the Trustees nucleus fund, Harrison F. Dunning as chairman of the major gifts committee, Emil Mosbacher Jr. and Lawrence Marx Jr. as co-chairmen of the national alumni committee, Robert S. Oelman as chairman of the corporation committee, and Professor Kemeny as chairman of the foundations committee. President Dickey, although not formally a part of the campaign leadership, was counted upon as an important factor in the campaign's success. He was not overly fond of the fund-raising part of the President's job, he admitted, but he always faced up to that responsibility and was especially willing to make clear the ways in which financial support would advance the mission of the College and the cause of liberal learning.

The major component of the Third Century Fund was $25-million for faculty and staff compensation. This was divided into $15-million for College endowment, $5-million for professional-school endowment, and $5-million as an expendable sum. The second largest allocation was $7-million for library acquisitions, $6-million as endowment and $1-million expendable. Other objectives of the campaign were $5-million for undergraduate scholarships and graduate fellowships, $2.25-million for student programs, and $11.75-million for various facilities, including a physical sciences center, renovation of Silsby Hall and Dartmouth Row, an undergraduate dormitory, a 4500-seat ice arena, permanent stands on the east side of the football stadium, and new facilities at all three associated schools, where expansion of programs, enrollment, and faculty was planned.

In keeping with a recommendation of the Trustees Planning Committee, the college year began with a new Department of Personnel, responsible for the institution-wide direction and coordination of personnel policies and procedures. In a ten-year period the number of regular College employees had grown from 800 to 1,700, and when part-time and summer employees were counted, nearly 3,000 were on the payroll. Not only had the numbers grown, but the complexities of administration had grown with them. Clarence Burrill, who had come to Dartmouth the previous fall as Director of Employee Relations, was named head of the new department, reporting to Vice President Meck. Donald W. Cameron was promoted to Associate Director of Employee Relations, while continuing to be in charge of student placement. Two other administrative changes at the time were the appointments of Frederick L. Hier to be Director of Public Programs and Josiah F. Hill to be College Editor. Mr. Hier succeeded Nichol Sandoe Jr., who left after nineteen years with the College to be director of public affairs for the Claremont Colleges in California. A new college chaplain also took up his duties on September 1. He was the Rev. Paul W. Rahmeier from Oberlin College, where he had been director of student religious activities. His coming to Dartmouth filled the vacancy created by the death of the Rev. George H. Kalbfleisch.

Things were also happening on the academic side. Drama became a separate department within the division of the humanities. Headed by Professor John Finch, the new department drew its faculty from the Hopkins Center theater staff, particularly Rod Alexander and Henry Williams, and from five cooperating departments. It began with eleven majors, all of whom were required to be active in theater in Hopkins Center. In another curriculum development, Greece was added to France, Germany, and Spain as countries where Dartmouth undergraduates could spend time, usually summer and the fall term, in the foreign-study program. This feature of the College's educational program was enjoying a considerable growth. For 1967–68 approximately one hundred students were studying abroad, compared with sixty-five the year before, and it was estimated that during 1968–69 three hundred would be overseas, most of them engaged in the new program of intensive language study introduced in the fall. While the foreign study program, in operation since 1958, called for independent research in a variety of fields, the intensive language training concentrated on the language and the literature and culture of the host country. In both cases, study was pursued in a center where university courses could be taken, and for language students there was the added advantage of living with families where the language being studied was spoken constantly. The striking feature of the language program was intensive training at Dartmouth before the student went abroad. The method created by Professor Rassias for training Peace Corps volunteers was adopted for the College's own undergraduates. It was strenuous, consisting of five hours a week in small sections, with a faculty teacher; another five hours of intensive drill, under apprentice teachers; and four hours in the language laboratory. This, plus the time abroad, produced remarkable language proficiency, satisfying the College's language requirement. Thus equipped, the student had the option of going abroad again to undertake a project in the foreign study program, where language training was not the prime objective.

The position of College Librarian is almost as old as Dartmouth College itself, going back to 1773 when Eleazar Wheelock named Bezaleel Woodward to the post. To be the fifteenth librarian in the Woodward succession, President Dickey in November appointed Edward Connery Lathem, then the Associate Librarian. Mr. Lathem was scheduled to take over the position on July 1, 1968, upon the retirement of Mr. Morin, who had administered the College libraries for seventeen years. Mr. Morin during his tenure oversaw a great expansion of library collections and services. The number of volumes at the College grew from 665,000 to 930,000, adding solidity to Dartmouth's reputation of having the finest undergraduate college library in the country. Mr. Lathem had joined the Baker Library staff in 1952, after graduate work in library administration at Columbia University. He later received his doctoral degree at Oxford University and actively continued his productive scholarship, with particular interest in Dartmouth history and in the work of his close friend Robert Frost, a comprehensive collection of whose poetry he edited.

Another important administrative appointment announced by President Dickey at about the same time was that of Professor John W. Hennessey Jr. to be Dean of Tuck School at the start of the next academic year. Professor Hennessey succeeded Dean Karl A. Hill, who had tendered his resignation after eleven years in the top position at the business school. During those eleven years the school increased its enrollment from 170 to 220, and underwent a marked change in the make-up of the student body, increasing the enrollment of students from other colleges from twenty percent to seventy-five percent. For most of its history, Tuck School, like the associated schools of medicine and engineering, had drawn its students almost entirely from the College. Dean-elect Hennessey, a Princeton graduate with advanced degrees from Harvard and the University of Washington, was chairman of the TPC sub-committee on advisory and counseling services, and as chairman of the Tuck faculty committee reviewing the MBA curriculum he was the leading figure in setting goals for Tuck School's long-range academic development.

The curriculum study directed by Mr. Hennessey was financed by a grant from the Alfred P. Sloan Foundation, which in December made a major gift of $1.5-million to the Thayer School of Engineering to continue the curriculum innovations aimed at revitalizing and updating professional education for engineers. (These innovations had been initiated with a Sloan Foundation grant of $1-million in 1962.) Thayer School's "pilot plant" program was credited with influencing engineering education far beyond Hanover. Its emphasis was on creative design at both the undergraduate and graduate levels, on concern with the needs of society, and on a linkage of professional studies with industry. Dean Myron Tribus stated that the second Sloan Foundation grant would enable Thayer School to increase its student body by one-third, from seventy-five to one-hundred, and its faculty from twenty-two to twenty-seven. It also would finance new equipment and some plant expansion. The first Sloan grant had great impact on the school, enabling it to increase the faculty from fifteen to twenty-two and the technical and supporting staff from nineteen to thirty-four persons. It also made possible three new graduate programs, laboratory and shop renovations, and a doubling of sponsored research, to $750,000 annually.

The $1.5-million from the Sloan Foundation was the second major gift credited to the Third Century Fund. The first, announced shortly after the three-year campaign opened in October, was $750,000 from the William R. Kenan Jr. Foundation of New York, to establish an endowed professorship that would encourage an outstanding member of the faculty to give his primary interest to undergraduate teaching. The first holder of the chair was Professor John W. Finch of the English department, who shortly before had been named chairman of the new drama department. The professorship was named for William R. Kenan

Jr., a chemist and former president of the Florida East Coast Railway Company, who established his foundation for the support of education.

As the fall term was getting into stride, Selective Service Director Lewis B. Hershey sent a shock wave through the academic world by issuing a directive that, in effect, threatened military service as a punishment for those engaging in "illegal demonstration" against recruiting or the draft. Students, faculty, and administrators at Dartmouth, as elsewhere, denounced the directive as a denial of free speech and academic freedom. Provost Rieser and Dean Seymour, pending a December 11 meeting of the faculty, recommended that all scheduled visits by military recruiters be postponed until the directive was clarified. This, they made clear, did not represent any change in Dartmouth's policy of open recruitment on the campus. At its December meeting the faculty supported this open policy, but passed a resolution urging President Dickey and the Trustees to exercise their influence for revocation of the Hershey directive, to do so in concert with other institutions, and to suspend recruitment if necessary to achieve revocation. General Hershey's action, the faculty declared, "constitutes a serious, immediate threat to free speech and to academic freedom in America," invites draft boards to exceed the powers granted to them by law, and "tends to produce an atmosphere of fear and inhibition on the American campus." In a December 21 letter to President Johnson, the presidents of the Ivy Group institutions asked that he make it clear that there was no intention to make induction a punishment or to make draft boards extra-legal judges of the legality of acts of protests. The White House released the letter and the reply from Presidential Assistant Joseph Califano, who agreed with the principles enunciated by the Ivy Group presidents. Most importantly, the exchange was distributed to draft boards throughout the country. At Dartmouth, the scheduled visits by military recruiters were, by mutual agreement, postponed until the winter term, and the College issued a statement saying that the campus was open to recruiters as long as they acknowledged the rights of free speech and dissent. Palaeopitus and the chairman of the student-faculty Committee on Freedom of Expression and Dissent were unhappy with the statement, but it stood as College policy.

Prelude to the Bicentennial

WITH the Dartmouth bicentennial less than two years away, the planning committee headed by Professor Frank Smallwood released in January a tentative schedule of anniversary events. It announced that the period beginning with Commencement in June 1969 and ending with a Third Century Convocation in September 1970 would be designated as the Bicentennial Year. The focal point within the year was Dartmouth Day on December 13, 1969, the actual 200th anniversary of the granting of the Dartmouth College Charter by King George III of Great Britain. In each of the three terms of the year a symposium was to be held on the general theme of "Liberal and Professional Learning in a Changing Society," with sub-themes related to the sciences in the fall, the humanities in the winter, and the social sciences in the spring. As a prelude to the Bicentennial Year the planning committee listed an observance in Washington, on February 9, 1969, of the 150th anniversary of the U.S. Supreme Court decision in the Dartmouth College Case; also a program in Columbia, Connecticut, in May, remembering Moor's Indian Charity School, where Eleazar Wheelock's idea of a northern college had its genesis. Among the other things planned were special glee club tours, a New York art show, bicentennial events at the two Commencements occurring within the Bicentennial Year, and a celebration on August 23, 1970, of the 200th anniversary of Wheelock's arrival in Hanover. It was hoped that Lord Dartmouth would come from England for the 1969 Commencement and that a commemorative postage stamp would be issued for the 150th anniversary of the Dartmouth College Case—both of which wishes were to be fulfilled. The planning and carrying out of the Bicentennial Year events were entrusted to a twelve-man committee of faculty, staff, and students. The chief aides to Chairman Smallwood were presidential assistant Alex Fanelli as executive secretary and Professor Arthur Jensen, who upon his retirement in June 1968 assumed the role of coordinator.

Plans for the Bicentennial Year were one of the reports made to the Trustees and members of the Alumni Council when they held a joint meeting in Hanover in January 1968. The single discussion topic for the joint meeting was the financial future of the College. In his role as chairman of a five-part presentation of the subject, President Dickey opened the discussion by saying, "I know it is increasingly held throughout the community of higher education and in the foundation world that the genuinely critical consideration on both the qualitative and quantitative aspects of American higher education at present and in the foreseeable future is on the income side. Although, as in every business, there is a need to be disciplined with respect to cost, the demands of our society on American higher education are such that the problem has got to be solved on the income side. This may seem to be heresy to many of you who are accustomed to solving many a crisis by the control or reduction of costs, and I do not wish to minimize that as a heavy necessity in this enterprise. However, you've got to realize that our purposes today embrace our relationships with secondary schools and range up through the most advanced levels of scholarship. We are engaged in professional education at the advanced level in the three most critical areas necessary to the service of today's American society—health, managerial skills, and technology.

"Dartmouth is an institution of comprehensive purpose and Dartmouth today is moving into, for her, an essentially new area of purpose, certainly in extent and emphasis; namely, the purpose of making the institution a continuing, systematic servant of American society as well as an institution carrying out the educational needs of individuals who attend. Dartmouth today has the intellectual muscle in her four faculties—the faculties of arts and sciences, engineering, medicine, and business—to provide this kind of service to the American community, regionally, nationally, and indeed, internationally. Only if one understands this broad range of purpose can one understand this institution today."

After President Dickey's introduction, financial strategy for the next decade was discussed by Vice President and Treasurer John Meck, who concentrated on tuition and endowment income; Provost Leonard

Rieser, who dealt with public and semi-public funds, including foundations; and Vice President George Colton, who discussed philanthropy.
Mr. Meck, going back a decade, stated that operating income (not
counting auxiliary activities) for 1956–57 was $6.7-million and grew to
$21.4-million by 1966–67. The projection for 1976–77 was $38.5-million,
leaving $4.7-million of estimated expense unfunded. This gap could
be reduced or eliminated, he explained, by endowment income from
the Third Century Fund, tuition increases greater than projected, federal funds, and philanthropy. A last resort would be a cutback in budget
allocations.

Provost Rieser, making the same comparisons by decades, explained
that operating income from public sources had grown from $330,000
in 1956–57 to $5.75-million in 1966–67, and that such income from
foundations had grown from $170,000 to $450,000. His projection for a
decade hence was ten or eleven million dollars of operating income
from public and semi-public sources. A good portion of this estimated
gain of approximately $4.5-million would be in support of computing,
he predicted. Income from public and semi-public sources, he concluded, would continue to be given mainly in support of educational
innovations and public service.

Mr. Colton found it difficult to make a prediction about operating
income from private sources, because of the unknown nature of gifts
and bequests, but he reviewed the steady upward climb of private
support over the previous fifteen years and saw an opportunity to
accelerate it in the decade ahead. The Alumni Fund's role in future
financing was discussed by Ralph Lazarus, chairman of the fund; and
Trustee Thompson, chairman of the Third Century Fund, concluded
the five-part presentation by bringing the joint meeting up to date on
the capital campaign. On that January date, he reported, the fund had
pledges of $11.85-million toward its $51-million goal. Mr. Thompson
referred to President Dickey's all-important part in the campaign and
said, "Before I ever dared assume this marvelous opportunity, I was
assured that the President put the Third Century Fund first on his
calendar. The most important man in this whole effort is John Dickey.
He stands for Dartmouth College. He has made a record of which we
are all so proud. Without his leadership we never could get off the
ground."

The Alumni Council at its own, separate meeting in January was primarily concerned with the report of the special committee it had named to review Dartmouth's alumni relations and make recommendations for bringing them up to a new peak of effectiveness, in keeping with other efforts looking ahead to the College's third century. The gist of the report was to move toward more intellectually oriented programs, to give younger alumni a greater say in alumni affairs, including membership on the Alumni Council; to devise new ways of meeting the growing alumni interest in continuing education, particularly through club-sponsored events bringing the faculty to the alumni; and to make sure that the College kept the alumni thoroughly informed about its plans and programs.

While the Trustees and Alumni Council members were concerned with weighty matters, undergraduates were agitated about parietals, the rules and regulations governing the entertainment of women in student rooms. Probably no other campus issue has a longer history, unless it be complaints about food. The history is one of increasing liberalization as mores changed—from no visitors at all, to a 7 p.m. curfew in the Forties, to midnight and then 2 a.m. on Saturday night. Liberalization also took the form of allowing women upstairs in the fraternity houses. Now it was proposed that students be allowed to make their own rules in the dormitories and fraternities. The Committee on Administration took a dim view of this idea, particularly the proposal that a student be permitted to house a female guest in his room "for not more than a few days." Its official response is something of a classic: "The Committee on Administration has been asked to approve a series of proposals which would allow a student to house a woman in his bedroom, on the condition that the woman and his roommates consent and that the woman stay no more than a few days. On this issue the Committee is anxious that its response be unambiguous. It is for this reason that we use a simple word which has gone out of fashion in this age of meaningful dialogue: No."

New Hampshire is the only state in the nation in which student dormitory and dining facilities are subject to the property tax. As a means of getting a clarification of the state law, the College in April filed with the Grafton County Superior Court an appeal for a property tax abatement that had been denied by the town of Hanover. Under a reappraisal of all town property the year before, the fair market value of dormitory and dining properties was increased from $2,664,300 to $5,724,950, resulting in a 1967 tax increase for Dartmouth of $67,586, which was a percentage increase higher than for town property in general. Vice President Meck, arguing the case for the College, not only opposed the tax as contrary to almost unanimous interpretation throughout the United States, but also complained of the lack of an objective, stable method of applying the tax. The appeal was denied by the Superior Court. Later, Phillips Exeter Academy, with the blessing and support of Dartmouth and other independent educational institutions in the state, carried the case of the dormitory and dining hall tax to the New Hampshire Supreme Court, but here again the state law was upheld, since residence halls and dining facilities were not viewed as buildings serving an educational purpose and entitled to tax-exemption. At the time the College filed its appeal with the Superior Court, its total tax bill in Hanover for 1967 was $316,900. This, plus taxes paid by the fraternity houses, accounted for more than one-fourth of the property taxes collected by the town.

The Board of Trustees, meeting in June, elected two new members to the board. Harrison F. Dunning, Class of 1930, was chosen to succeed John L. Sullivan, who completed his second five-year term as Alumni Trustee, and Ralph Lazarus, Class of 1935, was chosen to fill the unexpired term of John C. Woodhouse, who had reached the compulsory retirement age of seventy. Mr. Dunning was president and chief executive officer of the Scott Paper Company, and at the time of his election was chairman of the major gifts committee for the Third Century Fund. Mr. Lazarus was chairman of the board of Federated Department Stores, one of the country's largest retail chains, chairman of the 1967 and 1968 Dartmouth Alumni Funds, and a member of the national executive committee for the Third Century Fund. His educational interests had involved him with the Peace Corps, the Harvard School of Education, urban studies at Harvard and M.I.T., and the National Committee for the Support of Public Schools.

The Trustees' most important educational action was their approval of reviving the M.D. degree at the Dartmouth Medical School, contingent upon the availability of the necessary new financing. This was something toward which the School had been moving ever since Dean Carleton Chapman took office in September 1966, and the Trustees were encouraged to vote such approval by four major gifts totaling $4.25-million, given to the Third Century Fund and designated for the Medical School.

President Dickey, in his valedictory to the Class of 1968, spoke in the somewhat despondent mood in which he had opened the year in September. "Traditionally, graduation from college has had something of the exclamation mark about it," he said, "but today, with so much at issue, it must also be a question mark.

"It is fitting that, in our last meeting as the 1968 Dartmouth academic community, we should acknowledge that this has been one of those years when events become the great teacher of mankind. We gathered last September in the spreading darkness of warfare in our cities, in Vietnam, and—perhaps most portentously of all—in those inner sanctums we call our 'souls.'

"We end the year in the gloom of two ghastly acts of renunciation of man's pretense to being human. Since last September the contagion of violence in thought and speech and deed has spread to every corner of the earth where man presumes to reign."

Not only had city riots continued during the year, and not only had the whole country been shocked by the assassinations of Martin Luther King Jr. and Senator Robert F. Kennedy, to which Mr. Dickey referred, but on the Dartmouth campus student protests, even if kept within reasonable bounds, were more frequent and were drawing larger crowds. What was developing at Dartmouth was not to President Dickey's liking, and his disappointment, particularly with some of the younger faculty members, and his discouragement were plainly seen in these final years of his presidency. The seeds of more radical protest had been planted during 1968, and they bore unwanted fruit in the following academic year.

It was in tune with the times for the valedictorian of the graduating class to throw the Commencement proceedings into disarray by his address. James W. Newton, a Quaker pacifist, outraged a great many in the audience by denouncing the U.S. involvement in the Vietnam war and by urging his classmates to refuse to fight if drafted. "Take the path that seems appropriate for you," he said. "It may be conscientious objection, draft resistance, or escape to a country of greater freedom in the north." His remarks drew boos and catcalls from his older listeners, and it may have been in reacting to that criticism that a sizable portion of his classmates applauded him. Senator Jacob K. Javits of New York, following him as the Commencement speaker, felt impelled to add an impromptu commentary on Jamie Newton's valedictory, calling it "quite an act to follow." He came prepared to argue that, despite the understandable impatience and anger of young people, particularly those in college, non-violent, Constitutional means were the only effective way to bring about change. In making his case forcefully and persuasively he won a standing ovation, from the seniors as well as the general audience.

Retirement from the Dartmouth presidency had been on John Dickey's mind for a year or more and he had discussed it with the Trustees, both as a group and individually, a number of times before a definite time was settled upon. At the close of his Convocation address of September 1968, he announced that he would cease being "the fellow on this job" after the observance of the College's bicentennial. "Finally," he said, "may I use this occasion to note that the bicentennial year, 1969–70, will bring me to my twenty-fifth year as Dartmouth's twelfth president—one-eighth of the life of this venerable institution. Some time ago I informed the Trustees that at their convenience during the 1969–70 bicentennial period I'd like to cap my stint in the effort to bring Dartmouth to a running start as she enters her third century, by passing the baton to another and retiring, shall we say, to the green pastures of Hanover. God willing, with lots of help and a little bit of luck, that's the way it will be. But enough of that for the moment. This is the beginning of another fresh year for all of us; it is assuredly not the time for a valedictory. There will be opportunities later to say a few of the things that these Dartmouth years have meant to me as the man on one of the world's wonderful jobs."

To President Dickey's Dartmouth friends and colleagues it was unthinkable that anyone but he should preside over the celebration of the College's 200th anniversary, after his years of leadership and his central role in the fifteen-year effort to advance Dartmouth to a new level of excellence as she began her third century. John Dickey himself undoubtedly wanted to see the College through the bicentennial period, and he did, but his closest friends noted that he was tired, both physically and mentally, from the pressures of his job. The problem of protesting students was an added burden in his final years, and one that was personally hurtful, because he felt that the students had turned against him. The participation of some of the younger faculty members in demonstrations was a particular annoyance, Mr. Dickey later stated in an oral-history interview, and "the deepest disappointment of my entire Dartmouth experience," he added, was the failure of the faculty to maintain free speech on campus. At the fortieth reunion of his Class of 1929, at the end of the college year in which student rebellion had been the most disruptive, he told his classmates that being President of Dartmouth College was not fun any more. Except for the desire to see the bicentennial through its climactic days, John Dickey was indeed ready to pass the baton to another. The decision to delay retirement until early 1970 turned out to be a happy one, because the bicentennial observance and the success of the Third Century Fund provided the note of triumph and celebration on which Mr. Dickey's remarkable administration deserved to end.

In the 1968 Convocation address which ended with the announcement of his retirement, President Dickey picked up the subject of his address of the year before and reiterated his rejection of the idea, prevalent among students across the land, that good can be attained and error righted "by any means necessary." He broadened his concept of the turbulence in the academic world by saying that "we are dealing with something more profound and far more pervasive than the popular diagnosis of a 'generation gap' or a revolt of youth." The same tide was running against governing authority and even against church authority, he noted. The war in Vietnam and inequalities of opportunity and justice at home might provide issues for demonstrations and defiance, he said, but more than issues was involved. "I suggest for continuing consideration," he went on, "that the most significant underlying factor in all of this, as in many other continuing contemporary situations beyond mentioning here, is a mounting—although, often, unarticulated—rejection throughout all human affairs of the role of authority. In particular, I think, we can detect a worldwide, contagious downgrading of what might fairly be termed the authority of experience—or even the relevance of experience—as it is embodied in the institutions of the human community." Yet, authority, along with responsibility, is essential if anything is to get done, he declared.

At Convocation, President Dickey made the first public announcement of the establishment of the Dartmouth Campus Conference, a new agency for ongoing, face-to-face communication among undergraduates, Trustees, faculty, administrative officers, and the President, to discuss matters of common interest about the College. Proposed by Mr. Dickey as a partial answer to the lack of any real student government, the forum held an organizational meeting on September 22, 1968, under the chairmanship of Trustee F. William Andres. Two other Trustees serving as members were Mr. Zimmerman and Mr. Braden. Four students, three faculty members, four administrative officers, and President Dickey rounded out the membership. Financial support for the Conference was provided by the Joel Benezet '66 Memorial Fund, which previously had financed an annual weekend retreat at which a dozen or so sophomores met with Mr. Dickey and a few faculty members and administrators. The organizational meeting of the Conference was followed in November by the first regular meeting, held at the Hartness House in Springfield, Vermont. There, as typical of the sort of discussions to be held, the group talked about College governance, student representation on various official committees, residential life, the College's budget and financial strategy, and coeducation. The Dartmouth Campus Conference was the latest move by the Dickey administration to give undergraduates more of a voice in the conduct of College affairs. The previous spring, for instance, four students were added, for an experimental period, to the Committee on Administration, which ruled on major disciplinary cases and matters of academic standing. A year earlier, three students were added to the Faculty Committee on Educational Planning, and undergraduates also were named to the Bicentennial Planning Committee and to *ad hoc* committees which drew up policy statements about dissent and drugs. The high-water mark of "student power" was the allocating to students of four of the nine places on the newly formed Campus Committee on Standing and Conduct, which replaced the Undergraduate Council's Judiciary Committee and the Faculty Committee on Administration as judges in cases of misconduct or of petition for changes in academic requirements and standing.

The new academic year 1968–69 opened with the first Ph.D. program in the social sciences. It was in psychology, bringing to five the number of doctoral programs in the College proper. Four candidates for the psychology Ph.D. were enrolled at the start. With four or five more admitted each year, maximum enrollment in the four-year program was expected to be about twenty. The primary aim at Dartmouth was to produce psychologists who would go into teaching, and to that end a seminar on teaching and a sequence of supervised teaching experiences were made a part of the department's graduate curriculum. The new facilities of Gerry Hall and a sixteen-man psychology faculty were the quality assets that encouraged the College to extend doctoral work into the social sciences division for the first time.

The year opened also with the news that Thaddeus Seymour, Dean of the College, would remain in that office only one more year and then, after rounding out ten years of deaning, would return to teaching in the English department. "It is my observation," he contributed, "that this position is one that calls for periodic infusions of new enthusiasm, energy, and resilience." His plan to return to teaching did not work out. In the spring he was elected president of Wabash College in Indiana, to take office on August 1. The news of his impending departure led to a whole string of tributes, begun by President Dickey, continued by the Boston alumni, the Dartmouth Alumni Council and the executive committee of the faculty, and concluded by the Class of 1969, which honored him at Class Day exercises in June. The faculty, with unwonted informality, sent the dean off to Wabash with this declaration: "Whereas our student revolutionaries vow simply to unhinge the institution, your departure threatens to unravel the entire Upper Valley. We put it to you straight that we do not lightly face the loss of a 1929 Packard from the Fourth of July parade, the High Striker from the Norwich Fair, or Batman from Variety Night!" Dean Seymour's versatility as crew coach and star performer at extracurricular happenings, on top of his competent deaning, made him a special personality to the whole Dartmouth community.

When the Christmas recess was over and the College resumed its work in January 1969, all hands were aware that the bicentennial year had actually arrived, and preparations for the scheduled calendar of events were accordingly stepped up. Word had come that Lord and Lady Dartmouth would be pleased to be guests of honor at the Commencement weekend formally opening the Bicentennial Year. Signed into law by President Johnson was a bill passed by both houses of Congress, authorizing the U.S. Mint to strike a medal commemorating Dartmouth's 200th anniversary. And the Postmaster General announced that one of the four commemorative stamps to be issued in 1969 would be a six-cent stamp showing Daniel Webster and Dartmouth Hall and saying "The Dartmouth College Case 1819." The design chosen for the stamp was by John Scotford, Assistant Director of Hopkins Center, and the color, naturally, was green. These developments were announced by Mr. Fanelli, who had taken over the chairmanship of the Bicentennial Planning Committee from Professor Smallwood, newly appointed Associate Dean of the Faculty and chairman of the social sciences division. Professor Jensen, who had by now joined the ranks of the emeriti, assumed Mr. Fanelli's previous duties as executive secretary of both the planning committee and the bicentennial executive committee.

The Dartmouth Trustees at their January meeting endorsed a far-reaching program recommended by the special Committee on Equal Opportunity, which the board had created in April to evaluate how the College was meeting its responsibilities in that area. The committee was chaired by John R. McLane Jr. of Manchester, New Hampshire, and was broadly representative of the faculty, administration, students, staff, alumni, and Hanover community. Its work already had one concrete result, in the conversion of the Nathan Lord House on College Street, once the home of Dartmouth's sixth president, into an Afro-American Cultural Center, where educational and social programs could be carried on for the benefit of the eighty-nine black undergraduates enrolled at Dartmouth for 1968–69. The center also provided headquarters for the Afro-American Society, which took on the responsibility for running it.

The program given Trustee approval in January recommended the strengthening of existing efforts toward equal opportunity and the introduction of new initiatives. The McLane committee urged the College to increase the number of qualified blacks and other minority groups in the student body, and to make a determined effort to recruit black faculty members, both for the permanent teaching staff and as visiting professors. On the curriculum side, the committee recommended the creation of an interdepartmental faculty committee to correlate the Afro-American course material already being offered in eight academic departments. Existing equal-opportunity efforts that the committee found praiseworthy included the ABC program, the "Bridge Program" whereby disadvantaged students admitted to Dartmouth could get special tutoring in English and mathematics during the summer before beginning freshman year, undergraduates working as tutors and teaching assistants in predominantly black schools in Jersey City, and student and faculty exchange programs with such colleges as Talladega, Fisk, and Morehouse. To coordinate the implementation of the McLane committee recommendations, the Trustees named Dean Dey of the Tucker Foundation, who was vice-chairman of the committee. They agreed to make more funds available for black enrollment and financial aid, for curriculum innovations, and for development of the ABC and Jersey City programs.

Financial aid for blacks and other minority students was a substantial part of the College's overall aid program, which for 1968–69 reached a record level of more than $2-million. The total broke down into $1.46-million in scholarships, $380,000 in long-term loans, and $200,000 in term-time employment. In view of President Dickey's determination, when he took office, to push financial aid to the limit of the College's means, the reaching of the $2-million record in his last full year as president was another mark of the successful way in which so many of his goals had been realized. Increased financial aid was one objective of the Third Century Fund, and at the joint meeting of the Trustees and Alumni Council in January it was disclosed by Chairman Thompson that the $51-million drive had passed the halfway mark, with gifts and pledges at that time totaling $25.5-million.

Following the January 10 meeting of the board, some Trustees were back in town a week later for an open meeting of the Dartmouth Campus Conference. The main topic for discussion was coeducation. After continuing the discussion in a closed session the following day, the

Conference adopted a resolution asking the Trustees to appoint a special task force to study the question of educating women at Dartmouth College. "The Dartmouth Campus Conference . . . agrees that the education of women at Dartmouth College is a subject of top priority," the resolution read, "and therefore recommends that the Board of Trustees take prompt action to undertake in-depth studies of this subject through a special committee or task force composed of students, faculty, Trustees, administration, and alumni and, based on the outcome of these studies, take whatever further action is indicated."

Action by the board followed soon after. Its executive committee voted to establish a study group to review Dartmouth's total existing and prospective program developments for the Seventies, with special attention paid to the question of coeducation. Trustee Dudley Orr, chairman of the Trustees' executive and planning committees, was chairman of the study group and Provost Leonard Rieser was co-chairman. Although coeducation was the most intriguing matter to be examined, it was by no means the whole of the charge given to the study group. The executive committee of the Trustees had in mind, also, educational programs and facilities, housing and boarding, site planning and land acquisition, financial resources, Dartmouth's heritage and purpose, and the views of faculty, students, alumni, and the community—in short, everything that would have a bearing on the College's development during the first decade of its third century. The executive committee took the position that coeducation had to be considered in relation to Dartmouth's commitment to educational excellence and its obligations in all the proposed areas of study.

Another committee looking ahead to the Seventies was the Presidential Analysis Committee, formed to consider the nature and role of the presidency during the coming decade and to make its conclusions known to the faculty-Trustee search committee that had been named to advise the board on the election of John Dickey's successor. Professor Walter H. Stockmayer was appointed chairman of the analysis committee. Here again, coeducation was one of the matters to be considered by the committee, which was asked "to identify those concerns and problems that Dartmouth will face in the next ten years, in order to enable the Search Committee to select the kind of man who can best serve the institution throughout this period."

Student advocacy of coeducation, meanwhile, was growing. It took its most concrete form in late January when a student-initiated program brought nearly a thousand women from eighteen colleges to Hanover for six days, to participate in the second annual Coed Week. The program was academically oriented, and the guests were given special course directories and invited to attend classes. The social side of the week was less appealing to some of the coeds, and they departed after a few days, but the majority stayed the course. *The Dartmouth*, which had been editorially advocating a coordinate college for women near Hanover, changed its mind after Coed Week and said, "It has become evident, from external sources such as the Princeton Report and from the changing mood on campus, that Dartmouth must become coeducational. It is our opinion that the sooner the better."

Much of the activity of Coed Week took place in Hopkins Center, which now had a general administrator in Peter Smith, who had come to Dartmouth in January from the University of California at Santa Cruz, where he was assistant vice chancellor. This new position at the College was in preparation for his taking over the full direction of Hopkins Center from Warner Bentley, who was retiring on June 30. Mr. Smith, a native of England, was actively engaged in theatrical work while attending the University of Birmingham. After administrative work at McMaster University in Canada and further graduate study at the University of Durham in England, he took up his post at the University of California at Santa Cruz. There, as chairman of the campus committee on arts and lectures, he was responsible for a variety of cultural initiatives and developed a drama program.

Before the busy month of January was over, the Dartmouth faculty held a special meeting and voted to phase out, over a three-year period, all degree credits for courses given by the three ROTC units on campus. This action, allowing students currently enrolled in ROTC to finish with course credit, was less stringent than that taken by the faculties at Harvard and Yale, where ROTC course credits and faculty status for ROTC instructors were summarily abolished. The Dartmouth faculty also voted, subject to approval by the Committee Advisory to the President, to limit faculty status to the senior officer of each ROTC unit. The faculty rejected the effort by some of its members to end ROTC completely as soon as possible. Preliminary to its January 21 meeting, the faculty heard and was undoubtedly influenced by a report from its committee on organization and policy, which found ROTC recruiting not incompatible with the purpose of liberal education at Dartmouth, but which faulted the training procedures of ROTC and suggested that they be transferred to summer camps. This latter suggestion was voted by the faculty as a whole, which urged the College to collaborate with other institutions in persuading the Department of Defense to take military training off the campuses. At the time of the action, slightly more than four hundred undergraduates were enrolled in the ROTC units, 220 in the Army, 175 in the Navy, and fifteen in the Air Force (which offered a two-year program).

President Dickey on February 27 announced that the new Dean of the College, succeeding Thaddeus Seymour, would be Carroll W. Brewster, Yale Law School lecturer and vice president of the International Student Center in New Haven. The 32-year-old graduate of Yale and Yale Law School was also a practicing attorney, United States Commissioner in New Haven, and secretary of the law school's graduate committee supervising foreign students. Before taking up his various activities in New Haven, Brewster had spent three years in the Sudan, where at the age of 26 he became legal assistant to the Chief Justice of that nation and pulled together for the first time all the important judicial cases and decisions from the national, provincial, district, and tribal courts, thus providing the first unified body of legal precedent available to Sudan since it gained independence in 1956. Although not officially assuming the deanship until July 1, Dean-elect Brewster came to the College in May in order to work with Dean Seymour for a brief period of time.

Another Dartmouth dean brought about an administrative change when Dean Myron Tribus of Thayer School, on April 1, became U.S. Assistant Secretary of Commerce for Science and Technology. He was granted leave of absence, but his departure for Washington turned out to be a permanent loss to the College. In his absence Associate Dean George A. Colligan assumed the duties of Dean. For two years before receiving his federal appointment Dean Tribus had been a member of the Commerce Technical Advisory Board, which advised the Secretary of Commerce on public policy and technology. His service at Dartmouth extended over eight years, during which time he became a national figure in engineering education, by relating it to the solution of economic and social problems and by emphasizing design at both the undergraduate and graduate levels.

Although not, strictly speaking, a part of the bicentennial, the observance of the 150th anniversary of the Dartmouth College Case in Washington on April 9, 1969, served to give tangible form at last to the string of events that had been planned and talked about for so long a time. The ceremony in the nation's capital took place in the old Court of Claims Building on Lafayette Square, with Chief Justice Earl Warren delivering the main address. The other principal speaker was U.S. Senator Thomas J. McIntyre of New Hampshire, who spoke on "The Union and Daniel Webster." Chief Justice Warren devoted his address to Webster's great influence on U.S. constitutional law and his unswerving support of a strong and free judicial system. In his remarks about Webster's appearances before the Supreme Court, he pointed out that Webster did not always win, but that in the Dartmouth College Case he was at his finest and made legal history, even though "there has long been, as we all know, a respectable body of opinion extant that the Dartmouth College Case came out the right way but for the wrong reasons." President Dickey presided over the Washington ceremony and was introduced by Judge Carl E. McGowan of the U.S. Court of Appeals, who was chairman of the alumni committee that arranged the program. Because of the small size of the chamber in which the ceremony took place, the audience was limited to 150 invited persons, representing the judiciary, Congress, alumni, and the legal profession. After the program, the College and the Dartmouth Club of Washington gave a reception in the historic Tayloe House, next door to the Court of Claims. In commemoration of the Dartmouth College Case, the Library of Congress mounted, in its main foyer, a display of pertinent material.

What might be called the most solid of bicentennial commemoratives was the bronze Dartmouth College Bicentennial Medal authorized by the Congress and the President of the United States and struck by the U.S. Mint in Philadelphia in time for the 1969 Commencement in June. The College ordered 5,000 bronze medals and (by permission of the U.S. Treasury) two in gold, one to be presented to Lord Dartmouth and the other to remain in the possession of the College. Designed by Rudolph Ruzicka of Norwich, Vermont, one of the country's most celebrated graphic artists, the medal featured the Old Pine and the dates 1769–1969, and on the reverse side combined the seal and motto of the College with the arms and motto of the Earl of Dartmouth (*Gaudet Tentamine Virtus*, translated as "Valor Rejoices in Contest"). The medal, three inches in diameter, was sold to alumni and others, and in this way the College expected to recoup most of the expense of having the medal struck.

In addition to the bicentennial medal and the Webster stamp, the U.S. House of Representatives took cognizance of Dartmouth's anniversary by adopting on April 29 the following resolution: "Resolved by the House of Representatives (the Senate concurring), That the Congress send congratulations and greetings to Dartmouth College on the occasion of the two hundredth anniversary of its founding, and extends the hope of the people of the United States that Dartmouth College will continue to grow and prosper in centuries yet to come."

While the approaching bicentennial was very much to the fore in College thinking, a potentially explosive situation was developing with regard to black students at Dartmouth. The Afro-American Society presented to the administration and certain faculty chairmen a letter that called upon the College to address the concerns of black students and then went on to list nineteen proposals to which the administration was expected to respond within a month, by April 3. Mindful of Afro-American agitation on other campuses, but primarily because of Dartmouth's genuine commitment to equal opportunity, as evidenced by acceptance of the McLane report, President Dickey and other officers of the College took the AAS letter seriously and promptly began a series of meetings with black student spokesmen. "As black students," the AAS letter stated, "one of our uppermost concerns is the College's social commitment to the black community as manifested in its recruitment and admissions policies and in the living circumstances of the black student on campus."

The nineteen things the Afro-American Society asked of the College were the following: (1) That at least 100 or 11% of each incoming freshman class, beginning with the Class of 1973, be composed of

Afro-Americans. (2) That the Admissions Office publicize and implement a pledge to modify admissions standards to accord with the socio-educational deprivation of the black community. (3) That ten to fifteen black students not meeting admissions standards under #1 be enrolled as "special students" with the option of entering a regular degree program if their performance proved satisfactory. (4) That the College hire a black admissions officer whose major duties would be the recruitment of black students. (5) That one black student each term be released from normal academic obligations, in order to work as a full-time assistant to the new admissions officer in recruitment of black students. (6) That Bridge Program students have the option of distributive course credit for summer courses preceding matriculation, if those courses are taught by Dartmouth professors. (7) That the Bridge Program be expanded to as many students as would benefit from it. (8) That the College hire a black guidance counselor who would counsel black students and assist them in their academic and psychological adjustments on campus. (9) That one black student each term be released from normal academic obligations, in order to work full time with the black guidance counselor. (10) That the financial aid office devise a form and a system of awarding financial aid packages geared to the socio-economic realities of the black family. (11) That adequate financial aid be assured each entering black student, on the basis of need. (12) That College rules and regulations creating a negative distinction between financial aid and non-financial aid students be eliminated. (13) That financial aid be independent of a student's academic standing, except in cases of flagrant neglect. (14) That the Afro-American Society be given a minimum annual operating fund of $5,000 and that subsequent financial arrangements be handled through the Tucker Foundation. (15) That a new site for an Afro-American Center be found before the present College Street site was eliminated to make way for College expansion, and that a black architect be hired for any new center that is built. (16) That the Afro-American Society have as much autonomy as every other recognized undergraduate organization, and that it be allowed to sponsor athletic teams in intramural sports. (17) That a "Black Studies" major be developed and offered by September 1970, and that instructors in the major include black persons who might not have the conventional requirements for college professorships, but who would be knowledgeable and articulate in the experiences of black people. (18) That the College make greater efforts to recruit black academicians, particularly for the urban-studies program. (19) That there be established a separate judiciary committee to deal with disciplinary cases involving black students.

To discuss these requests with representatives of the Afro-American Society, President Dickey named Provost Rieser, Dean Seymour, Dean Dey of the Tucker Foundation, and three faculty committee chairmen. More than a month of meetings ensued, with both sides showing a spirit of cooperation that finally produced an agreement that did not give the blacks all they asked for, but did go a long way toward shaping a new program supported by the Afro-American Society. The one point on which the College negotiators stood firm was that although adjustments and new initiatives were possible and reasonable, especially in connection with recruiting and admissions, nothing could be allowed to lower the standards of academic performance or the worth of a Dartmouth degree. The College pointed out that some of the conditions demanded by the Afro-American Society were essentially in existence already or were being developed in keeping with recommendations from the Committee on Equal Opportunity. Samuel W. Smith, a black graduate, had been hired as an admissions officer before the AAS letter was received, and the College for some time had been seeking to increase the number of blacks on the faculty. The final package of agreements, including the recruiting and admission of more black students, creation of a standing committee on equal opportunity, and establishment of an Afro-American Studies Program, was approved at a meeting of the full faculty on April 16. This was a decided turning-point in the place of black students at Dartmouth and has been the foundation of that relationship ever since.

The College's official response to the original AAS letter was an April 12 letter of its own, in which it answered each of the nineteen proposals. This prompted the Afro-American Society to write again, saying in part: "We are also encouraged by the fact that the College has recognized the urgency of our proposals and has seen fit to react positively and substantively as befits an institution of Dartmouth's character and quality. . . . We are confident that our present relationship, born of mutual awareness and sensitivity to solutions to the problems and needs of black people in America, will preclude even the consideration of violence and confrontation by any sector of the College community. . . . We are further confident that the past weeks have exhibited a spirit of cooperation that should make Dartmouth a model to which other institutions can turn for guidance."

In addition to the letter responding to the AAS proposals, item by item, the negotiating committee sent a letter from President Dickey reviewing what had already been done or was planned under the College's equal opportunity program, and expressing understanding of the problems faced by black students in a predominantly white college. As he saw it, the President wrote, "The specific concerns currently being discussed deal broadly with the need for more black students, more attention to black studies and culture in the programs of the College, more black faculty and staff personnel, and the desire on the part of your Society for more opportunities to further 'black identity' in the College community." He would not go back beyond the work of the committee on equal opportunity as appointed by the Trustees in April of 1968, he added, but "it is due a lot of people to say parenthetically that the College's concern and concrete efforts in a number of the specific areas as well as in the basic work of eliminating racial and religious discrimination from the campus go back well before your day." An intensified search for qualified black students, he reported, had resulted in two hundred black applicants for the current year, compared with ninety-four the previous year and thirty-nine five years ago. The most difficult problem of all to solve promptly, President Dickey told the Afro-American Society, was the development of "a substantial segment of qualified, mature black faculty and staff personnel." But he promised that efforts to find them would be redoubled. Finally, regarding opportunities to further black identity in the community, he offered the College's cooperation, but he pointed out that something like the Afro-American Cultural Center could not be operated on a segregated basis, because of the College's own historic principles and the federal law barring discrimination on the basis of race, color, or religion.

The Afro-American "confrontation" was something wholly apart from the agitation over ROTC fomented and kept alive by the Dartmouth chapter of Students for a Democratic Society; and the spirit in which it was settled was far different from the force used by SDS in an attempt to get its way. The seizure of Parkhurst Hall by SDS adherents on the afternoon of May 6 was one of the most traumatic experiences in the history of the College and was especially depressing for President Dickey. This has been covered in the chapter on student dissent in the Sixties and is mentioned here to place it in proper chronological order and to underscore the mature way in which the Afro-American issue was handled.

The student uprising in May and its aftermath were unfortunate in that they took so much of the time and nervous energy of College officials on the eve of the first big bicentennial event, the Commencement of June 1969. But for Dartmouth the long-awaited bicentennial was of such magnitude in the history of the institution that nothing could detract from it. The anniversary year officially opened on the afternoon of Saturday, June 14, 1969, when Lord and Lady Dartmouth, newly arrived from England, unveiled near Hopkins Center a bronze plaque recording the occasion of their visit. It was only the second time in two hundred years that an Earl of Dartmouth had visited the College. The first was in 1904 when the seventh Earl, accompanied by the Countess of Dartmouth and their daughter, Lady Dorothy, came to lay the cornerstone of a new Dartmouth Hall, after the original building had been destroyed by fire. He was the grandfather of the now-visiting Earl, the Rt. Hon. Gerald Humphry Legge, ninth in the line of Legges who held the title. Trustee Charles Zimmerman, chairman of the bicentennial committee, welcomed Lord and Lady Dartmouth at the afternoon ceremony, and greetings were then extended by Lloyd Brace, chairman of the Board of Trustees; Provost Rieser, on behalf of the faculty; Norman Jacobs, president of the graduating class; and Howland H. Sargeant, president of the Dartmouth Alumni Council. President Dickey at the conclusion of his brief remarks presented a gold casting of the Dartmouth Bicentennial Medal to Lord Dartmouth, who then spoke about the relations between the College and his family and read a letter from his aunt, Lady Dorothy Meynell, recalling her visit to Dartmouth in 1904. At the conclusion of his remarks, Lord Dartmouth said that he and Lady Dartmouth would like to present to the College a 200th anniversary gift from his family, whereupon he uncovered a large and handsome silver cup that had been made for the fourth Earl, some 120 years ago. President Dickey promptly named it the Lord and Lady Dartmouth Bicentennial Cup, and said it would join the Wentworth Bowl as a treasured possession of the College. The time had come for the unveiling of the Bicentennial Plaque, and this was done in consort by the two guests of honor from England. After Mr. Dickey had read the wording of the plaque, Chairman Zimmerman declared the Bicentennial Year officially opened and gave the signal for the raising of the Bicentennial Flag, which was to fly over the campus during the anniversary year and then be replaced by the College flag. Lord Dartmouth was surrounded by members of the audience as the afternoon ceremony broke up, and he seemed as pleased to chat with them as they were to meet him.

The evening part of the opening day was billed as a Fanfare. After aerial bombs and ringing bells had summoned the crowd, there was a torchlight parade around the campus, ending in front of Hopkins Center, where Governor Walter R. Peterson by proclamation declared the day to be Dartmouth Day in New Hampshire. Songs by the glee club and a fireworks display led to the climax of the evening. In the center of the campus, a giant hot-air balloon was inflated and, with its owner, Ralph W. Burgard '49, in the gondola, was sent aloft to float over the green with spotlights on it.

The weather outlook for Commencement morning was not favorable, but the graduating class, being desirous, like all classes before it, to have the exercises outdoors, urged College officials to take a chance on Baker Library lawn. It was the wrong decision. Only the class valedictorian was able to speak before the rain came pelting down. A half-hour recess was declared while everyone moved to the dry indoors of Leverone Field House, where five thousand seats were ready for just such an eventuality. The one good thing about the downpour was that a protest demonstration planned by SDS was thrown into confusion by the move to the field house and never did get itself reorganized. Governor Nelson Rockefeller delivered the Commencement address, and when he took his place at the podium a group of seniors, perhaps thirty or so, stood and turned their backs to him. Mr. Rockefeller took this in good humor and suggested that the men involved sit down with their backs to him so the people behind them could see.

The Governor was one of eight persons who received honorary degrees at the Bicentennial Commencement. His Doctorate of Civil Laws was added to the LL.D. conferred upon him in 1957, which made him and Robert Frost the only two men in Dartmouth history to receive double honorary doctorates from the College. Lord and Lady Dartmouth stood together to receive honorary Doctorates of Laws, the degree conferred also on President Kingman Brewster of Yale, who presented bicentennial greetings from the university of which Eleazar Wheelock was a graduate in 1733, and on Trustee-Emeritus Harvey Hood, who was chosen as the epitome of alumni service and generosity to Dartmouth. A certain bicentennial symbolism attached to all the honorary degrees. Professor John H. Wolfenden received the Doctorate of Science as representative of all the faculty members who had taught Dartmouth students for two centuries. The Reverend Lawrence L. Durgin, Class of 1940, received the Doctorate of Divinity as one who shared the Congregational ministry and religious vision of Eleazar Wheelock. Frell M. Owl, Class of 1927, a Cherokee Indian, received the Doctorate of Humane Letters for his work with the Bureau of Indian Affairs and for a life that validated Dartmouth's founding purpose.

Knowing that he was presiding over his last Commencement, President Dickey had mixed emotions. The first half of 1969, with its campus turbulence, had been a great strain on him and he was ready to turn the presidential burden over to someone else. But there was a lot of the Bicentennial Year yet to come, the Third Century Fund to complete, and his successor to be chosen. In his valedictory to the graduating class, John Dickey could not stay away from the subject akin to the one he had used at Convocation at the beginning of the college year. "The password at 1969 Commencements from coast to coast seems to be 'frustration'," he said. "The year itself, the world around, has been heaped high with frustration for everyone except perhaps our intrepid explorers of space and even they escaped only by 'getting away from it all' as no mortal man has ever done before.

"However it may be with astronauts, 'getting away from it all' is not the way out for the rest of us. You and I who bet our lives on awareness are required to know that few men walk the earth worthily, without learning that frustrations are mostly for managing, occasionally for banishing, but not for taking out on the other fellow." Was this an oblique way of saying that he felt the frustrations of student protesters had unfairly been taken out on him and other officers of the College?

His final words to the Class of 1969 were: "And now, as I prepare shortly to follow you, I bid you to join me in leaving our frustrations behind, to discover that in the Dartmouth fellowship there need be no parting."

After the Commencement exercises, President and Mrs. Dickey were hosts at a large luncheon party for the honorary degree recipients, Trustees, College officers, and guests. Lady Dartmouth, a well-known figure in the civic life of London, spoke at the luncheon and showed that she had acquired a good deal of the Dartmouth spirit during her short visit. A feminist somewhat ahead of her time, she was a lively and colorful figure at the events that launched the Bicentennial Year, and the women of Hanover remembered for a long time the stunning assortment of hats she wore during the weekend.

The Dartmouth Trustees had business as well as bicentennial events to attend to during the Commencement weekend. The most important action taken at the June meeting was the adoption of the concept of "total return" for determining the amount of money from invested funds to be used annually for operating expenses. The traditional procedure for countless years had been to use only the annual yield from College investments. The new concept was to add the appreciation in market value of investments and arrive at a "total return" for the year. With this information in hand, the Trustees were in a position to decide what percentage of return (usually higher than the percentage of yield alone) could be used for current operating expense or be budgeted for the following year. Treasurer John Meck, in writing about this new financial action, reported that for the ten years prior to 1969–70 the average yield rate was 3.6 percent, compared with a total-return rate of 10.7 percent. The Trustees chose 4.9 percent as a prudent rate in determining the amount of money for current operations to be taken from invested funds. Not all invested funds figured in this determination; the investments of life-income trust funds and some other special and restricted funds were excluded. At the time the Dartmouth Trustees adopted the total-return policy, it was being used by a limited number of educational and charitable institutions, but was being considered by a great many more. It has since become a prevailing form of financial management in the educational world and is still in effect at Dartmouth. Some institutions chose to apply the total-return concept to only a part of their invested funds, but Dartmouth elected an across-the-board approach, and this was supported in a Ford Foundation study of 1969.

John Dickey's twenty-fourth and final Convocation took place on September 22, 1969, and had he chosen to, he could have made this last gathering with the entire student body and faculty an emotional farewell occasion. But his address did not deviate from his characteristic pattern of dealing with serious issues of the College and the world. The audience was well aware, however, that within a few months, after the actual December 13 Charter Day, Mr. Dickey would be turning the presidency over to someone else. At the conclusion of his address he was given a prolonged, standing ovation that brought emotion to the occasion after all. In a reference to his retirement, near the end, President Dickey said: "At least until the hour strikes for me to be a little more 'retiring' in duty and utterance, you of the student body and you, my colleagues of our four faculties, may count on my company in mounting new responses of learning, to get at the great issues of peace and social justice promptly, adequately, and as humans whose ultimate commitment is to *both* the purposes and the processes of man's ancient quest for a civilized existence."

The title of the Convocation address was "The Transcending Great Issues," which Mr. Dickey defined as peace on earth and the cause of equal opportunity. Contrary to his expectations of twenty-five years ago, he said, peace was still "circumstanced with dark and doubt," but things were brighter for realizing equal opportunity. Of the latter, he said, ". . . we now begin a year in which Dartmouth's founding mission to the educationally disadvantaged of this land may come closer to fulfillment than ever before—closer, even, than in the heyday of Eleazar's hopes for his great design. Americans of every circumstance and color are today represented in the community of the College, as never before."

In any review of the major accomplishments of the Dickey administration, the Great Issues Course is always mentioned prominently. John Dickey himself always included it, and it is not without interest that in this last Convocation address he used Great Issues in its title and included this paragraph in his text: "From 1946 on, for a score of postwar years—long before 'relevance' became a cliché of educational philosophy—Dartmouth pioneered an institution-wide effort to make all her contemporary graduates a little more aware that 'great issues' are not irrelevant to liberal learning, but are, rather, the ladder on which humans climb to their liberation. That effort was little enough, compared to the endemic unawareness of those days, but in its way and its time it pioneered an approach to today's relevance."

The College's two-hundredth year opened with a record enrollment and no space to spare. The largest-ever entering class of 852 men, coupled with a reduction by forty in the number of students studying away from the campus and the one-year enrollment of seventy women as part of the ten-college exchange program, made the fall-term residential population exceptionally large (142 greater than the year before) and necessitated some trick logistics to get everyone housed. The grand total of all students was 3,878, made up of 3,252 undergraduates and 626 graduate students in the College and associated schools. As a result of the stepped-up recruiting efforts recommended by the McLane report and the work of the Afro-American Society, the freshman class included ninety blacks, a number far greater than the twenty-nine in the previous entering class and the seventeen and twelve in the two classes before that. The seventy coed exchange students, mostly juniors, were given a dormitory of their own, Cohen Hall. The largest contingent (twenty-five) came from Smith, followed by Mt. Holyoke, Vassar, and Wheaton. Courses involving the Hopkins Center were heavily elected and so were computer courses not available at the women's colleges. The exchange part of the ten-college program was a bit unbalanced. Only fifteen Dartmouth students elected to spend a term or more at participating colleges, with Smith (seven) and Vassar (five) the top choices.

Prior to the beginning of the bicentennial year in September, word reached the College that all three ROTC programs would terminate their units at Dartmouth after varying periods of time that would permit students to complete their training. The Air Force announced that its ROTC unit would end in June 1971, thus enabling juniors to finish the two-year program in which they were enrolled. The Army set the summer of 1970 for closing out its ROTC unit. Juniors would be allowed to double up in Army courses in 1969–70 and, thus, be qualified for commissions when they graduated in 1971. Sophomores could complete the Army's two-year basic course, but would have to transfer elsewhere for the final two years of advanced training. The Navy, with the longest extension of all, announced that it would honor its commitments to all Dartmouth men enrolled, including the twenty-eight freshmen who began the four-year Navy ROTC program in the fall of 1969. Following the faculty vote to reduce the status of ROTC and the student seizure of Parkhurst Hall, the Trustees had voted to bring ROTC to a close after meeting the College's commitment to the services. Summer action by the Army, Navy, and Air Force followed soon after this decision by the College.

The Trustees at their October meeting heard a report from the Andres Committee on restructuring the board's standing committees and approved in principle the inclusion of faculty, students, and Alumni Council members on some of them. However, at a meeting of the Dartmouth Campus Conference the following month, there was little enthusiasm for this proposal as a way of improving the governance of the College or of establishing closer working relationships among all parts of the institution. The faculty and student representatives on the DCC were as one in wanting more power in decision-making, rather than token membership on some of the board's committees. An actual enlargement of student participation in the College's governance was effected with the election of the first student member of the Dartmouth Alumni Council. This honor went to Brent Coffin '70 of Denver, Colorado, chairman of the bicentennial student committee and student head of the ABC program during the summer.

The growing push in the Sixties for more "student power" was related especially to social rules and the hearing of disciplinary cases. A student victory of some magnitude was achieved when the Trustees approved "home rule" in the regulation of dormitory life. This gave the resident council of each dormitory responsibility for "providing a quiet and orderly place in which to live and study and a suitable atmosphere for the entertainment of all guests." The Trustee action, taken upon recommendation of a special faculty committee, in effect ended parietals, which specified the hours when women guests could be enter-tained in student rooms. The Trustees were not about to set the sky as the limit, however, and they emphasized that there was still a regulation that students conduct themselves at all times in an orderly way and in conformance with the laws of New Hampshire. The final cautionary note was that the board reserved the right to reconsider "home rule" at any time.

Among October's noteworthy happenings, the General Electric Company gave Dartmouth title to more than $2.5-million worth of computer hardware, which the College and the company had been using cooperatively for three years in order to develop ways in which the computer could become accessible to large numbers of students and faculty. During that three-year period with the GE-635 computer the time-sharing system, pioneered at Dartmouth, was developed with great success, so that at the time of the General Electric gift nearly fifty colleges and schools were linked to the Kiewit computer center by teletype and were assured of almost simultaneous use of the Dartmouth facility. The National Science Foundation was helpful in providing a substantial part of the funds for the experiment, granting $142,500 in 1967, when twenty New England secondary schools were linked to the time-sharing computer system, and another $164,200 in 1968, when the first colleges were added. At the time that General Electric made the GE-635 system an outright gift, rather than a loan, it was announced that a new three-year agreement would continue the partnership between the College and the company. The College agreed to share its research findings with General Electric, and the company agreed to supply personnel to work with Kiewit in developing programs to meet the growing interest in being part of a time-sharing system. The international reputation of the Dartmouth system was attested in October by the three-day visit of eight Japanese government and business leaders, including three members of the Japanese Diet, in order to learn about the student and research programs operating in Hanover. Toshihiro Kennoki, former Japanese Minister of Education, was so impressed not only with the computer program, but with the College itself, that he said, on departure, that he was thinking of using Dartmouth as a blueprint for a new university that Prime Minister Sato had charged him to create in Japan.

In mid-October the College was host to one of the most distinguished groups of scientists ever to gather in Hanover. The occasion was the annual fall meeting of the National Academy of Sciences, scheduled as a tribute to Dartmouth in its bicentennial year. Professor Walter H. Stockmayer, an Academy member, was the local program chairman. Three public symposia dealt with chemical and biological warfare, manned versus unmanned space exploration, and new discoveries about water. At other sessions, papers were given by thirty of the seventy-five or more Academy members attending the meeting. Senator Thomas J. McIntyre, who was invited to give the traditional public address on science and society, made headlines when he departed from his subject and called for this country's immediate withdrawal from Vietnam.

At the concluding session of the three-day NAS meeting, Dr. William Shockley, Stanford professor of physics and a Nobel laureate, was scheduled to give a paper entitled "Offset Analysis Description of Racial Differences," enlarging upon his notorious and controversial thesis that the black race may be genetically inferior to the white race in intellectual ability. Under NAS rules, any member was entitled to deliver, at his own request, a paper at a regular meeting. But Professor Shockley was not given the chance to speak. After his introduction, a group of about thirty Dartmouth students, mostly black, began a sustained hand-clapping that drowned him out. The audience included only a few Academy members and was predominantly from the College. After efforts by Provost Rieser and others to stop the clapping failed, the session was adjourned and the chairman accepted the Shockley presentation in written form.

The aftermath of this incident was a strong difference of opinion about the culpability of the black protesters and the kind of disciplinary action, if any, that should be taken against them. Seventeen black students, the hard core of clappers who refused to stop, were charged with violation of the College's regulation on freedom of expression and dissent. The Judicial Advisory Committee for Black Students (JAC), which had come into existence in the spring, as a body to advise the College Committee on Standing and Conduct in cases involving black students, recommended to Dean Brewster that no penalties be assessed and that charges be dropped. The JAC argued that Dr. Shockley was trying to slander black people in a way that would endanger their status at Dartmouth and that the students' reaction was understandable and ought not to be condemned. The Committee on Standing and Conduct did not wholly agree. While respecting the JAC report, it found the disruptive conduct of the seventeen students a clear violation of the College's stated and well-known policy and, therefore, placed them all on probation for one term. If it were not for the extenuating circumstances, the committee stated, the discipline would have been more severe. This decision led to the resignation of all the JAC members, both students and faculty, who felt they had been arbitrarily ignored, despite several weeks of work and a 29-page report. The administration, on the other hand, was determined to uphold rigorously the College regulation on freedom of expression and dissent. President Dickey strongly backed this position and, as has been mentioned earlier, he was critical of a portion of the faculty for not being more outspoken in the defense of free speech on the campus. Another aspect of the Shockley aftermath was the disappointment of students that they hadn't had the full say in determining whether the seventeen should be disciplined. This led to much rhetoric about unequal justice and student distrust of the administration. It was, in essence, another example of the push for "student power" and the difficulty of getting it to the extent that students desired.

If black students were disappointed in the resolution of the Shockley incident, they had reason to take satisfaction in the introduction that fall of a Black Studies Program. A black alumnus, Robert G. McGuire III, came from Franconia College to be coordinator of the new program, which in general outline was put together in the spring by the Afro-American Studies Committee as part of the agreement that had been reached between the College and the Afro-American Society. The program, as described in the Bulletin of Regulations and Courses, was "designed to provide students with an understanding of the historical, economic, political, social, and artistic experience of people of African ancestry in the New World and Africa." It did not constitute a major, but students completing six course credits in the program would be granted certification in Black Studies upon graduation. In addition to relevant courses already existing in a number of departments, four new courses were created for the program. They dealt with the South in American history, urban economics, black America, and the black experience in theater and film. Field study in black, urban locations was to be part of the program, and Professor McGuire looked ahead to the possibility of sending a group of ten or twelve students to Sierra Leone to spend a term at a college there.

Anticipated dates do happen, and so December 13, 1969, the 200th birthday Dartmouth had been thinking about for fifteen years or more, did finally arrive, not in grandiose fashion, but with the air that attaches itself to something of historic importance. If the students had been on campus, rather than away for the recess between terms, the celebration of the actual bicentennial day might have begun at the crack of dawn and taken a noisier form, but as things were planned, the uncorking of Dartmouth's joy was delayed until evening, when a huge Charter Day dinner was staged in Leverone Field House. It was an event to be remembered. With all its space, the field house could accommodate only a "representative" guest list—which still numbered 1,200 persons, seated at 150 candle-lit tables. The Dartmouth Board of Trustees and the Alumni Council advanced their joint January meeting to the Charter Day weekend, and members of the board sat on a raised dais, amidst banners, shields depicting the fifteen planning years, and enlarged photographs of all the Dartmouth Presidents, from Eleazar Wheelock to John Dickey. In the audience were alumni class presidents, club presidents, and Third Century Fund area chairmen, along with men and women representing the faculty and administration, the staff, students, the town of Hanover, and friends of the College. Six college presidents were guests, bearing greetings from sister institutions. Before the evening was over, the bicentennial dinner had taken on the character of an enthusiastic and affectionate tribute to President Dickey on the eve of his retirement.

Trustee Zimmerman, chairman of the bicentennial committee, was toastmaster at the dinner. The first person he called upon was Third Century Fund Chairman Thompson, who announced that the fund had received $42.6-million in gifts and pledges toward its $51-million goal and that there could no longer be any doubt that the campaign would be fully successful by its closing date of June 15. He injected a bit of drama in his report by at first announcing a $39.8-million total, including an anonymous alumni contribution of $2.5-million. But, he went on, just that day Dartmouth had received two birthday gifts—one of $1.5-million and the other of $1.3-million—which boosted the total to $42.6-million. The first of these two gifts was made anonymously; the second was from Mr. and Mrs. Thomas G. Murdough, who had previously given $700,000 to the Third Century Fund. The funds they contributed were later used for constructing the Murdough Center, linking the Tuck and Thayer Schools. Mr. Murdough was retired vice chairman of the American Hospital Supply Corporation, whose founder and chairman, Foster G. McGaw, had with his wife shortly before given $1.5-million for a new medical science building.

A high point of the dinner was the announcement that President Dickey had been named the first Bicentennial Professor of Public Affairs, an action taken, without his awareness of it, by the Trustees only the day before. (He was to assume the professorship upon his retirement as President and hold it until his full retirement at the age of sixty-five). Professor Francis W. Gramlich, senior member of the Faculty Committee Advisory to the President, made the announcement of Mr. Dickey's faculty appointment, following which Professor Frank Smallwood, Director of the Dartmouth Public Affairs Center, presented Mr. Dickey with the key to the office being held for him in Silsby Hall.

The after-dinner program at this point developed into a flood of presentations to John Dickey. Harvey Hood, honorary chairman of the bicentennial committee, gave him a gold casting of the bicentennial medal, the twin of the one presented to Lord Dartmouth at Commencement in June. Representing the student body, Paul Gambaccini '70 virtually took the gold medal back, by presenting Mr. Dickey with a bronze version and drawing a roar of laughter from him by telling him that he was not really expected to keep the gold one—which Dartmouth would be glad to add to its prized possessions in the College Archives. Then came Judge William H. Timbers, president of the Alumni Council, who presented two bound volumes of personal letters from Trustees, former Trustees, Alumni Council members, and honorary-degree recipients who, he said, "want you to know that what you have done and been for twenty-four years has enriched us all."

As spokesman for all the non-academic, non-administrative personnel of the College, Frederick Schleipman, an instrument maker at the Thayer School of Engineering, thanked President Dickey for the respect and human consideration he had always shown toward staff workers. He presented to the President and to Mrs. Dickey a replica he had made of the sundial given to Eleazar Wheelock in 1773 for his garden. The audience was especially delighted by the tribute Mr. Schleipman paid to Mrs. Dickey, by saying that her support and influence behind President Dickey were important factors in the greatness he had brought to the College.

Lloyd Brace, chairman of the Board of Trustees, then spoke in behalf of the Trustees and gave Mr. Dickey a smaller version of a large color portrait by the famous Canadian photographer Yousuf Karsh, that was to hang in Parkhurst Hall, along with the oil portraits there of his predecessors. The Trustees, Mr. Brace said, wanted to make sure that when the Dickey accomplishments are appraised during future generations, Dartmouth men and women would be able to know what he looked like. Some of those accomplishments were recounted near the end of an historical chronicle of all of Dartmouth's presidents, which had been written by Ralph Nading Hill and narrated that night by drama professor Rod Alexander. The portraits of the twelve presidents, hung in the field house for the dinner, were spotlighted one by one, in turn, during the narration. The Dickey achievements, the narrative stated, "are unprecedented in the history of the College, but there has been an even larger growth in the values of Dartmouth's presence in the educational world."

President Dickey, invited to make some informal remarks at the close of the dinner program, thanked those who had heaped gifts and praise upon him, but made it evident that he prized above everything else the Bicentennial Professorship that came to him as a complete surprise. "If God had asked me what I wanted most, this would have been it," he said. He wished that his part in the Charter Day program could simply be silence, but since that was not vouchsafed to him, he would, he declared, "speak only a few pre-retirement words from the vantage of a no-longer-young man who learned much of what he thinks he knows sitting on a hot stove for twenty-five years, striving to make it hotter even as he counseled cooling down the rhetoric of our crowded, over-heated academic kitchens." He listed some serious subjects he might talk about and said, "Each of us might put these questions differently, but if there is anything I dare not not say to you after a quarter of a century of on-the-job learning, it is that these questions are more at issue in our daily doing than in any inaugural or farewell address. However these questions are put and however they are answered by any one generation, past, present or future, they must constantly be answered afresh if this place is to remain as it has now been for two hundred years a very special institutional person in the wide, wide world of institutions. That I take it is the meaning that abides in our motto *Vox clamantis in deserto*; that I take it is the abiding joy the Dartmouth family motto enjoins on us: *Gaudet tentamine virtus*.

"I cannot yet say my cup runneth over, but it surely is filled to what would be an unseemly overflowing if I were to attempt on behalf of today's Dartmouth, and the Dickeys, to say more than thank you, good and true friends, for lives sustained and lives enriched beyond any man's knowing, let alone my saying tonight."

The day before the Charter Day celebration, the Trustees and Alumni Council at their joint meeting devoted almost the entire time to hearing an interim report on coeducation, as presented by the special committee established under Chairman Dudley Orr to examine the likely developments at Dartmouth during the first decade of the College's third century. The main presentation was made in great detail by Professor John Kemeny, who headed the subcommittee on academic models. No conclusions were offered; the study committee was intent upon informing the Trustees and Council members about the sort of questions it was wrestling with and the way it was going about the job of seeking answers. Professor Kemeny presented three possible models concerning enrollment and the ratio of men to women, and he went on to discuss related problems of housing, dining facilities, faculty size, financial aid, and social life. He concluded by saying that Dartmouth had in the past not been afraid to go against the national trend. "We will look at all possible solutions and we will not copy other people," he said. "We will not be pressured into a solution, but we will try to work out Dartmouth's own destiny."

Mr. Timbers, the Council president, emphasized the importance of the coeducation issue to the alumni and recommended that their views be given proper weight. He reminded the meeting that whatever the recommendations of the study committee, the ultimate authority for making a decision rested with the Board of Trustees. He was confident, he said, that the alumni would back that decision if they knew that they had been fully consulted and if they realized the complexity of the question and the professional skill that had gone into its analysis.

The Trustees at their regular winter meeting (held one month ahead of schedule because of Charter Day) had to deal with the unpleasant news that the operating deficit for the current year would approximate $500,000, on top of a 1968–69 deficit of $603,000—the largest in the history of the College. In planning for the Third Century Fund it was expected that there would be a slowing down of operating income, so one component of the fund was expendable money, for a five-year period, that would cover compensation increases and other programs until the Third Century Fund benefits began to be realized and annual resources resumed their normal growth. Deficits were a new experience for the College, after eighteen consecutive years of operating in the black. They also were an indication that Dartmouth, at the beginning of its third century, would indeed be facing inflation and new financial pressures, like nearly all other institutions of higher education. The Trustees had raised tuition by $150 for 1969–70, bringing it to $2,350, and at their December meeting they voted another increase of $200 for 1970–71, along with a $100 jump in board and an average increase of $25 in room rent. That brought the basic cost of tuition, room, and board to $3,800, still within the lower range of charges among the Ivy Group colleges. Primarily for financial reasons, the Trustees also voted a halt in the Congregation of the Arts summer programs in music and theater, and they asked that the hiatus be used to make a study of what the scope of Hopkins Center offerings in the summer should be. Provost Rieser pointed out that the Congregation of the Arts had grown into something much greater than was foreseen when it was inaugurated in 1963, and its expense, requiring the use of general College funds, had grown accordingly. What was needed at that point, he said, was a period of planning, rather than of performance.

The naming of a new President is always a turning point in Dartmouth history, and such a point was reached January 23, 1970, when Lloyd D. Brace, chairman of the Board of Trustees, announced that

John Dickey's successor would be Professor John G. Kemeny of the College faculty. Mr. Kemeny, holder of the Albert Bradley Third Century Professorship and a man of formidable reputation in the mathematics world, had been in the thick of educational planning and development at Dartmouth ever since he arrived from Princeton, as full professor, at the age of twenty-seven. As chairman of the mathematics department for twelve years he had built the department into one of the best in the country, recruited an outstanding faculty, and initiated a doctoral program in mathematics, the first Ph.D. offering in the College proper. Beyond the campus, during this same period, he was a leading figure in the Mathematical Association of America, chairing its panel on teacher training and its Northeast Section, and serving on its board of governors. He also was chairman (1957–60) of the U.S. Commission on Mathematical Instruction. His book *Introduction to Finite Mathematics* was widely used in colleges and secondary schools.

As his mathematical studies shifted from logic to probability theory, Professor Kemeny became intensely interested in the potential—even the indispensability—of the computer in solving quantitative problems. This led to a second chapter of his educational fame. With Professor Kurtz of the mathematics department he was co-inventor of the simplified computer language BASIC and, then, of the time-sharing system that established Dartmouth in the forefront of colleges giving all their students the privilege of using the computer in everyday educational work.

When Professor Kemeny joined the Dartmouth faculty in 1953, he came as a teacher of both philosophy and mathematics. At Princeton, after being an instructor in mathematics, specializing in logic, he shifted to the philosophy department, and he was Bicentennial Preceptor in Philosophy when invited to Dartmouth. The biographical background he brought with him was most unusual. A native of Budapest, Hungary, he came to this country with his parents in 1940, in order to escape the Nazis. Despite his limited knowledge of English at the outset, he graduated from high school three years later, not yet seventeen, at the top of his class. As a Princeton undergraduate, he spent a year and a half in the Army and was assigned to serve as a mathematician in the theoretical division of the Manhattan Project at Los Alamos, New Mexico. He still managed to graduate from Princeton on schedule, in

1947, *summa cum laude*. While studying for his Ph.D. at Princeton, he was selected to be research assistant to Albert Einstein at Princeton's Institute for Advanced Study. With this background as well as Mr. Kemeny's Dartmouth record in mind, Trustee Brace, when he announced his election to the Dartmouth presidency, called him "one of the truly creative minds in America today."

It was widely accepted that President Kemeny would sustain the primacy of academic excellence established by John Dickey, also the emphasis on a professional faculty devoted to research as well as teaching. His academic experience at Dartmouth aside, Mr. Kemeny had accepted many responsibilities that gave him an uncommon acquaintance with administrative affairs of the College. He had a key role in designing the three-three academic year, and he was, at the time of his election, coordinator of educational plans and development, chairman of the College Committee on Equal Opportunity, a leading member of the Trustee-appointed committee to study coeducation and other questions facing the College in the Seventies, and chairman of the foundations committee of the Third Century Fund (in which role he achieved great success as a fund-raiser).

President Dickey's statement about President-elect Kemeny was full of praise for his Dartmouth colleague. "It is Dartmouth's great good fortune, and genuine happiness for me personally," he said, "that an outstanding member of our community is to be the next President of the College.

"Professor Kemeny knows well both the educational world and this campus and both have the highest regard for him as one of America's foremost teacher-scholars. He has served Dartmouth with singular distinction as a teacher, as the founder of today's fine Department of Mathematics, and as the moving spirit in establishing here one of the nation's pioneering computer centers.

"He is widely acquainted among the alumni and he has been one of the most effective workers in the current Third Century Fund campaign.

"Professor Kemeny has long since demonstrated his devotion to this College, and I make bold to assure him that all sectors of the Dartmouth community will make a response in kind to his leadership. It will be a high privilege of Mrs. Dickey and myself to be part of that response to the thirteenth President and his wife."

In speaking of the presidential search, in a taped interview some years later, Mr. Dickey recalled that the Trustees wanted him to be more involved in the selection than he wanted to be, or thought he ought to be. He had refused to anoint anyone, but was willing to be a consultant. President Hopkins, in his opinion, had been too much involved in choosing his successor, even though that choice, Mr. Dickey would have been too modest to admit, had turned out to be exactly the right one for Dartmouth at that stage in its history. Mr. Dickey also recalled that he and the Trustees made sure that the faculty had more input in this search than had been true when the Hopkins presidency neared its end. Final authority rested with the Board of Trustees, and there was no give on that point, but the faculty had no reason this time to feel that they had not been fully represented in the search for Dartmouth's new president.

March 1, 1970, was picked as the date when John Kemeny would officially become President. Mr. Dickey had only a few duties of a major nature to carry out before leaving his office in Parkhurst Hall. One was to preside over his last faculty meeting. The faculty was ready for the occasion, and they welcomed him to their ranks as Bicentennial Professor of Public Affairs by toasting him in champagne and by expressing their sentiment in a resolution, read by Professor Finch on behalf of the Faculty Committee on Organization and Policy, that clearly showed the affection and high regard the faculty had for him. As a summing up of that relationship, the resolution deserves to be quoted in full:

"It is time for teachers to say thanks to a teacher. For twenty-five years you have instructed us in the strict curriculum of leadership. From those first faculty meetings in which, with patience and passion, you began to make us see the future of this institution as you saw it, to this last year, when in an hour of doubt and confusion, you spoke to us once more with courage and clarity, your premise has always been the necessity for excellence.

"From that premise you have made large demands upon us, and encouraged us to meet them. You have shared your concerns with us, and treated us as partner. Always you have sought to instill in us your conviction that our great issue was Dartmouth's greatness. Finally, when some of us went out in search of your successor, we heard testimony from all quarters that the Dartmouth presidency is a position of national importance because you have made it so.

"Today we welcome you to our ranks with pride. Your credentials are impressive; we know because we have taken your course. You have taught us, by precept and practice, to define our obligations to our college, to our students, and to each other. Now, as you leave the presidency, we recognize that during your years on this faculty we have all been apprenticed to a master, and we are grateful."

With College in session, undergraduates formed a large part of the audience of 2,500 persons who saw John Kemeny inaugurated as Dartmouth's thirteenth president in an hour-long ceremony in Alumni Gymnasium on Sunday afternoon, March 1, 1970. Greetings from Governor Peterson of New Hampshire, the traditional transfer of historic symbols of office, and the inaugural address made up the announced program; but a surprise addition, after Mr. Kemeny had been officially installed, was the conferring of Dartmouth honorary degrees upon both John and Christina Dickey. Judged by the volume and duration of applause, the honorary degrees conferred on the Dickeys had the approval of everyone present. There was special satisfaction in the honor paid to Mrs. Dickey, who as the First Lady of the College presided over the President's House for nearly a quarter of a century, dispensing both mass and individual hospitality and warming the hearts of the Dartmouth family, as her citation stated, "with a gentle presence, a quiet competence, and an unfailing sensitivity to the feelings of others." The degree of Doctor of Humane Letters was conferred upon her, President Kemeny said, with gratitude and affection.

The citation for John Dickey's honorary Doctorate of Laws was a long one; it serves, in fact, as something of a recapitulation of the major achievements of his presidency and as an assessment of the pivotal place the Dickey administration will always hold in Dartmouth history. This was the citation:

"A quarter of a century ago you, as your first official act, awarded an honorary degree to the eleventh President of Dartmouth College. That quarter century marked the greatest progress for this institution in its entire history.

"Trained in the law, public official turned educator, you brought to the presidency of the College convictions about the responsibilities of an educated man. Your first priority was to awaken Dartmouth students to the Great Issues of our society. While students initially disappointed you by their lack of commitment, you finally met a generation whose commitment to great issues is, to say the least, overwhelming.

"Aware that the quality of the Dartmouth experience depends primarily on the quality of its faculty, you set out to recruit a group of outstanding teacher-scholars. You succeeded in building an undergraduate faculty second to none, committed to undergraduate education and to the continuing growth of their disciplines.

"Realizing the historical importance of the professional schools of medicine, business, and engineering, you strengthened them and built ties to the arts and sciences. Under your leadership we have seen the completion of the university functions through the introduction of Ph.D. programs, carefully balanced to supplement but not dilute the College's primary commitment to undergraduate excellence.

"Master of the art of infusing others with your own enthusiasm, you set the course for reassessment of the 'liberating arts.' We have seen a long series of sweeping revisions moving towards greater diversity and independence in learning for all students.

"You saw the College through its first two capital fund drives and you will leave a significant number of new physical facilities that will serve Dartmouth through its Third Century. Most notable among these was your bold plan to house the creative arts in a splendid building that serves as a memorial to your predecessor.

"In addition, you found the time to lend your counsel to causes beyond the Hanover community. You fought for educational institutions, you lent your counsel to great foundations, your voice was influential in the conduct of your country's foreign relations, and you championed the cause of your beloved North Country.

"Beyond these achievements we must note your constant concern for human rights. In 1946 you served as a member of the President's Committee on Civil Rights. Later your courageous action to remove all traces of discrimination from the Dartmouth campus made an impact on the Nation. You were also one of the first voices to call for an effective program to help with the education of disadvantaged students. Your call of conscience to the educational world was answered with the creation of A Better Chance, that set the pattern for a significant social breakthrough. Both literally and figuratively, yours has been a booming voice 'of one crying in the wilderness'."

"Dartmouth College owes you a debt that can only be paid by the historian. But this debt, even if unpayable, must be acknowledged. Therefore, as a token of our indebtedness, it is my rare privilege on behalf of the Trustees and Faculty of Dartmouth College to bestow upon you the degree of Doctor of Laws, *honoris causa.*"

President Kemeny's years at Dartmouth and his prominent involvement in College affairs during those years greatly facilitated the transition from one administration to the next. Mr. Dickey, in one of his oral history interviews, recalled that as he neared the end of his presidency he refrained from making any major personnel changes, except for the appointment of a new Dean of the College, a post that needed to be filled promptly. He also recalled that a decision on the revival of the M.D. degree at the Medical School, which the Trustees had already approved in principle, could not be delayed until the new President took office. The problem of Medical School financing was inherited by his successor, and so was that of implementing the plan to establish a closer relationship between the Tuck and Thayer Schools. The very important question of coeducation also remained unsettled. The retiring and incoming Presidents discussed these matters and many others during the period between the announcement of Mr. Kemeny's election and his inauguration, and their being together in Hanover made the transfer of authority much easier than would normally have been the case.

To make sure that the President's House would be vacant for occupancy by the Kemeny family, the Dickeys took a month's vacation in the South immediately after the inauguration and then spent some time at their cottage in Swanton, Vermont, until they could move into the new home that was being built for them on Lyme Road in Hanover. In addition to being Bicentennial Professor of Public Affairs at Dartmouth, which did not at first involve a regular teaching schedule,

President Dickey accepted the invitation of the Council on Foreign Relations to be the Whitney H. Shepardson Senior Visiting Fellow for 1971–72. This involved taking up residence in New York City for one year, a period which he found very satisfying in giving him a chance to "retool himself," as he put it, in the field of foreign affairs and to concentrate again on American-Canadian relations, which he had been forced to neglect in his final years as President. He had edited *The United States and Canada* in 1964, and the studies he resumed after retirement resulted in a book of his own, *Canada and the American Presence*, published in 1975 by the Council on Foreign Relations, as well as articles for *Foreign Affairs* and its Canadian counterpart, *International Journal*. In the post-presidential period, Mr. Dickey also became a public member of the boards of the Putnam mutual-fund investment companies and a board member of the Charles F. Kettering Foundation. Similar opportunities offered to him were numerous, but he made a point of accepting only those in which he was genuinely interested. The retirement years were so full, he recalled in an oral-history interview, that he could say, "I've had the happy experience of not looking back."

When he reached the retirement that he had so greatly looked forward to, particularly after the turbulence of the late Sixties, John Dickey left behind him a presidential record of more than twenty-four years' duration—November 1, 1945 to March 1, 1970—which is now seen as a truly pivotal period in the history of Dartmouth College. Central to all, the College faced up to the fact that it was a small university in everything but name, and from that acceptance flowed many of the changes and much of the growth that led to the pronouncement, contained in his honorary degree citation, that "That quarter century marked the greatest progress for this institution in its entire history." John Dickey will be remembered as the President who brought Dartmouth to its bicentennial and into its third century, but what is more important is the imaginative leadership he gave to the College throughout the years leading to that historic event. Like William Jewett Tucker before him, he set forth a great design of rededication for the College, and all the Presidents, Trustees, administrators, faculty, and students who come after him will reap the benefit of what he managed to bring to reality.

Index

by Virginia L. Close

293

LIBRARY OF CONGRESS CATALOGING-IN-PUBLICATION DATA

Widmayer, Charles E.
   John Sloan Dickey: a chronicle of his presidency of Dartmouth
College / by Charles E. Widmayer.
       p.   cm.
   Includes index.
   ISBN 0–87451–553–X
   1. Dartmouth College—History—20th century.   2. Dickey, John
Sloan, 1907–   .   3. Dartmouth College—Presidents—Biography.
I. Title.
   LD1438.8.W7   1991
378.742'3—dc20   90–23942
                                                       CIP

This book is printed on acid-free paper
and meets the guidelines for permanence and durability
of the Committee on Production Guidelines for Book Longevity
of the Council on Library Resources.